Painting Course

Painting Course

INTRODUCTION TO

Drawing
Watercolour,
gouache and tempera
Pastel and acrylic
Oil painting

Ronald Pearsall

CHANCELLOR
PRESS

CONTENTS

Published in 1996 by
Chancellor Press
An imprint of Reed Consumer Books Limited
Michelin House
81 Fullham Road
London
SW3 6RB

Copyright © 1991, 1993, 1996
Regency House Publishing Limited

ISBN 1 85152 973 X

Printed in China

INTRODUCTION TO
Drawing

CONTENTS

Introduction

Being able to draw something in front of you, whether it is a landscape, a figure, or a portrait, is one of the great pleasures of life. There is a challenge, that of representing three dimensions in two, but it is a challenge that should be taken up as it is a skill that can be easily acquired. Drawing is much easier than playing the piano; and, as with musicians, there are naturals. There are men and women – and children – who can look at an object and depict it as it is, not as they think it is, without thinking twice about it. And there are others who have to work at it.

If you can call it work! For the accent of this book is on fun. All you need to start is some paper and a pencil, but one of the delights of drawing is that you can expand your repertoire. You may move from pencil into charcoal, or into pastels or paints; and, if you do, your knowledge of drawing will prove invaluable. It is all very well splashing about with a paint brush, but you have to know what you are doing, even if you are dealing with masses and shapes and not lines and shading.

Drawing offers something for everybody. You may like to go into the countryside and sketch quietly by yourself, or you may prefer townscapes. If you are nervous, and don't want strangers looking over your shoulder, draw in the comfort of your car. Or you may like to join a sketching club. There are more of them than you may imagine. For there are a lot of you out there!

WHAT IS A DRAWING?

The dictionary defines drawing as the art of representing objects or forms by lines drawn, shading, and other means – that is a picture in lines. There are actually at least four types of drawing: trying to represent something in front of the artist; trying to depict something from memory; copying something in another medium; and creating something entirely from imagination. Drawing is usually carried out with a pencil or a pen, charcoal or a crayon, but it can also be done with a pointed instrument on metal (etching) or stone (lithography) or with something soft and flexible such as a brush.

WHAT MATERIALS ARE NEEDED?

Pencils range from the very hard (designated by H) to the very soft and black (B). There are 10 grades between 6B and 4H, the average office pencil being HB. Pencil lead is a mixture of clay and graphite, and the greater the proportion of graphite the softer and blacker the pencil mark. It is useful to have several grades of pencil for use in one drawing. Hard pencils can be sharpened with a pencil-sharpener, but 2B and upwards need to be sharpened with a knife. The point can be tapered or given a chisel edge (very useful for shading). Pencils should always be sharpened at the opposite end to that which shows the degree of hardness or softness; otherwise HB, 2B or 2H or whatever will be lost. Small pieces of sandpaper will keep the pencil point exactly as you want it; art shops sell these in little blocks. There is also an excellent range of coloured pencils in a multitude of shades, but there is little variety of hardness and softness, save between the products of the various manufacturers. These should not be confused with pastel pencils.

Pens also offer an immense range. Drawing-pen nibs are usually sold in sets of a dozen or so, and nibs themselves vary in size from mapping-pen nibs to those designed for doing posters. The larger nibs often come fitted with a kind of a tray, called a reservoir, so that there is a ready flow of ink. Lettering pens can be very useful, and so can the so-called calligraphic pens. Some people refer to pen-nibs as pens, which can be very confusing. For those who find it tiresome to dip the pen in the ink constantly there are of course fountain pens, especially those with interchangeable nib units.

Just as the steel nib replaced the quill, so today the steel-nibbed pen has been partly superseded by the Rapidograph, which has a range of nibs from 0.1 (very fine) to 0.8 (broad). The virtue of a constant flow of ink and a consistent line compensates for a lack of flexibility in the nib itself. A drawn line cannot be varied by pressing down on the point, as with the old-fashioned steel nib. When using pen and ink always have a variety of pens and nibs available so that you can change from one to another if the need arises. As pen nibs are now so little used other than in art, it is worth mentioning that they are vulnerable to ill-usage and have a limited life span. If the points 'cross over' reject them immediately; there is little profit in trying to restore them. A Gillott 303 nib is flexible and useful for both narrow and broad strokes. A 'J' nib is the smallest lettering pen, giving a hard line, and is very handy for flat patterns and hatching. It is a good idea to have a small round sable brush near at hand to use with the pen and ink. Although the brush can be used with full-strength ink, very pleasant effects can be created with diluted ink. An old toothbrush is also a handy accessory for spattering ink, if you rub a fingertip (or, if this is too messy, a piece of wood or an old ruler) down the bristles. Spattering ink onto watercolour can create amazing textures and effects. Rapidographs with a very fine nib do have a tendency to get clogged up, and the nibs need a good deal of care. Modern Rapidograph pens are cartridge-filled, a great improvement on manual filling from a small plastic bottle.

Inks come in numerous colours, though black remains the most popular. Indian ink is probably the best kind of ink to use. Ink can be waterproof and water-soluble, and coloured inks can be used to great effect in combination with watercolour, especially on a moist surface where the colours can run into each other. Nothing can be knocked over quite so easily as an ink bottle, so keep it on a saucer. A small flat cardboard box, of the kind used for cigarettes or chocolates, with a hole made in the lid is better still. The card at the edges of the hole can be pushed up to hold the ink bottle tighter.

Papers Anything which will take a pen or pencil line can be used for drawing. Artists of the past showed a particular fondness for the backs of old envelopes. The traditional art-school paper is cartridge paper, sold in various weights, and best bought in sheet form and cut in two or four. Decent cartridge paper takes watercolour well, and is a good substitute for watercolour paper as well as being less ex-

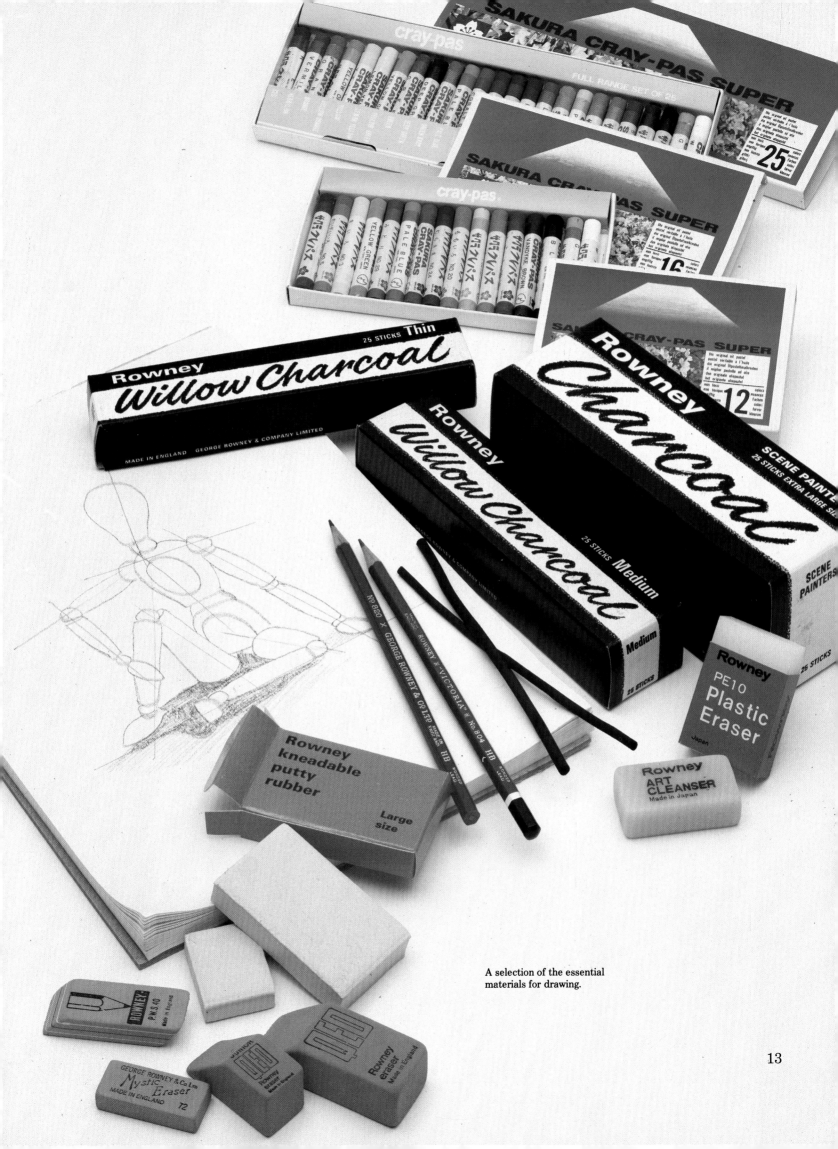

A selection of the essential materials for drawing.

pensive. Tinted papers, such as Ingres pastel paper, take pencil, pen and ink well, but almost anything can be used, though much depends on whether you are playing about with ideas, doing preliminary drawings, or intend to spend time on a finished pencil drawing good enough to frame. Sketchbooks are very handy, especially for on-the-spot work outdoors, as they usually have a thick cardboard back.

When sketching outdoors there is much to be said for having with you a variety of different papers, of various colours and thicknesses, some with texture, some smooth – some very smooth such as 'art' paper, glazed with china clay. A hard pencil such as 4H produces a crisp clear line on such paper. There are various smooth papers having trade names and sold in pads of different sizes, with perhaps the very best surfaces for pen-and-ink work.

For those who prefer pen-and-ink to pencil, who like the bite of a nib on paper, there is a stimulating and rewarding alternative – scraper-board. This is a prepared black board and when you draw on it with the point of a scalpel or craft-knife, or a rigid nib such as a 'J' nib, or the special instrument sold for the purpose, the lines are left in white, like a photographic negative. The final effect is stark and crisp, and it is a method which can give you a beautifully sharp and stylish result. Scraperboard is also made in white, so that an incised line shows up black (just like pen-and-ink). Of course, on scraperboard you have to get your light and shade by texture, by hatching, by stippling with

Far left: A selection of papers used for drawing, showing how the different finishes and textures affect the character of the drawing.

Left: Study of a nude girl, carried out freely and spontaneously.

Below: The various degrees of blackness achieved by pencils, ranging from 4H to 8B, charcoal and Chinagraph pencils.

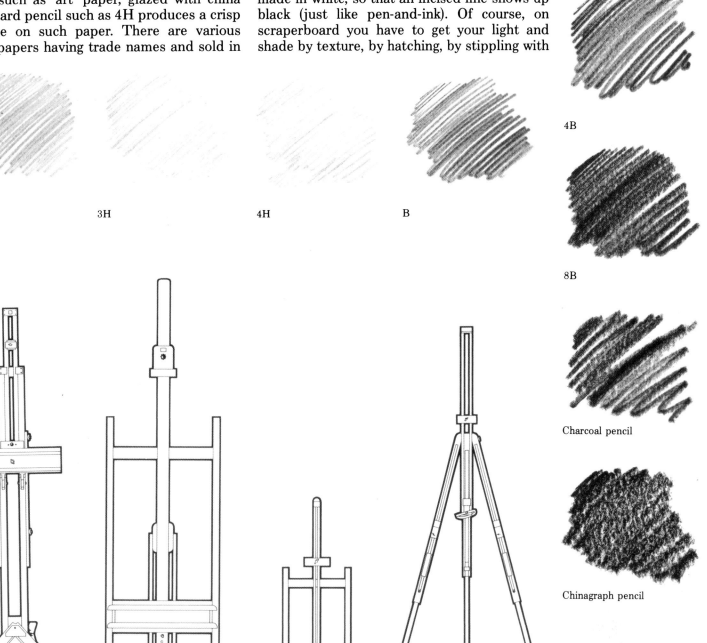

H

3H

4H

B

4B

8B

Charcoal pencil

Chinagraph pencil

Four different types of easel. The one on the extreme right is easily portable and ideal for outdoor work. The others are mainly used indoors.

15

dots, but it is worth while taking the time to get to know it as the final results can be dramatic. Scraperboard and the nib-like tool are very reasonably priced. No doubt those experienced in this kind of work can begin using the tool right away, but otherwise it is best to work out your subject on the surface in pencil or Indian ink. A marvellous effect can be produced by using watercolour on top of the finished scraperboard drawing.

Drawing Board The best drawing-boards are keyed, battened and proofed against warping and shrinking and all the other ailments wood is prone to. The most useful attribute of the drawing-board is that it takes drawing-pins, which alternatives such as a piece of hardboard will not. A drawing board of the traditional kind can be very useful in a life class where the drawing is on a vertical easel. A proper drawing board has just the right amount of give to a pencil point; a substitute may be too hard and shiny. Some people prefer to tape their drawings to a board with adhesive or masking tape (preferable, as it is easier to remove from the paper edge).

Easel Often looked on as an optional extra, an easel, especially a small portable one, can come in very handy, even for drawing. In out-of-doors situations it is often a good thing to stand back from the picture to see how it is going. Some artists never use an easel at all, even for doing oils, so it is very much a personal choice. Drawing at a vertical angle is altogether different from drawing on the flat or on a slope.

A very useful easel is the table-top type which works on the ratchet principle, so that the angle of the drawing-board can be altered to suit the artist. Some portable easels incorporate a fold-up stool. A fold-up canvas stool is better than a fold-up chair as, if the latter has arms, they tend to get in the way. An easel can always be improvised by using the back of a chair.

Erasers There are three kinds of pencil erasers on the market: the putty type, which can be very tiresome and crumble up into black pellets but which are ultra-soft and good for toning down blacks; the traditional office-type eraser; and the plastic type which has largely taken over from the second group as it is 'clean' and very versatile.

Charcoal At one time every art student wielded a stick of charcoal in the life class, and it has much to commend its use. It produces a soft black, which is easy to rub out even with a fingertip. However, it is not very suitable for fine detail and students are inclined to work on a larger scale than they would do with a pencil. This was considered a good thing by art masters, who had a paranoiac fear of niggardly work. Used on its side, it is very good for blocking in shadows, rather than hatching them in with a pencil.

Charcoal can be sharpened to make a point; small blocks of very fine-grained glass-paper are manufactured for putting points on charcoal and pencils. Soft bread kneaded between the fingers makes a good eraser. Try not to buy charcoal with a hard core, though this may be difficult as charcoal is normally sold in packets on a take-it-or-leave-it basis. The best way to hold charcoal is between the thumb and the first two fingers, with the thumb uppermost. Try to keep the hand off the paper and draw from the elbow. If you are using charcoal always keep a fixative at hand; an aerosol is the most convenient, but a fixative can also be sprayed on with a diffuser, which consists of two metal tubes hinged to make a right-angle. One tube is longer than the other; you dip this in the fixative, and blow through the shorter tube. A vacuum is created above the opening of the partly immersed tube, the liquid is drawn up and forms into a fine spray. Diffusers are cheap and efficient.

Conté Crayon This is not a school crayon, but a traditional artist's material made in France and used by the great French artists of the nineteenth century. It is sold in pencil form or in rectangular blocks and is used as it comes, not sharpened to a point. It gives a lustrous deep black, and has amazing covering capacity. Used with textured paper it gives a mottled appearance. It is very good with watercolour, but if used with what might appear to be its natural associate, pastel, it is inclined to slide as it is slightly greasy. It comes in a variety of colours, though black is by far the most useful. Many of the French artists used a colour called sanguine, a browny-red.

Torchon or Stump These are pencil-shaped articles of compressed blotting-paper or similar material, used for spreading charcoal, or cleaning up edges, and also useful in pen-and-ink work where they can tone down colours or blot out mistakes. Cotton-wool buds as sold in chemists can also be used, particularly for detailed work.

Of course other accessories can be added to the basic materials when needed. A toothbrush can be used in pen-and-ink work to 'spatter' ink on to a surface, and sometimes drawings develop into watercolours or pastels, so always have the necessary equipment nearby.

IS DRAWING DIFFICULT?

Learning to draw is like learning to play the piano, only easier. The classic form of drawing is reproducing something in front of you, whether it be a bunch of grapes, a nude or a landscape. In the art schools of yesteryear there was no chance of you touching a paintbrush until you could do this. This is why the artists of the past were very accomplished; whether they were imaginative or at all interesting is another matter. The first thing to do if you are drawing from life is to forget what you know; you are drawing what an object looks like, not what it is – unless, of course, you do not want to be representational, in which case you can draw what you like.

It is interesting to speculate on why prehistoric man made his cave drawings of animals. The most commonly accepted theory is that drawings were a form of magic, and that by depicting animals with spears in them he would be rewarded with success in the hunt. To the professional artists of the Middle Ages and after art was for the glory of God. When they painted Jesus and the Madonna they were not concerned with where the shadows went. Putting in a halo of gold leaf was more important than verisimilitude. When considering the present day, and ignoring for the moment that the Romans and the Egyptians could depict *exactly* on panels and walls what they saw, we

can see in children's art the wish to put down on paper what they know rather than what they see. A circle with two blobs, a vertical stroke, and a crescent shape at the bottom is a face, a rectangle with four squares, an oblong, and another oblong at the top exuding smoke, represent a house (even for those in tower blocks who only see a house once in a blue moon).

Some people, including artists, never lose this way of looking at objects, or, rather, pretend not to have lost it. The childish vision allied with a solid technique can often be a money-spinner. Art teachers are usually the first to try to eradicate the child's way of depicting external objects, and place before the class cubes and spheres and other dreary objects. No wonder that many children do not find much fun in drawing.

Some people, adults as well as children, may, when drawing a picture, put down an outline and then colour in the enclosed areas. This may be instinctive to them, though if you reflect a little you will realize that an outline does not exist 'out there'. An outline is only a dividing line between an area of light and an area somewhat darker. In other words, an outline is a convention. It is a convention that in drawing all artists will continue to respect –though not in painting, where changes in *tone* (not colour) are all important.

In drawing, except when using coloured pencils or coloured inks, all we have is outline and tone. Our aim is to depict with reasonable accuracy what we see. Success does not depend on manual dexterity but on looking and

Prehistoric wall paintings, which can be interpreted in many ways, as magic symbols or even as reminders of successful hunting missions. There is no mistaking their immediacy and verve. These early artists were not bogged down by methods and techniques but drew directly on the walls, using charcoal, earth or any material to hand. Here is an excellent example of freedom of style unfettered by too much discipline.

Left: This child's painting is totally uninhibited in its freshness, a quality which becomes more and more elusive with age.

In the above pencil drawing, the artist obviously wished to chisel out every small detail, starting with a hard pencil and finishing with a soft one to render tones.

Details.

assessing. By assessing we mean simply seeing how certain shapes relate to other shapes and how light or dark they are in respect of each other. Sometimes the shapes are simple, and can be looked at once and set down with something like accuracy. In landscape it can be a farmhouse set against a field. Sometimes the shapes are complex, such as the angle of a wrist in a life drawing. No shape is too difficult to put down. We do not have to know how the farm was built and its methods of interior construction. Nor do we have to be anatomists to find out why the wrist turns in one way and no other, though it is only fair to mention that artists of the old school needed to be well versed in anatomy (and sometimes robbed graveyards for specimens to dissect). These are the principles behind drawing, and after a time it becomes second nature to recreate on paper the external appearance of something. The next stage is using the drawing, either as a basis for something else or as a spur to further composition.

Once we realize that the outline is only a means to an end and that the effect of *solidity* is far more important than a pencil line surrounding a white silhouette, then the main barrier to accurate drawing is crossed. This may sound daunting for some, who believe that they will never be any good at drawing. Useful as the skill is, drawing is not the be-all and end-all. It is quite possible to be a bad draughtsman yet a good painter. There are a large number of short cuts that can be taken, and there is no need for anyone ever to bother drawing something from life if he or she does not feel confident about it, though it must be said that although it is a kind of discipline it is great fun, and it is fascinating to see a drawing gradually emerge from the first marks made on the paper, whether it is a bit of shading, a few squiggles to mark where the shapes come, or a fragment of line.

Before we pursue the practical side of drawing, a few words on the subject of perspective.

Perspective

Perspective is a simple matter. If you look at a straight road going towards the horizon it appears to narrow; a person walking along this road appears to get smaller as the distance increases between you and that person, losing height at the same rate as the road narrows. Telegraph poles will appear to shrink. If the road extends as far as the eye can see, the sides

The amateur artist needs to be aware of perspective. In this pencil drawing the avenue of trees recedes into the background, converging to a point where it disappears.

These diagrams show one of
the basic rules of perspective.
In a manner similar to that
shown in the previous drawing,
if one were to continue the
lines of the house roof they
would recede to a point in the
distance, i.e. the vanishing
point.

Diagram 1. Perspective as
seen when the level of the eye
is in line with the base of the
house.

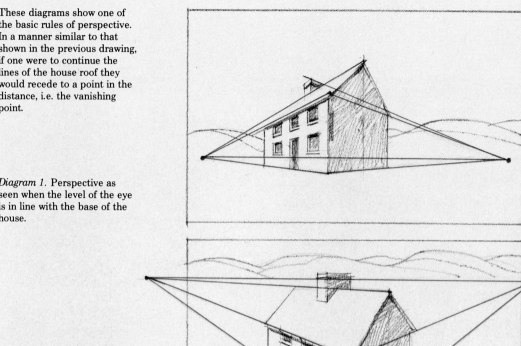

Right. Before starting a
drawing, decide where your
vanishing point will be.
Diagram 1. Choose your
vanishing point and draw in
the basic lines of convergence.

Diagram 2. Start to sketch in
the details. Guidelines can be
erased at this stage.

Diagram 3. Finished sketch.

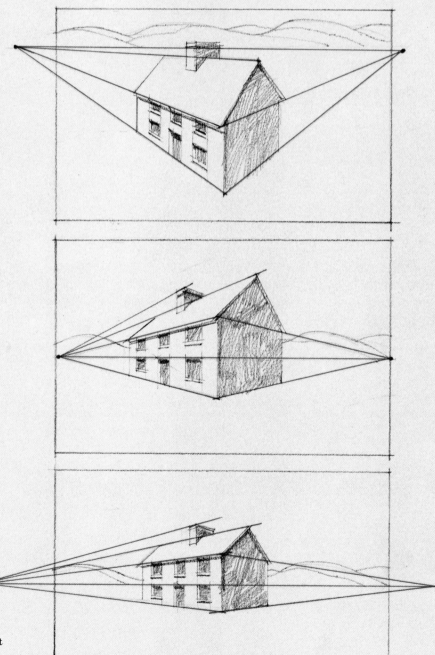

Diagram 2. As seen from
above the house.

Diagram 3. Looking at the
house on the normal level.

Diagram 4. When one looks at
an object from a distance, the
vanishing points are less
acute.

will appear to meet at what is known as the vanishing point on the horizon. The horizon is *always* at eye-level, and to prove it, sit or lie on the ground and watch how the horizon goes down with you. The horizon has *nothing* to do with the sky-line, and the only time to observe a true horizon is at sea where the sky meets the water.

Objects above or partly above the eye-level *appear* to go down towards the horizon and those below *appear* to go up. If you look at the roof of a house from any angle except directly in front, you will see it obeying the laws of perspective. If you extend the roof with an imaginary line it will lead to the horizon at its own particular vanishing point. There is only one horizon line, but there can be any number of vanishing points in any one scene. Without using perspective, a drawing or a painting will be flat, a mere pattern. Using perspective you get solidity and recession; you can place things in space with absolute certainty that you are getting the relative sizes right, because everything fits into the pattern.

In working from the imagination, the horizon can be as high or low as you wish. If you are doing aerial views it can even be off the top of the paper. But objects still recede towards it according to the rules. The laws of perspective must be used. Use perspective to help establish objects in space, and twist it if you need to get a better effect. The experts in perspective drawing are not usually artists, but architects. Their perspective has to be absolutely right, but if an artist's perspective *looks* right that is what matters. It is easy to imagine roads, roofs, and telegraph poles going conveniently towards vanishing points. Asymmetrical objects such as oval-shaped ponds also obey the laws of perspective, and nobody in their right mind wants to work out *exactly* how perspective works on them. If you are drawing from life, you can see; if you are not, but would like to put in an oval pond somewhere, you put one in and see if it looks right.

A brief mention should be made of accidental vanishing points. Surfaces which are tilted (academically described as 'surfaces which are inclined to the horizontal') *sometimes* converge on accidental vanishing points which lie above or below the horizon – and not on it. A good example of this is a road going uphill, where the sides will appear to converge at a point *above* the horizon, vice versa in the case of a road going downhill. This fact is another reason for not being too much in awe of so-called laws.

There is a useful tip: an object twice as far away from the viewer as another identical object appears to be half as tall; if it is three times as far away it seems one-third as tall; four

The New York skyline is a classic example of aerial perspective. Buildings in the front of the picture can be seen in detail, but the misty, blue quality of the background suggests distance.

times as far away, a quarter as tall, and so on. Another useful tip is: even in good drawings and paintings the clouds sometimes seem flat and uninteresting. This is because clouds are also subject to the laws of perspective.

Aerial perspective, oddly enough, does not have anything to do with ordinary perspective. You might think it means aerial views, and how objects on the ground have vanishing points outside the picture surface (or, if seen from directly above, have no vanishing point at all!) This is not the case. Aerial perspective is the effect of atmosphere. Atmosphere is full of moisture, dust, not to mention noxious fumes,

which tend to obscure the most distant objects. The more distant objects are, the more they are obscured, and the lighter or higher in tone they will appear to be. Distant features often take on a bluish tone, and 18th-century artists had a formula that was worked to death – dark brown for the foreground, green for the middle distance and blue for the far distance. This became a device for achieving a good effect without much soul-searching. In the early morning, distant objects can be as crisp and un-blue as you care to imagine. So aerial perspective is something we can take or leave, depending on the effect we want.

HOW DO I START?

In most cases, it is not a question of starting but of continuing. Most people have drawn at some time in their life, even if it is only a doodle on a telephone pad. The main question is: do I want a challenge or do I want to take the easy way? The challenge is to do *something* from real life and get professional or amateur opinion on your drawing as the work progresses – in other words, join an art class or a sketching club.

Lessons at art classes are cheap, especially if organized by the local community. The ultimate challenge for beginners is to join a life class, and paint the nude figure. The models in life classes have to stand still and be drawn or painted, which is actually very hard work. If you are worried about not being good enough for the class, do not be. Most adults who go to life classes are *not* very good at drawing, and some

of them never will be because they go simply for an enjoyable night out and because of the people they meet there. Many of them do not particularly want to improve, and others do not take kindly to any form of instruction from the teachers, who consequently have to be masters of tact and diplomacy (and usually are – the traditional stuffy ones are a dying breed).

Sketching clubs are usually concerned with landscape, which is easier than life drawing (in this context life is drawing from the nude). Experienced artists often go with sketching clubs, for the sake of companionship and comfort. For those sociably inclined, there is a lot to be said for sketching clubs, which usually include experienced artists as well as learners. There is no easier way to pick up techniques and tips almost by accident. Overlooking a good artist at work can be very rewarding, and it is amazing, by simply looking around, how many styles and methods of drawing and painting you find there are.

You should keep a sketchbook with you at all times as you never know when an opportunity will arise to sketch a friend or an interesting object.

Drawing at home, watched occasionally by a husband or wife, father or mother, or, more unnerving, children, may or may not be more acceptable, but it is important to give yourself something of a challenge. Do not spend too much time drawing something which bores you to distraction; if you feel that you ought to try a still life, set up an interesting group, and if the drawing is going badly finish it quickly and turn to something else which is more stimulating, whether it be the dog curled up on a carpet, a self-portrait, or a view from a window. There is no obligation to do pretty or picturesque subjects, nor any of those tiresome exercises middle-aged men and women remember from their school-days. If it is not enjoyable it is not worth doing; nobody is paying you, and if it becomes a chore you might as well settle down in front of the television screen.

The whole emphasis of this book is on pleasure. If you would like to go out with a sketchbook but feel that you will look foolish, go in the car and stay in the car while you

When out with a group – sketching landscapes, for example – it is a good idea to sketch some of your colleagues as they will invariably be standing still, deep in concentration on their own work.

24

sketch. You do not *have* to set up in the open air with all the paraphernalia associated with a 'real artist'.

But there is a lot to be said for outdoor sketching. It can be a means of gathering material for future work. Suppose you have decided to draw a quaint group of riverside cottages, not because of any deep interest in cottages but because it is a traditionally picturesque subject. Maybe there are boats on the river, and you decide to turn your attention to them as the cottages are beginning to seem rather dull. Suddenly you hear a clock strike in the distance and you realize that you have been busy sketching the boats for an hour, and in doing so you have found a subject you are really fascinated with.

Even if you go to the same place time and time again you will always find something different, for weather conditions are never exactly the same, and there will be details which you will see for the first time. Certainly at some time you will find a subject you will not

When sketching animals, speed is usually essential as they are constantly on the move, in contrast to the seated figure, lower right.

be able to let alone, and the sketch will eventually form the basis of a watercolour or an oil painting. If you had not been there at that particular time you would have missed it. If you had seen the view, thought it would make a good subject for a painting, but had not made a sketch, how much would you have remembered? Colour is fairly easy to retain in the memory, but not tones. Of course in drawing you have to express the tones with degrees or kinds of shading, but if they can be graded you can number them, from one to six for example, one for the lightest, one for the darkest tones. And tone is always far more important than colour; colour is to be used to make an effect. It does not or should not use you!

A substitute for sketching (if the idea is to have something to base an oil or watercolour on) is the use of a camera but, unless you are using filters, distinct tones which you can detect with the eye may be merged into one, as for example in a cloud, which is not a flat white blob but a subject having its own roundness and space. If you are taking a camera it might be better instead of colour, to use black-and-white film which will give insight into the tones.

If you feel that you will never be any good at drawing but want to paint, do not despair. There are any number of short cuts which will enable you to set down some kind of 'drawing' as a basis for painting, whatever the paint medium.

One of the greatest aids to artists is a collection of illustrations, photographs, photographs of people, landscapes, seascapes, prize-winning photographs, photographs in books and catalogues, snapshots, Polaroids and photographs of pictures, to mention only a few

The home is an ideal place to sketch children and pets. Children sometimes remain conveniently still while watching TV. The delightful West Highland terrier was captured on paper while fast asleep.

When the family have become accustomed to your sketchbook they will be only too pleased to pose for you.

examples. Most artists of the past accumulated illustrations; before the 1840s they were prints and paintings; between 1840 and about 1880 photographs were added to the collection, but these photographs were 'one-offs' as no way had been found to reproduce photographs in books except by sticking them in with gum. These photographs were all monochrome; colour photographs were not developed for a long time. Today colour photographs are available, and have been for over half a century. They form a valuable source of information, though black-and-white photographs can be even more useful as an aid because they deal with tone, which to an artist is more informative than colour.

Commercial artists rely very much on their photographic collection and are not shy to admit it. A number of the very best commercial artists keep photographs cut from newspapers, periodicals and magazines in folders, each labelled with its contents – men and women walking, action, games, children, uniforms, back

27

views of people, restaurants, shops, cars, trains, and so on.

Photographs can be consulted, and for those for whom drawing is their weak point, they can be copied – or even traced. If all you want is a basis for a picture, not a drawing to be proud of, there is much to be said for tracing. There is no need to trace an entire photograph – just the elements you want. Photographs can always be copied, and an advantage of copying is that the replica can be executed on a larger scale than the original by 'squaring-up'. Squaring-up is a traditional way of transferring a preliminary drawing on to a canvas, and all it means is that the drawing and the canvas are divided into squares. The numbers of squares on the drawing and the canvas are the same, but as the drawing is usually smaller the squares on the canvas need to be larger. The same can be done with a photograph.

A splendid short cut to squaring up is to make a grid. Take a small pane of clear glass

and divide it into squares – half-inch or one-inch as you prefer – by stretching thin strips of self-adhesive tape at appropriate intervals to divide the glass. Or you can paint the lines in by using a small pointed brush and acrylic paint. It is also a good idea to make a grid when you are using a home-made viewfinder (a piece of card with a rectangle cut in the middle). Stretch white nylon or cotton at the appropriate intervals across the aperture, so that when you look at your view it is conveniently divided into squares. Do not use the thinnest gauge cotton or nylon for if your eyes are focused on a distant scene you will not be able to see the grid properly.

Originals can also be copied, larger or smaller, by using a device called a pantograph, which is something like a flat wine-rack with interchangeable struts, a pointer to follow the lines of the original, and a pencil at the opposite end of the device for reproducing the picture. If you do buy a pantograph get a good one, and not a cheap plastic type which is no better than an irritating toy.

When using the squaring-up method it is simple to copy the material seen in each square, ensuring that the proportions are correct, which is vitally important in figure and portrait work. Many of the great painters of the past have used this method, and it is wholly acceptable. More artists than you might imagine have used tracing as a basis for transferring designs onto paper or canvas. The only problem with tracing is that unless one has a darkroom and photographic ability (or a good deal of money) photographic prints are relatively small, except in 'coffee-table' books, a source of illustration not to be overlooked. It is amazing how you can build up a picture using various photographs, even though it means altering the different areas of light and shade.

Among the most useful photographs are those you have taken yourself. A photograph not only jogs the memory, but is also valuable as a record; it can replace a sketch done on the spot for working-up later into a picture, or it can supplement a sketch. Using a Polaroid camera during sketching can be very rewarding, for bringing out features in landscape which you have overlooked, and establishing the exact look of a place, as well as the general colour and tone. Few professional portrait artists work without recourse to a number of photographs of their sitters. So it is not unreasonable to use a camera.

So far we have been dealing with photo-

Above: A home-made grid or viewfinder makes a good device for transferring a smaller image on to a large paper or canvas.

Far left: Squaring up a photograph or a magazine cutting is an excellent way to enlarge a drawing.

Below: A pantograph can also be used to reduce or enlarge an illustration.

Try to draw a subject in as
many different poses as
possible. This is an invaluable
method of testing whether
proportion and perspective
are correct.

Having quickly set down the basic shapes and forms, the artist has decided to make a further sketch of the head in some detail. This is a good idea in case you decide to do a full portrait at a later stage.

graphic *prints* as an aid to or a substitute for drawing, but colour transparencies can also serve a purpose. They are not so easy to flip through in search of subjects or information, but unquestionably they have their place. The image on a transparency is, of course, thrown onto a screen. Provided that you keep out of the way of the light source and substitute paper or canvas for the screen there is no problem in painting the picture as it is being projected –

painting-by-numbers with a difference. It is the procedure of highly regarded artists of the neo-realist school in the USA, and is no more reprehensible than collage, the use of silk-screen printing, and other dodges of contemporary art. If it suits you, and you like doing it, do it. You may think of other useful techniques.

Squaring-up is one of the traditional methods, and it takes time. There is also bound to be some deviation from the original. The slide

31

projector is limited because it naturally only uses slides, and invariably most of the slides are home-made.

The episcope is well worth considering. This is a device in which an illustration of any kind – black-and-white or colour – is placed face down on a window and projected onto a screen or other suitable surface by means of mirrors, a lens, and a strong internal light. The size of the image can be altered by adjustment of the lens, and the quality is as good as that provided by a slide projector. As with a slide projector, the picture projected can be drawn or painted on directly in almost any medium, though as the screen/paper/canvas is vertical any watercolour needs to be applied with discretion for otherwise it will run. Because the image stays perfectly still for hours on end you can spend as much time as you like drawing in or painting in, using small dots if you wish, every so often putting your hand in front of the lens to black out the light to see how the work is going. This avoids switching the machine on and off, which reduces the life span of the specialist bulbs. When setting up the episcope, place it so that you are not working in your own shadow – if you are right-handed have the episcope positioned on your left. For those who intend to do a lot of work with the episcope it is worth while considering fixing up a stand, so that the machine can be placed above the working surface with the lens pointing downwards.

Another method of drawing is by using computer graphics. Many home computers and word processors have 'add on' extras which make it possible to use a VDU (visual display unit – the television monitor) as a drawing surface. These computer-originated drawings can be printed out, and with the aid of simple inexpensive devices can be altered in all manner of ways – squeezed, enlarged, chopped about – and by using different coloured ribbons in the printer they can be coloured.

A casual mention must be made of video as an aid to artists. It cannot be used directly, but it can be a valuable source of information on every subject. In the old days an artist who wanted to study the sea and analyse the structure and pattern of waves had to go to the sea to look at it. If you are keen on doing maritime pictures, you can always find a television scene involving the sea, even if it is in the middle of a feature film. Such a section can be played over and over again, with certain episodes frozen to see exactly what waves look like. In today's world we can find out about almost everything without needing to go out-of-doors. How documentary-type artists of the past would have envied us!

Copying, tracing and reproducing are all

When making a tracing it is important to put in not only the outline but the shading as well.

Tracing the image.

Following the lines on the reverse side.

Retracing the lines.

32

shortcuts to painting, bypassing the process of drawing and the co-ordination of hand and eye. No one is going to award you a prize for diligently slogging away at a drawing when you are not really enjoying it, and if you happen to turn out a good painting very few are likely to enquire about the initial techniques you used. Copying, using the squaring-up method or freehand, needs little said about it; for tracing one needs a pad of proper tracing-paper as sold by art shops, not too thick and not too flimsy. When tracing, put in the tones as well as the outlines. There are two main methods of transferring the tracing onto paper or canvas, first, by using carbon paper. This is all right when using opaque watercolour or oils, but in watercolour proper the carbon lines are too dark and do not rub out easily. The second is to do the tracing, turn it over and rub the reverse of the outline with charcoal or soft pencil. Then apply the tracing paper right way up and go over the detail with a hard pencil (HB or H) or a ball-point pen. Charcoal has the slight edge on pencil as it is easily removed or obliterated by almost any medium from the lightest watercolour upwards. If there is a slight disadvantage with charcoal it is that the image can be a little 'fluffy'.

Let us suppose that you have not taken the easy option and are willing to draw something in front of you. Whatever you are drawing, you must decide whether to stand at an easel or sit down. If you are sitting down, you can have your drawing board or sketchpad on your knees, or on a table. If you are sitting down and want to work on a vertical surface but have not got an easel, two dining-chairs tied together by the front legs make an excellent substitute, if you sit on one and rest the drawing board on the back of the other. Large-scale work is better done standing up, as the action comes from the shoulder rather than the wrist so there is greater freedom.

The way you hold the pencil is a question of taste; in writing it is held between the thumb and the first or second finger. In drawing, try holding the pencil with all four fingers beneath it, thumb on top, and knuckles against the paper. This is for standing up. For sitting down, reverse the procedure, and in both cases it will give you flexibility if you hold the pencil loosely and not too near the point. For pen-and-ink work it is also worthwhile trying new ways of holding the pen.

In drawing any object, establish roughly what you intend to put in. In a still life, it is quite simple; you make the arrangement, so you put it all in. In a nude you will *try* to include everything, but sometimes the odd ankle just does not fit into the picture. Landscape has to

There are many ways of holding the pencil or other drawing instrument, and you will find the method which suits you best.

General sketching work.

Shading large areas.

Detail work.

Using the pencil as a measuring device to get proportions correct.

be cut off somewhere, and you may decide to put the most interesting features in the middle and let the rest take care of itself. Alternatively, you can make use of a viewfinder, which you can easily make yourself out of a piece of card, and it is nothing more or less than a small picture mount with a convenient-size rectangle cut out of the piece of card. A camera view-finder can be useful. In portrait drawing obviously the whole of the face must go in, and the rest you can leave rough or finished as you wish.

The very first step is to get *something* down on the virgin paper. There is nothing more demanding than an empty piece of paper. You may like to put in a few light touches indicating the size and position of the subject, or you may care to start by indicating the areas of shadow with the flat of the charcoal or by hatching with a series of parallel lines. If they are wrong, it does not matter; do not rub them out. As you become more certain that you are on the right track, lines and shadows can get firmer and more authoritative. Fashion designers usually put in the entire outlines, and then fill them in. If you have a good eye, you can do this but it is normally only possible with practice. It is usually easier to move from point to point, from drawing fragments you are reasonably satisfied with, whether they are bits of outline or areas of shade, to new sections.

Seat yourself at a distance from the model to enable you to draw your picture to the exact size of your visual image.

34

In the early stages it is very easy to come adrift on questions of proportion. A pencil held at arm's length is very helpful; the distance between point A and point B can be equated between the tip of the pencil and the top of the thumb nail. There is nothing to stop you using a 12 in wooden ruler for this task. Divergences from the vertical and the horizontal can also be figured out with the help of a pencil held at arm's length. It is easier to under-estimate an angle than over-estimate it.

Shadows come in all shapes and sizes, and because we are not really used to examining shadows, there are more varieties than we might imagine. There are shadows arising from the object part being away from the light source, there are background shadows, and there are cast shadows, in which one object is shielding another object or part object from the light. Cast shadows are darker than other shadows. If there is more than one light source, the shadows can be very interesting, and you may decide which ones you want and which you do not. The usual way to draw a shadow is to hatch it, but you can also use dots or scribbles; for strong shadow you can use cross-hatch, in which parallel strokes from right diagonally down to the left (or vice versa if you are left-handed) are overlaid by parallel strokes top left to down right. Or if you are using a soft pencil with a chisel point you can put the shadow in solid black. Try to build up the drawing with a combination of outline and shading; they complement each other. This applies to all types of drawing.

If you are setting up a still life at home or are drawing a husband or wife you can decide for yourself what source of light you want. The only advice is not to have the light source immediately behind the subject. A room with windows on one side only provides more comprehensible shadows than a room with several light sources; for really direct shadows, nothing is better than electric light with an unshielded standard lamp or adjustable lamp better than an overhead bulb or fluorescent tube.

In landscapes we have to depend on the sun, and if we are interested in drawing for drawing's sake it is better to go out when the light is good, as well as in the early morning or late afternoon when the shadows are at their most interesting. Needless to say, there are no hard or fast rules about this; atmospheric drawings can be made on occasions when a photographer would hardly get a reading on his light meter.

Place your model near to a window or other good light source if you are looking for a dramatic effect with light coming from a specific direction.

HAVING STARTED THE DRAWING, HOW DO I CARRY ON?

Your drawing may at this stage look like tea leaves in the bottom of a tea cup or automatic writing at a spiritualist seance. It does not matter if you have bits of outlines and areas of shading as long as you have an idea, however vague, what is going on and are not merely putting in strokes and blobs at random. It is more important that you can see a way to get to grips with the subject, and can assess it as a whole, knowing from which direction the light is coming and what will be the stumbling blocks needing extra effort. If you find it difficult to work out the tones, and cannot decide which areas should be darker, half-close your eyes and look at the subject again.

Every drawing exercise has its difficult aspects, and sometimes it is a good idea to tackle these separately, on a separate sheet of paper or on the corner. In still life, it may be the curvature on jugs or bowls and how to put in the graded shading as the curve moves into the dark, or it may be that you are tackling a vase of flowers and wondering how to manage those flowers partly in the shadow of blooms above them. In landscape, it may be the problem of depicting trees so that they do not look like overgrown cabbages. In life drawing, a common disaster area is the hand and wrist, and even great artists can come unstuck. In portraits, you may have a problem in preventing the subject looking cross-eyed. Each of us has a particular area which we find fraught with difficulty, even if there is no sensible reason why this should be so. However, you must persevere and try to crack it. If a hand looks like a melon, rub it out and start again, though it may be that you have already gone over it a dozen times and the lines and indentations are beyond redemption. If the rest of the drawing is going well, it is much more convenient to paste a piece of paper over the offending part and carry on over that (adhesive envelope labels are ideal for this purpose).

There is no substitute for looking *hard* at something which is proving intractable, and this is where a photographic collection can be invaluable. Examine what the difficult object *really* looks like and how painters and draughtsmen of the past have managed to make their efforts believable. It is sometimes a good idea, even if you are a dedicated non-copier, to copy a detail from another picture and in so doing realize where you went wrong. Many of the problems of drawing derive from the fact that

36

A fully worked-out drawing of a seated man, with details of the shoe and head. The light is coming from the artist's left, giving sharp shadows.

you are trying to interpret a three-dimensional object in two dimensions, and that parts of an object are nearer to you than others, sometimes quite dramatically. This is most evident in life drawing, and *foreshortening*. Imagine a fist extended towards your face; the knuckles of the hand will take up most of the image, and the shoulder at the back will be very insignificant indeed. Sometimes problems will fall away if we remember about perspective, and that *everything* is set in space and is subject to its laws. Even in a still life it is sometimes helpful to put in an eye-line, and insert vanishing points.

There is nothing more rewarding than working away through your own personal drawing problem, but here are some tips to make it easier.

Figure Drawing

It is traditional in old-fashioned teach-yourself books to emphasize that beneath clothing is a nude and beneath the nude is a skeleton, not to mention muscles. There is nothing more off-putting than anatomy. As we are not going to draw skeletons, we can take it as read that they are there and influence the shape and movements of the body. The proportions of the various sections are much more useful. A man is eight heads tall, a woman six heads; bearing in mind the fact that we are all different, the half-way point down a man is the crutch or thereabouts. Some professional artists and fashion designers have the women at eight-and-a-half heads tall, with longer legs than is natural (or often seen). A one-year-old child is four heads high; a nine-year-old child is six heads tall. Regarding the shape of the torso, that of a man, broad of shoulder and narrow of hip, can be represented by an equilateral triangle upright from a tip, that of a woman by a straightforward triangle. Tricky areas for novices are connecting the head with the shoulders in a convincing manner, the hands and the feet. The neck, unless the head is thrown back, tilts forward; a man's neck slopes slightly *outwards*, a woman's neck slightly *inwards*. The neck does not stick on *top* of the shoulders, but is slightly below. A fist is harder to draw, though there is less of it, than an outstretched hand, and always be aware of the angle and relative smallness of the wrist. You can practise drawing your own hand, preferably with the aid of a mirror. It is far more important to get hands right rather than feet, as feet usually have shoes on. The fingers of a hand are not on the same plane as the thumb unless the hand is fully outstretched. When the hand is held casually the thumb droops. It is very easy for a novice to make a hand look like a flatfish. The main difficulty with feet is getting the

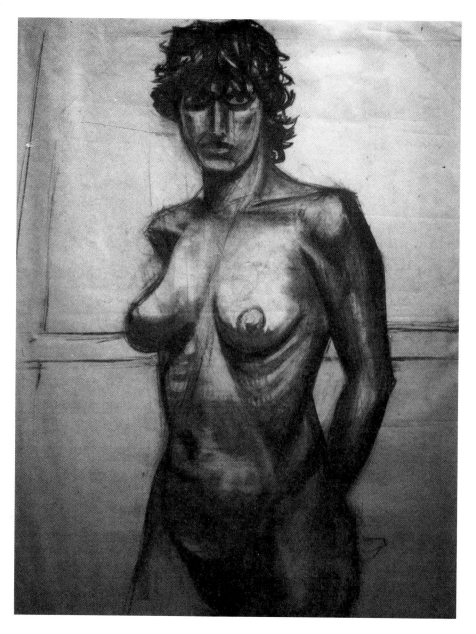

Above: It is important, when drawing the figure, to have an understanding of how the body is formed and how various parts are joined. In this study of a nude, the artist has shown that he understands the underlying forms and clearly defined bone structure. He has used a Conté-type crayon to make this powerful drawing.

Detail of the head.

In complete contrast (to the drawing on the left) this lovely reclining figure has been drawn softly and with tenderness.

Drawing a head in profile can
be a most satisfying exercise.

A fully worked study of a
couple, taken from a family
photograph. The drapes and
folds of the clothes have been
particularly well drawn.
Remember that clothes
generally follow the form and
should suggest the body
beneath.

41

Quick rough sketches can
often be just as rewarding as
detailed studies.

ankle in the right position. If you are drawing a nude you can start where you like, though it is easier to begin somewhere on the torso where there are shadows to give you starting-off points than at the end of a leg. With the torso reasonably accurately drawn it is possible to add the appendages in a convincing manner.

If you have some experience of drawing the nude then it helps when drawing clothed figures. The folds in clothing can be divided into four kinds, occurring in hanging materials, pulled materials, heaped materials and crushed materials. Folds are expressed by shading, but be selective, only putting in those which you think important. Do not be tempted into trying to express pattern or texture in black-and-white, unless the pattern is very aggressive.

At the life class in art schools it is customary to have a longish session doing one drawing followed by 'quickies', five-minute poses, which can be more enjoyable as you will have no time

to quibble over nagging difficulties. These five-minute studies can best be done with a soft pencil (say 4B) or charcoal, and sometimes even a newcomer can get the pose absolutely right by not thinking about it too much and letting the hand do the work, drawing intuitively rather than intellectually. So if you have completed a drawing which you are really pleased with and want to take it home rather than screw it up and sling it into the nearest waste bucket, what do you do – if it is in charcoal which will partly slide and smudge in transit? You fix it. So when you are using charcoal always keep nearby a can of spray fixative, or a fixative with a diffuser.

If you are using charcoal for a quick nude study it is also worth while keeping some pastels at hand. As with charcoal, you can cover a sheet of cartridge paper in five seconds flat, and for expressing shadow a short length of pastel in a grey or a brown applied on the flat

These quick sketches amply demonstrate that the artist has understood the shapes and movement of the figure.

can be perfect. Always remember that it is your choice regarding the medium to use. Sometimes a drawing that started off as a pencil piece demands to be treated with ink.

Always take a variety of different papers with you when drawing nudes or costume studies – cartridge, watercolour, Ingres pastel paper, even brown wrapping paper. You may not use all of them, but they are there if wanted.

Two interesting studies, one in sepia wash and pen, the other in crayon.

44

Right: Moving figures present a variety of difficulties which can provide a rewarding challenge to overcome.

Below: Detail of the left arm and legs; these are likely to present the most problems but, with close observation, even the most outlandish movements can be set down accurately.

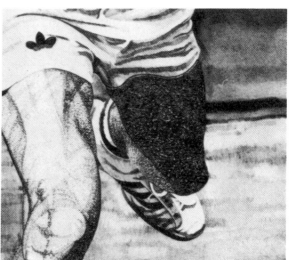

In this illustration the artist
has carefully studied the head
and hands and has drawn
them in some detail. The rest
of the figure has, rather
cleverly, been merely
suggested.

Portrait Drawing

If you think about it, the ability to draw portraits is one of the most highly regarded talents. It is also one of the hardest tests of ability since a portrait, to be of any merit, must be *a likeness*, and there is no harsher critic than your nearest and dearest. Getting a likeness is not as difficult as you might imagine, and there are far fewer problems associated with this branch of art than life drawing – in the first place you do not need to go to a life class; using a mirror you can draw yourself.

What are the first steps?

First of all get your materials together – drawing-board, paper pinned on with drawing-pins, easel or a chair converted into an easel, an eraser which you may not use, and a pencil or pencils, HB or 2B being the most useful, with an assortment of pastels in reserve if you feel that they are necessary. The best distance for the sitter is about six feet away, the head held at a three-quarter angle, and the light coming from left or right and throwing good shadows. The paper should be level with the sitter's head and the nearer to life size the drawing is the better. If you draw too small you won't be able to see your mistakes. The traditional way is to draw the contour of the head; it doesn't have to be absolutely exact – that can be dealt with later. A dividing line is put in between the hair and the face. Draw a faint line down the middle of the face, and put in three lines, one marking the distance from the hair to the eyebrows, another under the nose, and the other at the bottom of the chin. Then mark in the eyes; the distance between them is usually about the length of an eye. Observe whether the upper lip is long or short and fix in the position of the mouth. Mark the ears. The neck is important; observe the pit in the neck, and how it helps set the head on the shoulders.

Every so often lean back, or get up and take a stroll, so that when you return to the drawing it will say more to you. Continually compare one shape with another, if necessary doodling across the paper with the pencil. When drawing the nose try not to make the nostrils too narrow for otherwise they will appear pinched, and from certain angles the nostrils are not ovals but slits. At all times draw what you are seeing, even if a likeness seems to take a long time in coming, and do not read details into the portrait which you cannot see. For example, when you come to do the ears portray the ear-hole and the ridges of flesh as they seem, perhaps just as shading, not as scale drawings.

Another method is to start from the eyes, putting these in and working from there, and there are certain proportions that are useful for all methods of approach, the straightforward

Top: Use your colleagues in the office or at work to make a variety of quick sketches.

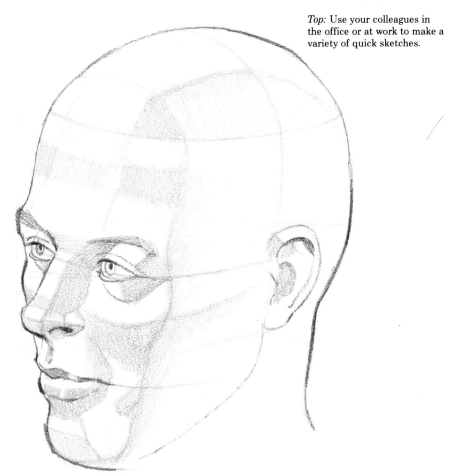

When drawing a head, divide the surface up into contours and planes as illustrated. This is the best method of achieving the correct angle and perspecive.

and the oblique.

The eye, conveniently, is situated about half-way down the head, and other useful measurements are these: the distance between the top of the forehead and the top of the nose is approximately the distance between the top of the nose and the bottom. The same distance lies between the top of the upper lip and the bottom

1

2

3

4

5

6

This selection of portraits offers a wide variety of techniques and methods.

1. A simple pen-and-ink sketch drawn from life.

2. The kind of sketch one can readily make from a photograph.

3. A detailed sketch chiselling out various planes and features.

4. A direct portrait from life.

5. A quick pen sketch with the sitter totally unaware.

6. A similar sketch but pencil instead of pen.

7. Pen-and-ink is a good medium for studying individual features.

8. A light and shade drawing, that can be seen in a magazine, with the detailed rendering of an eye.

9. A quick pencil sketch of a child.

10. A good expression captured in pen-and-ink.

11. This is an obvious, good likeness in pen-and-ink.

12. Simple line and tone can give a good effect.

13. Features spelt out in an obvious likeness in pen and ink.

The gradual building-up of a
portrait, dividing the head into
planes, areas and lines.

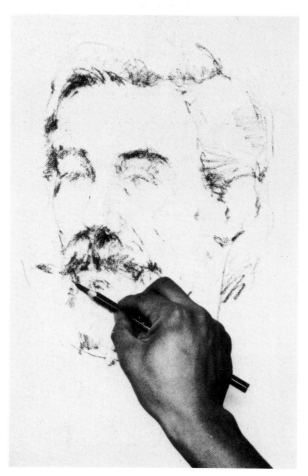

A finished drawing, achieved
in approximately ten minutes.

51

The building-up of a portrait of a girl. In this case the artist began with the mouth and nose and used these as starting-off points; other artists prefer to begin with the eyes and then move on to the nose.

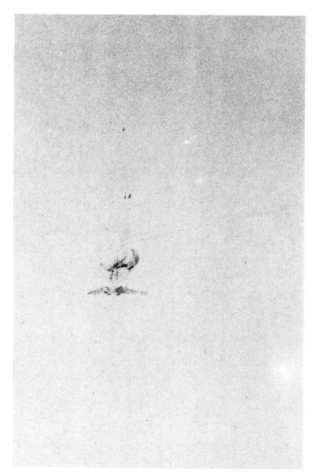

of the chin, and between the top of the ear and the bottom (though ears vary enormously). The top of the ear is on the same level as the eyelid. Newcomers doing a face from memory will simply forget that an eye-unit consists of three parts, the eye itself, the eyebrows and the eyelids. Eyes are the key to a good portrait.

Of course it is not obligatory to start with the eyes. Some artists prefer to begin with background shadows, using these as a guide to the features. This is not a bad idea for newcomers, for shadows are shapes which do not have meanings and there is no temptation to read more into them. Shadow areas can be built up bit by bit with hatching, and this helps when the time comes to put in more determined lines. There are many ways of doing a portrait, and no one best way. The aim is to get a likeness, and a well-drawn face means nothing at all if it is not like the sitter. Of course, the sitter may not like it, but that is a matter for him or her.

The slightest shift of angle will dramatically alter the look of a face, and amateur sitters may find it very difficult to keep the same pose for any length of time. If you are doing a serious portrait, even in pencil or pen-and-ink, it is advisable to use a camera to establish the pose – preferably a Polaroid so that it can be referred to and any change of position noted and rectified. The usual pose for a portrait is a three-quarter, which is without doubt easier than a full frontal. With full face there cannot be any divergence between the left and right sides. Profile used to be a very popular position, but the slightest error is noticeable. Uptilted and downtilted heads do not present many problems provided that you look at what you are doing and are aware of the foreshortening.

When drawing a face, try to forget what the individual features are. You are not playing some guessing game. It is easy enough to draw a pair of lips by themselves and get them recognized as such, but in doing a portrait the lower lip may, in certain light, be merely a protrusion with a shadow underneath. There may be nothing to show the lower lip is there; *except* the shadow underneath. Again, the nose may only exist in the form of a shadow.

As you are working only in black and white, you will have to ignore the colour of the hair. Black hair need not necessarily show up as black where the light is on it. The amount of detail in hair depends entirely on you. You obviously cannot put every hair in, but if you wish to suggest hair by a pattern of parallel lines, by all means do so, especially if the rest of the face has been done with attention to detail.

Although it may be difficult to say 'No!' try to

This delightful study
successfully captures the
warmth and softness of the
subject.

This self-portrait
has been quickly executed by
an artist in control of his
medium.

The success of this sketch lies
in the way the hand is
supporting the head and is
suggestive of its weight.

56

stop a sitter seeing work-in-progress. The merest final touch may make all the difference between a portrait being accurate or not. It might mean just a millimetre added on the pupil of an eye. When it is finished, who judges whether the portrait is 'like'? The famous portraitist William Rothenstein went to Oxford to draw 24 prominent citizens:

'I usually found that each of my sitters thought twenty-three of them excellent likenesses, the twenty-fourth being their own.'

The trials of a professional portrait-painter are illustrated by the fact that when Sir Joshua Reynolds, the first President of the Royal Academy, died, he had on his hands 300 rejected portraits.

Animal Drawing

If you are drawing an animal, even a pet, always remember that at any time it can suddenly move and the odds are against it moving back to exactly the same position. So if you are drawing from life, rapid sketches are more sensible than careful meticulous drawings. Charcoal is ideal for quick work, for you can swiftly brush off with the finger tips lines that are of no use when the animal changes position. Many professional wild-life artists have a collection of stuffed animals and birds (this sometimes shows in their finished work), but you may have to resort to photographs or a natural history museum.

Much that has been said about figure drawing applies to animal drawing. Do not bother too much about how the animal is built up, with skin on flesh and flesh on skeleton. Proportions are vital, but generally speaking animals are

Drawing animals can be quite a problem. Practise sketching them as quickly as possible.

57

Drawing several animals on the same piece of paper makes an interesting composition and is economical at the same time.

Horses and cows make good
subjects as they are fairly
docile and tend to ignore the
artist.

The head of a horse. Most animals have longer necks than one might imagine, but painters of the horse in previous times have shown a tendency to elongate the neck to a ridiculous degree in order to give an impression of speed.

The torso and legs of an animal within a square – well illustrated in this drawing of a horse.

easier to draw than human beings because they are more of a piece and have a limited repertoire of actions. For example, cows are either standing up or lying down. They do not lie on their backs, or have one leg in the air, unless there is something wrong with them. The cow is an ideal animal subject for when it moves it moves very slowly and it is chunky and compact. It is easy to relate one shape to another, and as the legs are relatively short it is easier to get them in proportion, whereas a horse has long legs, with consequent difficulty in getting them the right length.

Professional artists have probably drawn more horses than any other animal because it has paid well, and the horse artist, even if not very good, has never been short of commissions. Many 18th-century painters of horses seem never to have looked at a real horse, and persisted in painted horses in gallop with their four legs outstretched at the same time. Eventually photography showed artists that this was not right, but if the early painters had used more observation they would have known the correct sequence of legs. A moral of this is to draw what you see, not what you think is there. But the 19th-century Frederick Remington and Charles M. Russell, for instance, were notable for their accuracy.

The more compact an animal is, the easier, and an animal in repose makes a more convenient model than one astir. Animals with the same all-over texture are less difficult than those which have a mixture of smooth hair and long hair and rough hair, such as a dog. Novices would do well to start with cats and rabbits.

Draw only those animals which are of interest to you. If you like cats draw cats, if you like dogs draw dogs, and if there are technical problems, struggle with them. To judge by amateur drawings which turn up – not at auctions but at jumble sales, boot sales and the like – more people draw dogs than any other animal, and even if there are faults in the execution the affection shows through. There are certain errors which are repeated in drawing after drawing. The ears are in the wrong place, the back legs don't look right, and there is no animation in the eyes (to avoid this, put in a highlight in the pupil, in the centre so that the dog does not appear cross-eyed). This applies even if, when drawing the dog, there does not appear to be any highlight. With drawing cats, the main difficulty seems to be the nose and

Here the artist has immortalized his favourite pet.

'Shona' 26-7-82

the nostrils and in indicating the mouth without having the cat grinning. The coat of a cat is easier to draw than that of a dog as it 'flows' in a more consistent way.

The men who drew the most lively and realistic dogs and cats were not the high-flying painters of the academies but the cartoonists of magazines such as *Punch* in the 19th century, with its Charles Keene and John Leech. Bound volumes are in libraries and for sale second-hand and it is worthwhile looking at them and discovering how animals should be drawn.

It is often overlooked when drawing animals from memory that they have necks, and that the legs are set further back than you would imagine. A useful guide-line is that in many animals, and in most of the familiar ones such as cows, horses and dogs, the distance from the front of the forelegs to the back of the rear legs is the same as the distance from the ground to the top of the body. In other words, the torso and legs of a standing animal are contained in a

perfect square. If there is any part of an animal that presents difficulties, it is the leg, especially the back leg. The curious shape of a dog's back legs is obvious, but those of other animals are not so straightforward as you might remember. When drawing animals in herds, it is not usually necessary to make a study of each of them. This is more apparent in paintings, where sheep (simple animals to draw) are often represented by landscapists as blobs with a bit of black at one end and four sticks as legs.

Birds are delightful to draw because they have so few component parts, and it is not difficult to relate wing length to body length. There is however little point in trying to draw them in real life. The wild-life programmes on television are a boon to bird artists, as they are to all wild-life painters, giving close-ups we would never experience otherwise.

The main problem with drawing birds lies in depicting the feathers. These are not fixed on in a haphazard manner but have a structure.

An atmospheric drawing of a graveyard. There is a brooding quality of neglect suggested by the overgrown foliage, which has been strongly suggested through the use of pencil work.

The simplest way to describe this is that the feathers occur in overlapping segments of feather batches, each of which throws shadows on to those lying beneath it. The feathers of the tail lying over and shadowing the body can be seen clearly. The legs of a bird are very slender indeed, and when the bird is on the ground it is very tempting to draw the legs when in fact they cannot be seen.

Perhaps the easiest creatures to draw are mice, hamsters and jerbils and similar small animals. There are several reasons for this. One is that they can be taken in with one glance and it is simple to relate one part of the body to another. Two, their legs are small and partly hidden so that it is difficult to get them out of proportion, and three, the coat is usually of a consistent texture.

Landscape

Landscape-drawing and painting are among the great pleasures of life, even for those who are just setting out on their artistic career, whether 16 or 60. It is easy to get dewy-eyed on the subject of nature, and we tend to take it for granted, along with Wordsworth and his daffodils. We may look at nature at its most spectacular if we are told to in a guide-book, but too often it is something we pass by.

Nature does not move very much, so you can spend as much or as little time drawing one subject as you wish. However, the lighting does change, often dramatically, though this is of more concern to painters than to those who are just using a pencil or pen-and-ink. Shadows change gradually with the passing hours, and not too quickly to put down. Once again it is important that a house is not seen as a rectangle with four squares in it for windows, but as a pattern of light and shade. Remember what you are looking at and forget what it is, and watch for groupings. Draw something interesting to *you*, not something which you feel is a right and proper subject for the Artistic with a capital A. If you like bungalows, draw bungalows rather than the local church. If ordinary landscape bores you, stick to the town – many famous artists have built up their reputations from their pictures of the suburbs.

As with all kinds of art, you have a multitude of choices, not only with the particular view you have selected out of countless options, but whether you decide to do it 'straight' or refine it. In other words, making a composition.

The first thing to do after you have settled down, whether you are sitting on a convenient bench with your sketchbook in hand, or standing in front of an easel, or sitting at your car

Pylons and power stations always provide interesting shapes to draw. Rather than try to draw each individual line and cable, the artist has selected the main features and his loose approach gives the feel of the massive complexity of the installation.

*Dungeness
Power Sta.*

window, is to draw the horizon and the eye-level. You must bear in mind perspective, and remember that all things above the eye-level lead down to the horizon and all things below lead up. The horizon may be obscured by hills or trees, but that does not matter. A pencil held up at arm's length in line with the eye will give you the horizon. Do not change position half-way through a drawing, as this will alter your eye-level.

Everything which reaches the eye is really of the same importance. Do not pick out the features which seem of most concern and emphasize them unduly, keep windows and doors the right size and do not go overboard on detail, unless that happens to be your style. If you want to count the layers of brick on a building, by all means do so, but there will be more than you think, and painstakingly putting in every single brick can be tiresome. Too much detail on the light part of a drawing can counteract the shading. If there is detail, the foreground is the best place to put it, and do not *imagine* detail in the middle distance or far distance.

Trees are most likely to be a stumbling block in a simple country view, and it is very easy to make them symmetrical. Mostly they are not.

Right: In complete contrast to the illustration above, the eye level is above the subject.

Every artist has an individual way of doing trees, but very few of them past or present put on every leaf. A suggestion of leafiness is the main thing. The basic shape of the tree is best seen in winter when except for evergreens they are leafless, and the way the branches go is often very interesting. The variety of leafage on a tree is not, as often depicted, expressed in a change of colour, but in light and shade. Leaves usually grow in masses, each of which has a light and dark part, and the shadow of which will fall on some other group of leaves. It is important to make the tree seem solid. The trunks are much simpler to do than the leaves, and the characteristics of the various kinds of tree can be demonstrated with shading. A tree is one of the few landscape objects where shadows do alter dramatically, and too much time spent drawing-in infinite detail is time wasted. The shadows and the entire disposition of light and shade will have altered by the time the drawing is completed.

Bushes should be looked at closely, for the changes of tone need not be dramatic. Half-close the eyes and try to compare the various tones inside the bush. If the bush is in the foreground you may find yourself looking into it from above. Sometimes the bottom of the bush in deep shadow is enlivened by grass and plants which are in the light, and these silhouette themselves against the shadows. These can be depicted in drawings by taking an eraser and, holding it by the edge, 'drawing' in the blades of grass with a corner of the eraser, lining in the shade of the blade of grass with a precise pencil line. Hedgerows are very good to have in the distance or middle distance, as they can be used to define fields and establish relative sizes of features such as barns and cottages.

If you are going to use trees or tree parts in the foreground it is not a bad idea to collect a few typical branches and take them home and draw them, but do not pick any wild plants. Expanses of grass can be a minor difficulty. Except in the immediate foreground individual blades of grass are not seen, and can be best registered with shading. Tufts have a shaded side, and cast shadows on to the ground. In the middle distance grass can best be represented by grading the tone as the surface of the ground rises and drops. The ground itself is important, and by the use of shading you have to specify which way it is going, whether it is tilted, what happens when it dips. Whereas in much landscape detail we have to forget what we know in order to see accurately, when we are dealing with the surface on which all the features are positioned the only way we know which way the ground is going is by the light and shade.

A selection of plants can be gathered and taken home to be drawn or to make a pleasing watercolour.

Landscapes, like townscapes, naturally involve all the problems of perspective, both linear and aerial.

The artist has employed a variety of techniques to produce this delightful drawing. Note the use of white paint to raise the highlights out of the cream-tone background.

In a drawing (but of course not a painting) the sky and the clouds are of minor importance, and if clouds are put in they should be put in lightly as otherwise their presence will overwhelm what is happening on the ground below. Water in a landscape is always a plus, and the reflections in water can add great interest to a picture. It is necessary to really *look* at reflections, and not put in replicas of what is above the water level. Rippling water makes nonsense of mirror images. There is a weird sort of perspective in reflections, and there is also the question of refraction, in which the reflections do not make sense. It is important to look and digest.

It is very easy to make a stream or brook look like a path, and even when using a watercolour it does not help to paint it blue. Sometimes a stream needs to be suggested, its existence noted with waterside reeds, so that the viewer picks up the clues.

No matter where you go, always take a sketch-book with you. Those with a spiral back are the best, and the small postcard size will get you into the habit of making thumbnail sketches. Draw anything that appeals to you, even if it might seem outside your technical ability. If you are going out, work out the potential sketching possibilities – a cup of coffee in a place where there are secluded side seats and nooks and crannies so that you can sketch without someone peering over your shoulder, a country car-trip where there are parking places convenient to good sketching territory, a visit to a friend's house where there are good roof-top views from a convenient window and there may be interesting subjects to look down on. Even if you feel the sketches are failures, do not throw them away. At the very least they will be an indication in the future of your progress. And everybody gets more proficient, never less.

Townscape

Most books on practical painting do not mention townscape, which is a pity because it offers much to those who live in towns and who find the countryside somewhat alien. Although it does not always do to generalize, a townscape is usually simpler to draw and paint than a landscape, especially for those who have come to grips with perspective. You are also not diverted from looking for the differences in light and shade by too much colour. Townscapes can merge into landscapes, but the gaunt industrial towns of the north have their own kind of sombre beauty and even, as in the paintings of L. S. Lowry, a wistful charm. Many of the recommendations for country drawing apply to townscapes – do not let the detail in the middle distance get out of hand, draw when there are interesting shadow-shapes about, let the features stand out for themselves and do not over-emphasize important features. Sometimes a townscape looks odd without figures, and although this will not matter much in a drawing which is meant to represent what you are seeing, if the drawing is worked up into a painting, figures – inserted according to the rules of perspective – do add interest to a townscape. No need to go mad with them, as Lowry did. They also serve as splashes of colour in paintings, and are useful for setting

The people and traffic are mere suggestions in this sketch, but the bustle of the street is well captured and contrasts well with the grandeur of the building behind.

69

On this spread, the artist has demonstrated some of the problems you may come across when drawing a townscape with people.

Cars *(above)* are always difficult to draw in perspective as they have few straight lines.

This interesting perspective drawing *(right)* has the front of the car below eye level, with buildings receding dramatically in the background.

the scale of the adjacent buildings and other features. As with traditional landscape, water adds interest; in townscapes it is usually a river or a canal. Many of today's canals are derelict and consequently picturesque – and usually situated in the inner suburbs and run-down areas. What with traffic and hordes of people, it is often advisable to carry a camera with you when searching for townscapes.

When you are adding figures to a landscape or a townscape, always remember that they have shadows which must go the same way as those already in the picture. Shadows can be useful if you are putting in groups of people, and cast shadows, where one person is standing obscuring or partly obscuring a neighbour, can depict figures as certainly as line. Look on

groups of people not as a collection of distinct individuals but as a tonal block – adjoining rectangular shapes with protrusions on top (the heads). Legs are less evident in groups of people, especially if there are strong shadows. For townscapes to be really believable, they need to contain objects we take for granted and hardly notice are there, for example, cars, moving and parked. As with figures, they often add colour to a picture or an accent in an otherwise empty spot, but if you draw a car from memory you will find it an odd experience. You will probably over-emphasize the upper part of the car, which is actually little more than a glass box on top of the solid bodywork. The wheels also pose a problem; how much is hidden under the wings? You need to *look* at

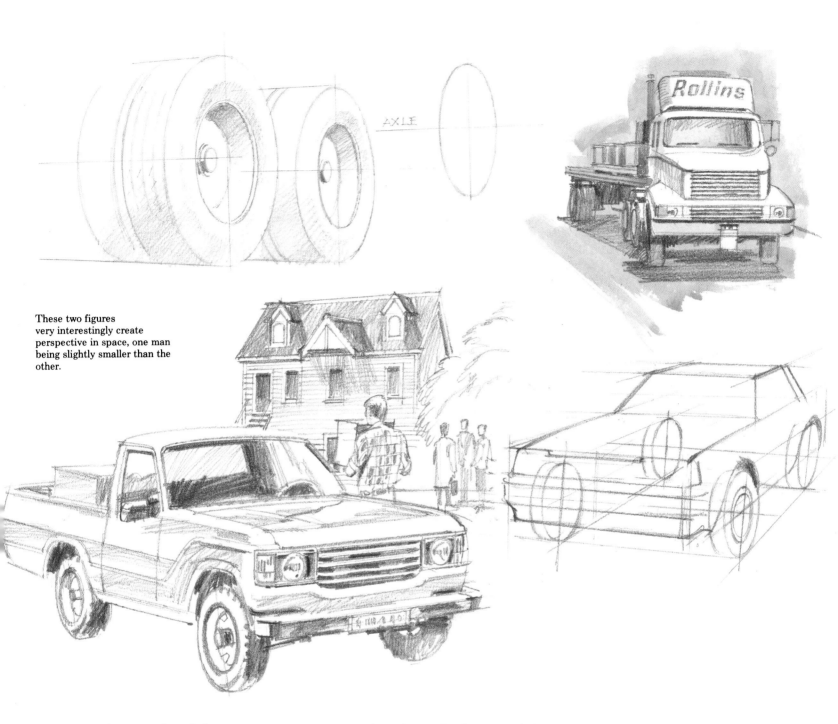

These two figures
very interestingly create
perspective in space, one man
being slightly smaller than the
other.

Practise drawing wheels and
perspective lines on vehicles.

cars or at photographs of them.

When drawing cars, shadows are very important, for if there is any light at all the area beneath the wings and the car itself will be in dense shadow. Although it does not matter so much in drawing, the metal of the car will throw off highlights, and in paintings these highlights can be employed very effectively. Drawing cars is a good way of getting to know how to draw other mechanical objects, and coming to terms with circular objects which turn into ellipses as they turn away from us or to us. Whether the angle of the ellipse is *exactly* right is of less importance than the need to keep it symmetrical, and not have odd bulges on one side. By all means use aids to get your wheels right. Stationers keep a stock of stencils of various

sized circles and other useful shapes, and these stencils can also be used for ellipses by tracing down one side, and then the other, leaving out the section in the middle and joining the two arcs together by freehand. It will not be a perfect ellipse, but it should prove convincing enough and that is the object of it all – what looks right, is right. If you are putting imaginary cars into a townscape, or, for that matter, a landscape, work out whether the windows will look transparent or opaque. One of the main points to remember about cars is that they are not very high; a man of reasonable height can stand by a car and rest his elbows on the roof. So in a street scene with pedestrians and traffic, pedestrians' heads will always appear well above the roofs of the cars.

Still Life

A drawing of a landscape, townscape, portrait or figure will often stand by itself as a work of art. A still life rarely does. Still-life drawings are usually used as a basis for a painting or as an exercise, and even the most accomplished still-life drawing is not intrinsically interesting. The one great advantage of still life is that you are in control of the composition, arranging the lighting as you want it, getting the shadows you like, and grouping the objects in the most acceptable manner.

Naturally you collect what objects you want when setting up a still life, and although fruit and jugs are the obvious things to select they can be impersonal. So why not build up a still life with objects which have some connection with you, have pleasant associations, or present some interesting but not insoluble problem? It can be anything from a small statuette, a seaside ornament, to a book. A book is an ideal thing to draw because it is symmetrical and can act as a perspective guide to other items in the assemblage.

It is good not only to have a variety of shapes but a variety of textures as well, so drape some material around, letting it partly obscure some of the objects. The items do not have to be in the middle of the picture, nor do they have to be piled in a heap all at the same distance from the artist. Something placed in the foreground will make a picture more interesting.

When drawing the various objects which surround you, try to suggest their intrinsic qualities of hardness, softness and texture with the use of tone.

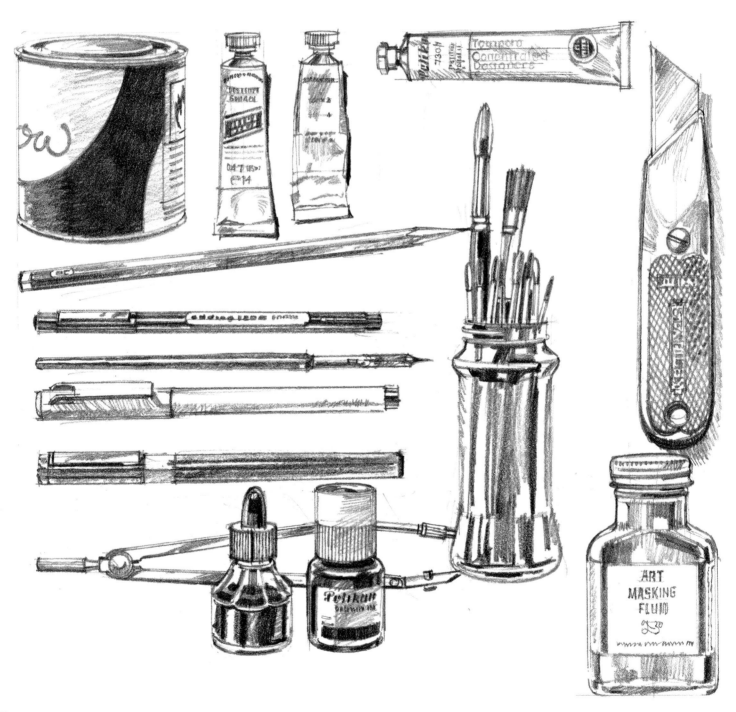

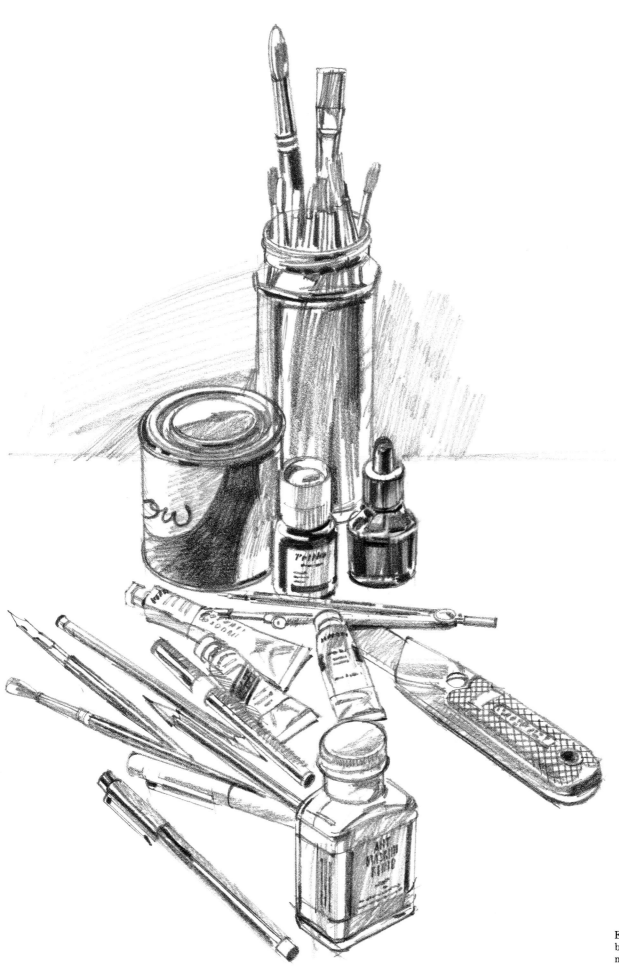

Exactly the same objects as
before but arranged in a rather
more pleasing composition.

Let the eye roam around the still life, examining the possibility of turning it into an interior drawing. Look at the window, which may be your light source; notice how it is much darker in the area immediately around the window frame. Where there are deep shadows, put them in in deep black, using charcoal or Conté crayon, smudging with the finger tip if you like.

Flower painting comes into the general area of still life, if the flowers are set in a vase or a bowl on a table. They are not in their natural habitat, and can be manipulated as desired. Flowers demand colour, and perhaps pencil is the least suitable medium except as a try-your-skill exercise. Unlike many other objects in nature, there is a change of colour in flowers and not just tone, and when doing a drawing it is important to decide what is happening. In flowers there are many varieties of shadows, and although the drawing of petals and leaves presents few problems in itself, these petals and leaves cast shadows on other petals and leaves, and so on and so on. So before even putting pencil to paper it is necessary to study such shadows, moving the light source around and seeing the result.

Some flowers are easier to draw than others. Those with a multitude of small shapes such as a hyacinth are more difficult than flowers with a fully comprehensible structure such as a rose.

Quick washes laid down as above can be brought to life with pen and ink.

74

Seascape

Much of what has been said about landscapes applies to seascapes and, if anything, seascapes are easier, provided you put the horizon in *exactly* the horizontal position – otherwise the sea will appear to be slipping downhill. Ships are fine subjects for drawing, but it is best to get them right, for it is incredible how many people know about ships and which way the sails should go and why that mast is two metres (or should it be a furlong?) too tall. In a landscape, it does not matter if the tree is the wrong shape; in boats it does.

Boats are usually entities in themselves and, unlike some landscape features, they make sense, and can be summed up at a glance. Boats in the foreground or tied up together at a quay can also be figured out, even though you may not know what all the ropes are for. The shadows on boats are also comprehensible; if the shadow is on one side of the boat, it will apply to *all* that side and, as the superstructure is usually in one block, cast shadows are not much of a problem. Do not get bogged down with all the ropes and lines unless you are doing a very detailed drawing.

Seascapes are usually more interesting if there is subject matter in the foreground (even if it is only a few rocks or an extra-special wave). Painters of the old school often put in a red marker buoy to add interest to the foreground.

It is often an advantage to have an indication of land in the distance. This will rest on the

All the ingredients of the sketch *(above)* can be practised before arriving at the final picture.

75

This pleasing seascape can be finished off at home provided you have remembered to make on-the-spot visual references in your sketchbook.

horizon, not intrude into the sea-space unless it is in the middle distance.

If you are trying to do waves in pencil you are tempting providence; it is sufficient to get the *feel* of waves, and not be precise. Waves are good for painting, but not for pencil work, and seascapes in pencil can never be really convincing. They should be regarded as sketches for paintings. Seascapes are among the most enjoyable type of pictures to do.

It is very restful to look at the sea, and if you have a seascape in mind remember how waves react, how they form and break, and how, very important, they fit into a pattern of other waves and water movement. The *look* of the sea is far more significant than the accuracy of the odd wave. Nowhere is reference to photographs of other artists' work so useful as in depicting the sea; everyone has their own method. The Venetians such as Canaletto used an unconvincing pattern of flat U-shapes, but others have done really convincing seas, even quite minor artists now almost forgotten.

Photographs of seas are useful but not as much as photographs of other artists' endeavours, who somehow had to express the constantly moving. Television and video are enormous helps in letting us see, via the freeze frame in video, exactly what water in motion looks like.

Waves, too, obey the laws of perspective, and recede according to the rules; they also have shadows, but judging by the blobs of blue and green in the paintings of real novices they are often forgotten.

Right: There is no perspective in the sea. Waves become smaller and eventually disappear on the horizon. This can be seen in the Turner seascape *(below): Calais Pier: An English Packet Arriving.*

78

PICTURE MAKING

It is easy to get preoccupied with the various kinds of paints, watercolours, oils, acrylic, pastels and other materials and think they are divided into exclusive compartments. They do require different equipment, but if divisions are to be made there are just two – paints which go with water and paints which go with oils. However, even this division is not sacred. For example, the sculptor Henry Moore used oil pastels and watercolours for his drawings, which do not mix. That is why he used them. His aim was to make the oil-pastel drawing stand out from the background, so he used the oil pastel first for his main features and then covered the paper with a watercolour wash, which, being repelled by the oil pastels, filled in the area not covered by the initial drawing. The

work done in pastel therefore came through boldly.

So when you start off a picture, do not have too definite a view of the end product. If it is a drawing it might be advantageous to develop it into a watercolour or a pastel, or if it is a watercolour it can turn into an acrylic or, if you size over watercolour, into an oil painting. Similarly a drawing in oil pastel can turn into an oil painting. If this seems about to happen, you do not always need to size the paper, but let the oil paint soak into the surface. This results in a flat matt rather intriguing surface.

When you are working outdoors you have to be careful about how much equipment to take with you, but indoors there is a lot to be said for having *all* your painting equipment within easy reach. This can be a glorious muddle, and if you have a large table or working surface so much the better.

In picture making you have a number of

Salisbury Cathedral from the Meadows by John Constable. Places of architectural interest have long been a favourite subject for painters.

A typically adventurous painting by Turner in which the oil paint is used almost like watercolour, allowing the canvas to show through. This painting gives the impression of having been formed from accidental blotches and blobs of paint, though Turner was the last man to reveal the secrets of his techniques.

choices. You can use pencil sketches made beforehand, or you can build up the painting as you go along, leaving some of it to chance. The 'blob' school of watercolour painters who included many good English watercolourists of the turn of the century laid down small splashes of colour and then meditated upon them until they could see an embryo picture – rather like looking at pictures in the fire. In some of his watercolour work J. M. W. Turner did much the same.

If you use preliminary sketches you can either reproduce them more or less exactly, or you can shift the subject around to make the picture hang together better – in other words making a composition of it. But there are certain subjects you may want to set down accurately. If you are doing a picture of your house you do not want to shift around the chimneys, alter the disposition of the rose bushes in the garden, or change the shapes of tree branches to make them look more artistic. You want a record, just as you do if you undertake a portrait. Similarly, if you are doing

a well-loved landscape you do not want to move the elements around to make it pretty. You want it as it is, warts and all.

Remember that you are doing the picture for yourself. A visual autobiography can be enchanting to look back on, charting not only past events but your increase in expertise. If this is the reason you paint, nurture it – and *do not throw anything away!* Even if the picture does not quite come off, it may bring back memories. No one is going to give you a prize for a better-than-average picture.

If the picture you are doing is imaginary, even if based on a real subject, you can include anything in it, including the improbable and impossible. Fantasy pictures are immense fun to do and may have some therapeutic benefit. If you know the rules, it is sometimes refreshing to forget them, and have different perspectives in the same picture, or even eliminate perspective altogether.

Reference has already been made to composition. This is something you can take into account or discard. At its simplest, composition

80

All the right ingredients are here to make a nice little drawing.

Here, the same ingredients are used in two dimensions.

Again, the same ingredients, but here they are used three-dimensionally to make a satisfying composition.

Two lively high-toned illustrations. Mediterranean scenes of this nature benefit from a fluid technique with the colour loosely applied.

is making an interesting picture from a boring subject, and there is a good analogy in photography. Every photographic album contains architectural views – the White House, Empire State Building, or Stonehenge. How utterly boring most of these photographs are, the building set in the middle of the snap, nothing in the foreground except grass or a loved one. When we look at a professional's photograph of the same subject, what a difference! The professional looks at angles, the light, foreground interest (and is concerned with keeping the camera still).

When you are sketching or painting on the spot it is sometimes difficult to decide which is the best vantage point (and sometimes you will not be able to get at the best vantage point because there is already something there such as an intrusive building). If you do not particularly want an exact visual record, then you can alter things when you get home.

The most important point about composition is to get the spectator to look *into* the picture and not *across* it, to focus on an area of interest, not necessarily in the centre. The part of the picture that attracts or pulls the eye towards it is sometimes known as an anchor. Degas often had his focal point at the extreme edge of the picture. If you can get the eye to come to rest on something in the picture so much the better. The most obvious way is to use perspective, the receding lines leading into the focal point, and in some way blocking them so that they do not lead out again. You can improve composition by raising or lowering the horizon, and you can use shadows to direct the attention. Foreground detail can also draw the viewer in, and if overloaded can keep the attention there – though it may be that this is what you want.

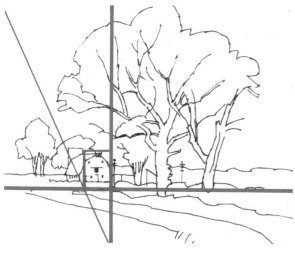

Composite drawings showing use of the Golden Section.

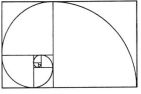

The Golden Section

Beauty can be a matter of mathematics as well as aesthetics, and something that is designed on mathematical principles will also look right. An example of this is the Golden Section, which the ancient Greeks used in the design of the Parthenon in Athens, and which is aesthetically very pleasing. It is a particular ratio between height and width, in the approximate proportion 13 : 8, though this cannot be expressed as an exact fraction. A rectangle constructed according to the Golden Section can be divided into a square and a smaller rectangle, and this smaller rectangle will have exactly the same proportions as the original one (see the diagram). Of course, this smaller rectangle can also be divided into a square and a yet smaller rectangle of the same proportions, and so on for ever. The pattern obtained by joining corresponding points on the rectangles drawn by this division is exactly the same spiral as you see in seashells, which shows that the Golden Section can be found in nature as well as architecture.

In this charcoal drawing, on a grey-blue washed background, the artist has cleverly used a paint brush to highlight the road and barn.

In the charming little seascape *(far right)* the artist has first of all quickly sketched in the areas he wishes to paint, over a blue-grey washed background. He has then simply blocked in the patches of colour and finally used a charcoal/Conté-type pencil to draw over the top to produce this pleasing effect.

In the old days there were reckoned to be golden rules of composition, and much time was spent by theorists in analysing the works of the great masters of the Renaissance to see how they behaved or how they fell short. To some of these self-styled experts, painting was geometry in action, and joy was unconfined when they found this or that painter using rules, especially when the subject of a well-known picture was in the form of a triangle (in Virgin and Child pictures it would have been difficult to avoid). Even better when one triangle on its base was balanced by an inverted triangle, or there were intricate interrelated triangles to glorify.

It is probable that artists such as the 15th-century Italian artist Piero della Francesca used a geometrical scaffold to base pictures on, and many artists, such as Hogarth, have published their ideas, though Hogarth does not seem to have acted on his theory of the 'curve of beauty'. There is therefore a lot of weighty theory about classical composition, and it can

be satisfying to sketch in a geometrical figure and use it as the basis of a picture. But what is good composition to one can be boring to another. If composition can render a service, it is to stop the subject matter 'leaking' out of the edge of the picture.

One of the questions that arises if you are doing a watercolour (but not an oil) is whether to put in the outer limits of the picture when you start, in other words rule in a border. With a canvas you naturally cover the whole area. There are no hard and fast rules about a border; it helps some, hinders others, but if you are keen on composition and a balanced scheme then a border can be an asset. If you paint in a fantasy or formal style a decorated border can be an advantage – if it is carried out systematically. A geometric border which gets tedious because of the repetition and is skimped is worse than nothing at all. If the edges of a watercolour are getting ragged and inconclusive remember that you can always hide them under a mount – or cut them off.

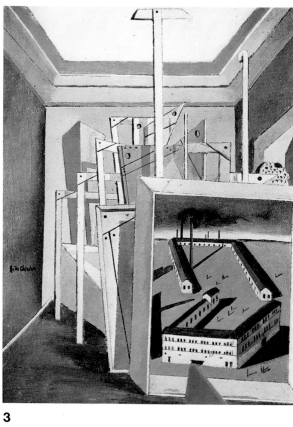

The fifteenth-century artist Piero della Francesca based most of his compositions on geometrical principles, as in his *Madonna and Child* (1) and *The Flagellation of Christ* (2). In stark contrast to the medieval beauty of Piero della Francesca is de Chirico, whose fantasized paintings (3 and 4) demand natural inquiry and attention to hold the viewer. He totally abuses the laws of perspective in order to distort one's senses. Salvador Dali's amazing skills and draughtsmanship in his paintings, such as *Christ of St John of the Cross* (5), can produce the magical uniqueness that should be the aspiration of any artist, whether exploring simple drawing techniques or as in the advanced classicism of the Virgin and Child in the frontispiece

5

If you are embarking on a fantasy or surrealist picture in the style of Dali or Chirico, try and keep to the same technique throughout. You can mix your mediums, but a medley of styles in the same picture never really works. It can be great fun working in someone else's style, doing a pastiche.

You must not feel you are being curtailed, and that certain techniques are artistically out of bounds. Not everyone has the egotism of certain famous painters who feel that even their thumb print is of value to someone. There are still numbers of techniques waiting to be found: so far as I know, nobody has yet experimented with painting on polystyrene ceiling tiles.

If you are one of those people who embark on a project with a set idea and are reluctant to be diverted from your path, you may think it trivial to doodle or to let the painting take over.

A bit of doodling, if you happen to be a name, can be worth a fortune.

On 23 March 1983 there was a sale of modern and Impressionist art at Sotheby's, London. One of the pictures on show was *Nocturne* by the Spanish painter Joan Miro. The estimate was £150,000–£200,000, and in the event it made £270,000 (about $500,000). This is how Miro himself – a charming artist with a rich vein of invention – described the origin of the painting, in 1940–41:

'After my work (on oil paintings) I dipped my brushes in petrol and wiped them on the white sheets of paper from the album with no preconceived ideas. The blotchy surface put me in a good mood and provoked the birth of forms, human figures, animals, stars, the sky, and the moon and the sun. ... Once I had managed to obtain a plastic equilibrium and

Human and animal figures can be drawn realistically using a variety of techniques, and sometimes, through caricature and cartoon, humorously.

90

bring order among all these elements, I began to paint in gouache, with the minute detail of a craftsman and a primitive.'

So when you have conquered the art of drawing to the best of your ability, or have decided that you have mastered it sufficiently to go on from there, there is a whole world of adventure and colour waiting for you. You may find that drawing is so fascinating in itself that that is sufficient, and you decide to pursue it, perhaps going into cartooning and caricature, the art of exaggeration and compression. It is up to you. But the ability to put something on paper which is not an aimless doodle is priceless, and easily come by. As I said at the start of this book, it is like playing the piano – only easier.

91

FRAMING

A good drawing is worth framing, and the instant that it is framed and stuck on a wall it gains an added prestige. 'It must be good if it is worth framing', visitors will think. Professional framing can be expensive, and it is worthwhile shopping around as prices vary enormously. One framer may charge twice as much as someone else for exactly the same job. The most reasonable are those who do framing 'for the trade', and they will be the best qualified to decide what colour or size of mount is the best.

Framing kits are widely available, but it is much cheaper to resurrect secondhand frames, bought at junk shops, garage sales, jumble sales and boot fairs for very little money. If you are framing watercolours, and only watercolours, do not be tempted to buy dozens of frames without glass, for although glass is not expensive it will mean going to a hardware store to get it cut or cutting it yourself as odd pieces of glass that you have lying around will rarely fit the frames you have.

If you buy a secondhand frame, clean it thoroughly and if some of the moulding is missing be firm and get rid of the whole lot. When the frame is clean it can be sanded down and painted, varnished, or if pine or a light wood, treated with linseed oil or wax and burnished with a soft cloth.

When cleaning the glass use detergent or a glass-cleaning agent, and perhaps a scrubbing brush. Flymarks may need to be picked off with the blade of a knife. When washed and dried the glass should be placed on a sheet of white paper and examined to make certain that it is clean. There is nothing worse than putting a picture in a frame and then seeing a smudge on the glass.

The glass will have been kept in place by almost anything – pins, nails, drawing-pins, Scotch tape – and there is little point in trying to reuse these. All old nails, etc., need to be taken out; if any are left there is a danger of breaking the glass by forcing it against nails which have been left in or have broken off. Professional framers use a stapler which pushes slivers of flat metal into the frame with great force but, for the occasional frame, brads, (headless tacks), are as good.

Drawings are seen at their best if mounted, and the mount itself should be bigger rather than smaller. A tiny drawing which does not look very exciting by itself can be transformed by placing it in the centre of a mount very much larger than itself. The equipment needed for cutting a mount are a surface such as a piece of thick card or wood – not a drawing-board as the knife will bite into the surface and ruin it; a craft knife or a scalpel; a steel rule, preferably of the safety kind; an ordinary rule, preferably transparent, for measuring; and a medium pencil such as HB.

Mounting-board is not expensive and comes in large sizes. Cut the size you want to fit the frame reasonably accurately, though absolute precision is not necessary as the mounting-board will be held in place by the brads. Measure the drawing to be framed, top to bottom, side to side, remembering that there must be a little overlap to go inside the space cut in the mount, and then divide in two the difference between the measurements of the mount and those of the picture. Put in your lines so that you have a grid; the intersecting lines should overlap slightly as they are then easier to see when using the knife. When cutting the mount keep the finger tips away from the edge of the steel rule; the rule will stay rigid if you splay the fingers. Never use a wooden rule or straight edge in association with a knife as no matter how much care is taken the knife blade will bite into the wood.

Three or four medium strokes with the knife are better than one deep stroke, and have the 'showing' side of the mount uppermost, otherwise there will be 'drag' and little flecks of card will stick up. If the piece cut out is 'sticky' go over the corners where the trouble is likely to be. Try not to cut past the intersections, though it will not show when the picture is framed.

Lining – putting lines round the aperture where the picture is to be – should be done carefully, and if not well done should not be done at all. If there is a risk of messing it up with a brush use a coloured pencil or pen and ink. The best kind of brush to use is the 'liner', made to do such work. Sometimes the spaces between the lines are colour-washed. Mounts for drawings are traditionally light in colour, but it is all a matter of personal preference.

A well-mounted drawing is sometimes spoiled by the addition of a picture title on the mount. A good artist need not necessarily be a good calligrapher. Or the wording might be ill-balanced, not lined-up, or on a slant. Use a ruler to set in the proportions of the letters, work out how long the words are, put them in lightly in pencil, and if you are not experienced do not use fancy lettering. A very good substitute for hand-lettering is Letraset. But a drawing need not necessarily have a title. It is a good idea to look at drawings and watercolours in galleries to see how they are framed, mounted, and entitled; even if the pictures in commercial galleries are uninteresting the owners know that good presentation can help enormously in selling them.

INTRODUCTION TO
Watercolour, gouache and tempera

94

CONTENTS

The White House by Thomas
Girtin.

Previous page: Shady Pool by
J. S. Cotman

96

Introduction

Painting in watercolours offers an immense scope for everybody. There is no end to the number of methods you can use, and watercolour can be used not only by itself but with pastels, coloured pencils, pen and ink, and acrylics – anything which is compatible with water.

You may wish to restrict yourself to what is known as the English method of watercolour painting, which means using the paints without the addition of white, as you use the white of the paper by allowing it to show through. Or you may wish to use not only thin washes but thick paint, and you have it in gouache. Gouache is well known to children in the form of powder paint, but refined it comes under a variety of names, such as designers' colours, poster paint, etc.

You work out the style which suits *you*. If you are good at drawing, you may like to create a picture meticulously and then colour it in. For added crispness, you may care to go round the shapes with a very fine pen. If you are no good at drawing, don't be alarmed. You can paint a perfectly good watercolour, without ever needing to touch a pencil, by relying on changes of colour and tone.

The accent of this book is on enjoyment. Nobody is paying you for painting a picture. But the satisfaction of creating something which only you can do can be unbelievable. Every person has the seeds of an artist in him or her. We just need encouraging!

WHAT ARE WATERCOLOURS?

Pigment mixed with a gum which acts as a binder; this binder is soluble in water. The traditional gum was gum arabic (which naturally came from Arabia) but it has been largely replaced by gum from a species of acacia tree grown in Africa. Gouache or opaque watercolour varies in quality from ordinary distemper to designers' colour.

Watercolour painting is older than oil painting, and was used by monks for illustrating manuscripts before they found that gouache, mixing their watercolour pigments with white, provided a better base for the inevitable gold embellishment. In the 17th century Dutch painters added a little colour to their drawings to liven them up; tinted drawings then became fashionable, the colours limited to blue, yellow, green, brown and rose madder. Among the first English artists to use the tinted drawing style was Francis Barlow (1626–1702). Watercolours were not regarded as at all important, but were records, notes for oil paintings, or sketches for engravings. Early papers were thin and fragile, and artists were obliged to scrape them to make them serviceable. Many artists made their own inks, sepia or black, and diluted them so that they could supplement pen-and-ink work with a thin ink wash.

Topographical artists commonly used a single wash, but the more adventurous found there were great possibilities in several washes, and different ways of applying paint, in dabs as used by David Cox or stippling where the paint is applied in the form of dots, as exploited by Birket Foster in innumerable village cottage scenes. Lifting the colour from the paper to expose highlights was done extensively by using rag, India-rubber, blotting paper, or dry bread. Francis Nicholson anticipated the use of masking fluid by applying a mixture of turpentine, beeswax and white, over which he painted his washes. When the wash had dried, he would lift his mixture with turpentine.

Shadows were put in with prussian blue and brown ink, and later by darker tones of the local colour. John Sell Cotman and Turner achieved their highlights by taking off the wet paint with the wooden end of the brush. This left a hard dark edge by creating a kind of canal at the edge of the highlight, an effect impossible to get with the brush and less brutal than lifting the colour off with a knife. John Varley's device was to paint upon thin paper laid on white card, and when he wanted a highlight he would scratch right through the paper so that the white of the card would show through.

Those watercolour artists who also did engravings found that they could duplicate drawings very well by taking blacklead impressions from an etched plate. It was very convenient for those who worked to a formula. Each watercolourist had his favourite colour scheme; John Cozens (1752–1799) used a basic palette of greys and blues with a very restricted use of brighter colours. John Webber (1750–1793) used blues, greys and light yellows.

Many 19th-century artists applied the paint to the paper without pencil drawings, using the splashes and blobs as a basis for a composition, others used rich watercolour to make a mosaic, and others returned to the tinted drawing format, with a difference. The works of Arthur Rackham and Edmund Dulac are tokens of what can be done in book illustration and are superb watercolour paintings in their own right. Watercolour lends itself equally to atmospheric suggestiveness or precision, and can do almost anything required.

WHAT MATERIALS ARE NEEDED?

Watercolours come in tubes or pans, sold in sets or separately. Artists' colours are a good deal more expensive than students' colours, which can be slightly grainy (though this can be an advantage as it provides interesting textures). Opaque watercolours, under whatever name, are sold in tubes, pans or jars; designers' colours are the best, though poster paint sold in jars is useful for covering large areas as it is cheaper. White gouache is sometimes known as process white and is sold in jars, and is extremely useful for eradicating mistakes on pen-and-ink work and pencil drawings. It can also be used to accompany ordinary transparent watercolour, either to provide highlights,

Watercolours provide a perfect medium for the artist to express himself by the quickness of technique and to capture the mood and atmosphere of his subject, as in this painting *Hurricane Bahamas* by Winslow Homer

or as a mix, when it is known as body colour. Watercolour in tubes is very concentrated, and a little goes a long way. For outdoor work a paint box with pans is the most convenient.

Mediums Normally the only medium needed is water, but gum arabic can be added, and so can megilp, which gives added brilliance and retards the drying.

Above: At first glance Alfred Jacob Miller's *Trappers Resting on the Trail* is of tightness and detail. Closer examination shows that it is just a collection of simple washes which make up the whole.

Right: The Needles by J. S. Cotman. A limited palette has produced this remarkable watercolour with only the boats in the foreground to give details.

Liquitex® Artist Water Colors
Tube Size ½″ x 3¼″, 6 per box

Color No.		Series 1841 Per Tube 6 tubes/box
110	ACRA® Crimson	●
112	ACRA® Red	●
114	ACRA® Violet	●
116	Alizarine Crimson	●
127	Burnt Siena	●
128	Burnt Umber	●
150	Cadmium Orange	●
152	Cadmium Red Light	●
154	Cadmium Red Medium	●
155	Cadmium Red Deep	●
160	Cadmium Yellow Light	●
161	Cadmium Yellow Med.	●
162	Cadmium Yellow Deep	●
164	Cerulean Blue	●
166	Chromium Oxide Green	●
170	Cobalt Blue	●
172	Cobalt Violet	●
186	Dioxazine Purple	●
190	Emerald Green	●
214	Green Earth	●
220	Hansa Yellow	●
224	Hooker's Green	●
225	Hooker's Green Light	●
240	Indian Red	●
244	Ivory Black	●
250	Lampblack	●
252	Lemon Yellow Hansa	●
258	Light Red Oxide	●
272	Manganese Blue	●
310	Payne's Gray	●
312	Permanent Green Light	●
316	Phthalocyanine Blue	●
317	Phthalocyanine Green	●
318	Prussian Blue	●
330	Raw Siena	●
331	Raw Umber	●
344	Rose Madder	●
360	Sepia Umber	●
380	Ultramarine Blue	●
388	Ultramarine Violet	●
390	Van Dyke Brown Umber	●
398	Viridian	●
413	Yellow Ochre	●
430	Zinc (Chinese) White	●

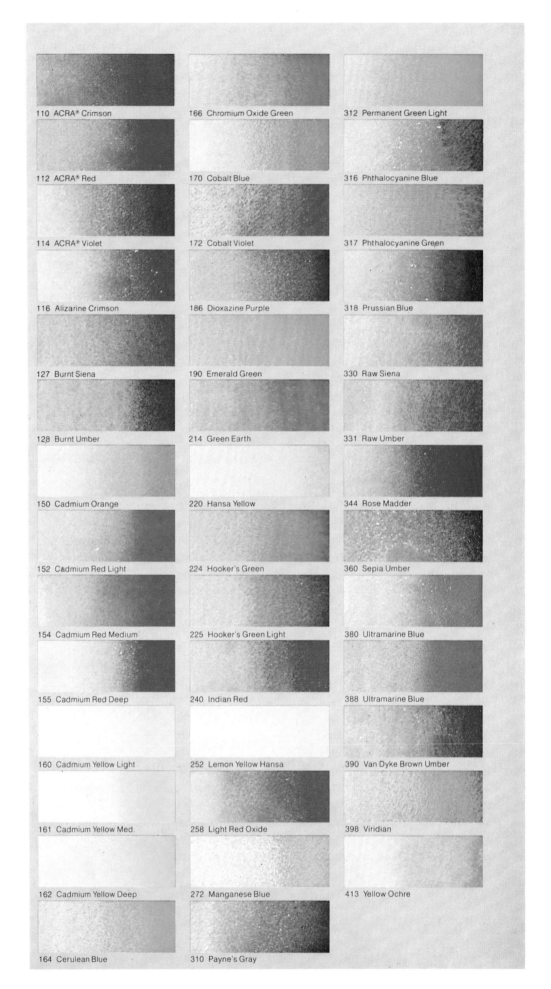

110 ACRA® Crimson
112 ACRA® Red
114 ACRA® Violet
116 Alizarine Crimson
127 Burnt Siena
128 Burnt Umber
150 Cadmium Orange
152 Cadmium Red Light
154 Cadmium Red Medium
155 Cadmium Red Deep
160 Cadmium Yellow Light
161 Cadmium Yellow Med.
162 Cadmium Yellow Deep
164 Cerulean Blue

166 Chromium Oxide Green
170 Cobalt Blue
172 Cobalt Violet
186 Dioxazine Purple
190 Emerald Green
214 Green Earth
220 Hansa Yellow
224 Hooker's Green
225 Hooker's Green Light
240 Indian Red
252 Lemon Yellow Hansa
258 Light Red Oxide
272 Manganese Blue
310 Payne's Gray

312 Permanent Green Light
316 Phthalocyanine Blue
317 Phthalocyanine Green
318 Prussian Blue
330 Raw Siena
331 Raw Umber
344 Rose Madder
360 Sepia Umber
380 Ultramarine Blue
388 Ultramarine Blue
390 Van Dyke Brown Umber
398 Viridian
413 Yellow Ochre

Brushes To an artist a brush is as important as a violin to a violinist or a chisel to a carpenter, and this applies just as much when you are a beginner. A great range of sizes and shapes is available and care is required when making your choice. Sable brushes are regarded as the best for watercolours, so it is wise to invest in these even if they cost more at the outset. If treated well they will last for several years. Cheap brushes (ox hair, camel hair, etc.) are a false economy, though some nylon ones may be satisfactory for some purposes. Do not stint on the number of brushes in your watercolour kit, and get a good range from size 00 upwards, including pointed brushes, flat square brushes, and the long thin brushes known as 'liners' (used for drawing lines but ideal for any kind of detailed work). 'Fan' brushes are also useful and excellent for blending in washes. To test a pointed brush wet it, shake out the excess water, and roll it on the palm of the hand to form a point. If the point is thin and weak, reject it; if there is too much 'belly' the brush may hold too much water and be difficult to handle. If any hairs come out during this test, the brush is past redemption. Oil-painting brushes can also be useful and so can old toothbrushes (which give a good 'splatter' effect) and shaving brushes, for texture and for loading a paper with water.

Some professional artists use soft Chinese and Japanese brushes which often have cane handles. These were intended for calligraphy and they are used as writing instruments in their countries of origin and not for washes.

When brushes have been used they should be washed in water and left to dry at room temperature, with hairs uppermost, in a jar or other container, and although during a painting session brushes are frequently and unconsciously dropped hairs – down in the water container this is not to be recommended for any length of time. Some colours clean off the brush easier than others; greens always seem to lodge in the hairs and bristles.

For artists who like to do outdoor work special containers are available so that they can carry their brushes around without damaging them; but even better is to fix the brush, with an elastic band, to a narrow piece of card which is slightly taller than the brush. Then use another piece of card, the same size, as a cover. Many small sable brushes when sold have little plastic covers over the hairs, and these could be well worth keeping for outdoor excursions.

Palettes Paint boxes usually have three depressions in the lid to serve as a palette, but these are not very practical, and divided dishes are better. As you will not be standing up to paint with watercolour (and therefore you will not need an easel) the dish for your paint should be by your hand rather than in it. Tin and plastic containers divided into up to eight sections are excellent, but ordinary household saucers can be used, as well as dinner plates.

Far left: Watercolour chart showing the large variety available.

Below: A selection of watercolour materials, a few of the vast range available.

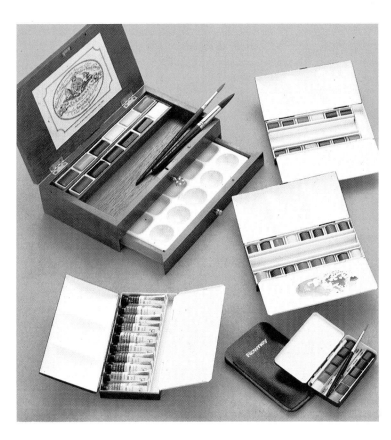

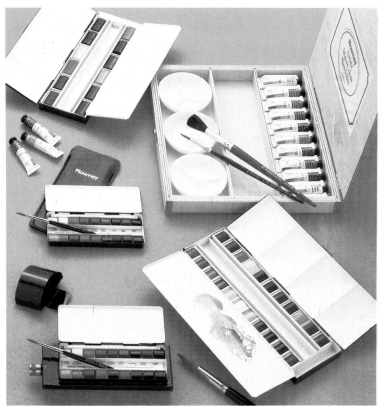

Paper Watercolour paper comes in different weights and textures, so you have a good range from which to choose. A good medium paper is 60-pounds; at 200-pounds it approximates to cardboard. The surfaces of paper are known as 'hot-pressed', which is very smooth, 'not' (not hot-pressed), which is medium, and 'rough', which has a very marked tooth. Unless the paper is thick (above say 72-pounds) sketching blocks are not altogether suitable as the paper is apt to bubble up. Watercolour board, which sometimes goes under the name of fashion board, is usually smooth, and of excellent quality, suitable for all finishes. Cartridge paper is much cheaper than watercolour paper, but unless of good quality is inclined to let the user down, as it puckers up if there is too much water. You can use watercolour paper as it is, pinned to a drawing board, but the best method, though it may take a little extra time, is to 'stretch' it, not nearly so formidable as it sounds. Purists make use of a stretching frame, but far simpler is the method where you wet the paper, lay it on the drawing board face up, and tape it down with masking tape or brown adhesive tape (Scotch tape is all right but sometimes tears the paper immediately beneath it). When dry the paper will be drum-tight, a perfect working surface, and if need be the paper can be dampened slightly again before painting. Stretching is more necessary when the paper is light. A further short cut is to dampen the paper and fix it to the drawing board with spring clips (sold by art shops). For outdoor work where you may not need paper drawing-board size, a smaller panel of wood can suffice, and where you intend making several pictures you can put down several sheets of paper, wetting the top one in turn, painting on it, and then taking if off, leaving the others in the clip for further work.

When the picture is completed it is better to cut it out from the tape which is holding it to the drawing board. If the tape is pulled there is always the danger of tearing the paper and ruining the work. Of course, the adhesive or masking tape can be left on if the artist intends to frame the picture. If a mount is being used (as it really must be for a watercolour) the tape-covered edges of the picture will be hidden under the mount and provide more of an overlap for the part of the picture that is actually showing.

Drawing Board There is no substitute for a drawing board when painting in watercolours. If you wish to have a more resilient surface, you can place a pad of newspaper between the paper and the board. A *T-square* is an accessory to a drawing board that saves measuring up

when you are drawing horizons, and a *set-square* used in co-ordination with a T-square enables you to get verticals absolutely upright.

You will add other ingredients to your basic kit as you find them necessary, some of them obvious such as *pencils* (a variety from hard to soft), *pastels* (which mix if water-based), *dividers* and a pair of *compasses* (an intended circle which is not quite right sticks out like a sore thumb). Dividers are used to compare distances and are useful if the watercolour is to be meticulously accurate. *Blotting paper* can be very handy for soaking up a watercolour wash which has got out of hand, to take out areas (creating clouds in sky and waves in water) and to tone down colours. *Sponge* is also a help in evolving textures, taking out surplus water, and applying paint where the use of a brush is not suitable (where you want a mottled finish). A sponge can also be used instead of a large brush when applying water to the watercolour paper when it is being stretched prior to being worked on. For fine work, *cotton buds* are excellent for taking off surplus moisture in a very small area. Although there is not much mess associated with watercolours, household tissues and rags are useful.

You can use coloured inks in association with watercolour, therefore *pens* with nibs of dif-

Stretching paper is essential for achieving a final flat surface for a watercolour. You can either sponge the paper wet or leave it to soak in a sink or bath. It is advisable to cut the gum strip into appropriate lengths before you begin the stretching.

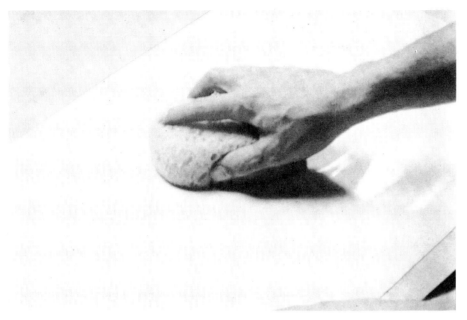

Soaking the paper.

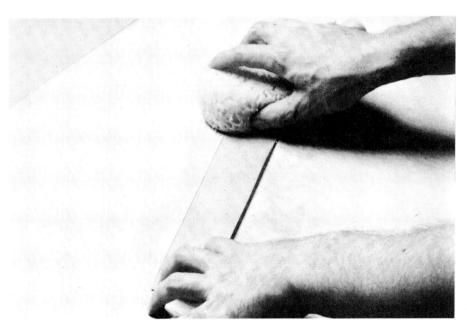

Wetting the pre-cut gum strip.

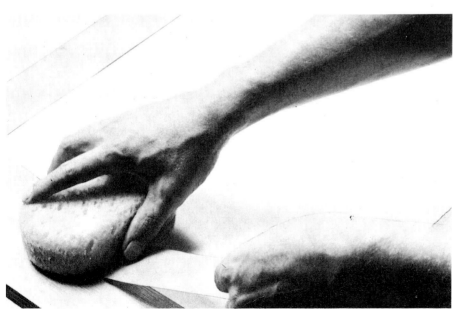

Applying the gum strip to the edge of the paper.

103

ferent sizes, *Indian* and *coloured inks* should all be kept in mind and within reach, as well as containers for water. Pens and nibs come in a very wide variety of shapes and sizes, ranging from mapping pens to lettering pens, the nibs of which often have reservoirs to hold the ink. Among the most useful are Rapidograph pens, which have a range of 'nibs' from 0.1 upwards. 0.1 is almost as fine as a spider's web. The great advantage of Rapidographs is the even line and the constant supply of ink provided by a cartridge, though those with a very fine point do have a tendency to clog after a while. Calligraphic fountain-pens with interchangeable units can be a great asset. Ordinary steel nibs, now mostly used in artwork and not for writing letters, have a limited life and if the points 'cross over' there is no point in trying to rescue them.

Erasers are a valuable accessory if they are not used too energetically, for damage may otherwise occur to the paper. Plastic erasers are the most versatile but, for charcoal, a putty rubber or a piece of bread is advisable. Erasers can not only be used to rub out intrusive pencil work but also to tone down the paint areas.

Applying a Wash The most important thing in watercolour painting is to know how to apply a wash. There is nothing easier. A wash is a smooth and even transparent tone of diluted colour. You need to have sufficient colour mixed, because you will rarely get the same tint again if you run out half-way. Use a large brush, fully loaded, and with the paper at modest slant (a book under the back of the drawing board is ample), carry the brushful of colour lightly across the top of the paper, left to right, or right to left, but keep the direction consistent. The wet colour will gently roll down like a wavelet, and when it gets to the bottom, or the place you want it to stop, mop off the surplus wash with a dry brush or blotting paper. If you want to graduate your colour, darker at the top, lighter at the bottom, you will add water to your brush after each line of wash so at the bottom you will be using almost pure water. This is excellent for skies. If you want washes darker at the bottom than the top, start with water and add the wash gradually or, alternatively, simply turn your paper upside-down. You can introduce washes of a different colour into a wash in progress, or even touches of pure colour from the tube or pan.

If you wish to apply a wash over a large area such as a sky it is advantageous to wet the paper beforehand with a sponge, waiting till it is just moist before applying the wash (you can hurry up the drying process by dabbing with a clean rag). Rough paper will take more water than smooth, and watercolour board least of all.

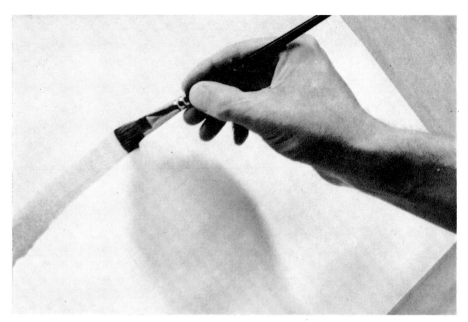

Applying paint with a fully loaded brush.

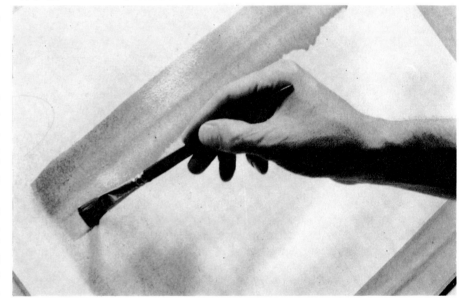

Applying the wash gradually.

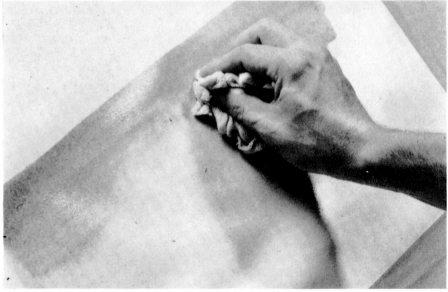

Dabbing with a soft rag or blotting paper.

A variety of different washes on a fairly coarse paper.

This interesting landscape (*below*) employs the techniques described in this part of the book.

105

Above: An Ancient Beech Tree,
by Paul Sandby, 1725–1809.

A full range of sable
watercolour brushes.

Far right: A selection of
watercolour papers:
1. RWS 90;
2. Green's Pasteless;
3. Whatman's Rough 200;
4. Fabriano NOT 90;
5. Whatman's HP 140;
6. Ingres;
7. Bockingford.

106

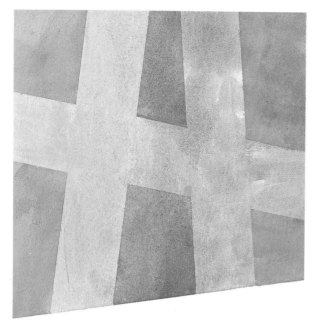

You can lay a wash over a small area, and the only thing to remember is to keep the direction of the brush strokes consistent, and never, for a wash, up and down, Once a wash has been applied, it is better to let it dry out thoroughly before doing anything else, and it is more effective to put strong washes over weak ones than the other way about. You can apply as many successive washes as you want, but after four or so there is a chance of them becoming lifeless as the watercolour paper begins to disappear. But of course it depends on what kind of picture you are painting. Many great artists have loaded wash upon wash. In art, nothing is firm and fixed, and if you do not want to do what someone says you should do, what does it matter? You are the person who is painting the picture.

Sometimes you may wish to lay an 'incomplete' wash, a wash where there are objects to be painted which are *lighter* than the wash. The beauty of the colour wash is that it is smooth. You do not want to go round the edges of anything. On the other hand, if this feature is to be lighter than the wash, there will be no way through the wash except by adding white to the mix and making it opaque. This is where masking fluid can be so invaluable. Masking fluid is a creamy sticky substance which, with a small soft brush, you paint on to the area you do not wish to be covered by the wash. It rapidly becomes tacky, and then dry, and you can apply your wash over it. When the wash is dry, you peel off the masking fluid, either with the point of a knife or by rubbing it with the finger tips, whereupon it will come off like rubber solution. Beneath it the virgin paper will be ready to be painted on. Masking fluid is most suitable on smooth surfaces, as it is inclined to pick up fragments from rough or hairy paper. Do not rely too much on masking fluid. It is not a magic material.

When using watercolours it is always advisable to have at least three jars of water, one clean for light washes, one fairly clean, and a general purpose jar for washing out the brushes. If you are using a paint box with pans, there will always be certain pans with vestiges of other colours on them, as at some stage you will mix the colours on your brush rather than in a dish, especially if you are using the colours at full or moderate strength. It is a good idea to clean off the pan surfaces periodically, so that the colour is what it purports to be.

It is quite possible to paint a watercolour using washes only, and indeed many of the great watercolourists of the past have done just that, overlapping the washes to suggest shadow and distance and not needing anything stronger such as paint straight from the pan. Many of these early artists never used white as a colour, preferring to let the white of the paper show through for their highlights. This was known as 'the English style'. 'The French style', somewhat frowned upon, incorporated white paint – though it might be mentioned that the Chinese white found in most paint boxes is not a very powerful covering agent; process white or designers' white gouache is much more effective.

Most teach-yourself-painting books advise using watercolours light to dark, as opposed to oils where dark to light is reckoned the better. Of course you cannot make much of an impact with light washes over dark washes, even if they can be seen; but, despite all this, when using watercolours you can put the darks in first if the very dark colours are not used thickly. A wash of brown or diluted black can easily be modified when need be, though it may be necessary to dispel another taboo – that freshness is all in watercolours, and that the spontaneous touch is a must. This is not so. You can use the technique you want, and you can even modify the 'flat brush' technique of oil painting by rubbing the moist watercolour surface horizontally with the flat sable or nylon brush to get the same kind of texture you can achieve with oils. When you do this, naturally you will not be able to use the white of the paper; so you will use white gouache for your highlights.

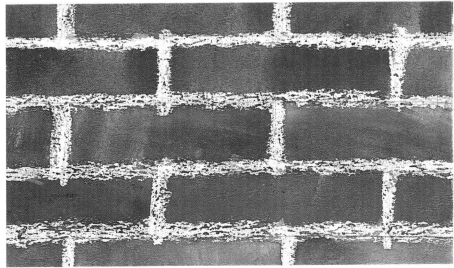

In this group, use of the wax-resist method is illustrated. A candle has been used to draw in portions of the pictures prior to actual painting.

Here the artist has chosen a picture postcard as his subject matter.

First of all, he has decided in his own mind what to put in and what to eliminate. Then he has drawn in the different areas in simple outline.

With the application of simple flat washes a feeling of distance is starting to emerge.

110

Some artists doing outdoor work prepare their paper beforehand with a colour wash – blue for sky, some dark colour for the ground – and no doubt it suits them. But it means that their imagination is restricted by what they have already down before them. They are being programmed to do a certain kind of picture. It is supposed to save drying time, as if five minutes or so makes any difference when sketching outdoors. A way to help watercolours dry more quickly is to add a little methylated spirit to the water. Or, if indoors, place the watercolour in front of a fire, preferably when the watercolour painting is on the drawing board as otherwise it might curl.

Watercolour straight from the pan or tube, with just enough water to make the paint flow easily, provides a satisfying counterpoint to washes already laid down. Watercolour paintings do not have to be loose and dreamy; they can be as tight and highly coloured as you like, and the textures can be worked up as diversely as in an oil painting, a prospect that would have horrified the 18th-century masters of the medium, especially those who worked to a formula and whose pictures now fetch big money simply because of the art market. One of these archaic formulas was to tint the paper according to the mood of the picture – nearly always a landscape. A wash of Naples yellow or yellow ochre was applied for a sunny lyrical scene, and a wash of grey or natural tint gave the right sense of foreboding for an overcast scene. There is nothing against this dodge – in fact it can make sense today – but it should not become a habit.

Watercolour paint can be applied in any consistency you wish. There is no need to use washes at all, as you can build up the picture with colour directly from the pan. This can be applied in a number of ways; in little dots with the point of the brush – you do not have to use the same colour; in small diagonal strokes, known as hatching; in small diagonal strokes going first one way and then the other, building up a tiny mesh (cross-hatching); in little moist blobs so that the colours melt into those next to them. It is sometimes recommended that newcomers to watercolour painting should use only medium or large brushes, but this can take a lot of the fun out of experimentation and it may also not be the artist's kind of thing at all. Some

111

people are born miniaturists who prefer to work on the smallest of scales, and if they are instructed to use large brushes and paint in a bold forthright manner they may never even find out where their talents lie. So if you wish to work in an area an inch square, go to it, and use a magnifying glass if it seems a good idea. Miniature sparkling pictures are just as 'good' (whatever that may mean) as big broad sketches.

Textures add interest to the picture surface, and there are many ways to achieve this. An interesting method is spattering the wash (still moist or dry) by loading a bristle brush with paint and running the fingers quickly through the bristles. You can put dots of colour by using a loaded decorator's brush and dabbing the tips of the bristles on to the surface. You can create the impression of foliage by dabbing at a green area with a sponge, blotting paper or tissues. A feathery texture can be achieved by holding a large brush, with not much paint on, close to the end of the bristles, and flicking the paper. The character of watercolour can be changed completely by being covered with blotting paper while still wet, and an even more drastic way is to immerse the watercolour in a bowl of water, swirl the paper slightly, take out, and treat with blotting paper. A watercolour which seems to be getting dull can be transformed by the use of pen-and-ink, pastel,

coloured pencils, and gouache. Gouache and true watercolour do not need to exist in self-contained compartments, but can be blended perfectly well on the same sheet of paper.

In laying a sequence of orthodox washes it *is* advisable to let each wash dry out in turn; however, remarkable effects can be obtained by painting wet-on-wet, guiding the changing colours with blotting paper. Paint straight from the pan can be put down moist, and then a loaded brush of water placed gently on top. Once again as you watch to see how chance is operating you have blotting paper or a tissue at the ready to control it. There is no way to predict how one colour will 'bleed' into another, but manipulating the transition takes away the element of chance.

There are so many ways of experimenting with watercolour that you will find your own method, and if you think you have discovered a winner go ahead with it despite failures, changing your brushes, changing the colours you are using, or turning to a different kind of paper. It is a far cry from the overlapping washes of the old masters, but they too were not averse to experiment, without having the variety of brushes, colours and papers that we have today.

All the methods described have been different ways of applying ordinary watercolour paint to the surface of the paper, but any

Right: A progression of illustrations in which masking fluid has been used. *Top:* Trees have been painted with masking fluid. *Middle:* A background wash has been applied. *Bottom:* Masking fluid has been removed and final details have been added.

Far right: Examples of different methods of applying watercolours.

Left: This interesting watercolour has been produced using the wax-resist method.

112

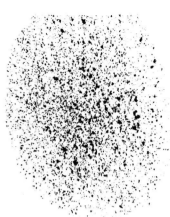

Flicking paint brush.

Dabbing with decorator's brush.

Dabbing over wash with tissue.

Dabbing dry wash with sponge.

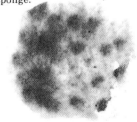

Dabbing wet wash with sponge.

113

outside medium, such as water-based pastels (or coloured pencils), is compatible with watercolour. By using the incompatibility of oil and water we can get amazing results. Mention has already been made of the techniques of using oil pastels in combination with watercolour, and this can be extended to using candle grease. If you stroke a candle across paper you will lay down a film, and when this is painted with watercolour the paint will slip off it or it will lie on top, unable to penetrate to the paper. Candle grease will not take the top off a wash, and further washes when applied will in all probability flow off it or settle uneasily on top, depending on how much candle grease you have put on. A further variation is pitting the layer of candle grease, either with a sharp object or by rubbing it with sandpaper. Where the paper is exposed the watercolour will take. Use the candle method with discretion; you are not making a candle-grease pie.

IS THE WATERCOLOUR WASH THE VERY FIRST STEP TO A PAINTING?

It can be – if for example you are going to have a large expanse of sky -- but not necessarily. You may wish to outline your design on the white paper, and then put in the first wash. At the other extreme, you may not want to put in *any* design, not even rough pencil marks, to show what is going where.

If you want to do a watercolour painting which is virtually a tinted drawing you put all your detail in, either with a sharp pencil or pen and ink, remembering that if you want additional effect and the ink to 'bleed' into the watercolour you must use a non-waterproof ink.

A simple exercise which will give you a chance to try out a simple wash is a sea scheme

An effective painting has been achieved by using the simplest of washes.

with a ship. Draw a horizontal line about two-thirds of the way down the paper, used upright or lengthwise. Apply your wash of diluted blue (ultramarine or Prussian blue), darker at the top, and stop it at the horizon, using blotting paper or tissue. If it overlaps slightly it does not matter as your sea will be darker than your sky. Mix a sea-colour wash, using what seem to be appropriate colours; blue and green are the obvious ones, but add other colours, such as a brown and, for extra drama, a touch of black. Lay down your wash from the horizontal line, letting the water go to the bottom of the paper and there mopping up the surplus. At any stage during this wash you can add further colours.

If you wish to have clouds, prod at the blue wash while still moist with a pad of cotton wool. If you wish to have waves on the water, use the edge of a piece of blotting paper, picking out wave shapes, but not excessively, indicating rather than describing. You can mix a darker wash, perhaps brown with a touch of blue, and put in land on the horizon, adding variety by giving light and shade with a small piece of blotting paper or a cotton bud. If you want a darker piece of land use paint straight from the pan. Unless the land is going to be elaborate you can place this in without preliminary drawing, though the boat will probably have to be drawn in (or traced in). It is easier to have the boat on the horizon, straddling the horizon, or not far below it, because if it is near the bottom of the paper you will be looking down on it, and the boat shape will not be so evident to a viewer. If you are tracing a boat on to the paper bear its logical position in mind. If the sky is fairly light you will find that birds in white will not show up very clearly, though they will on a green/blue sea. You can pick the bird shapes out (a flat V) with blotting paper, adding a touch of black at the front end to indicate the head and beak. Or you can put the sea-birds in with opaque white paint, such as process white. It must be emphasized that the Chinese white found in paint boxes is *not* a very solid covering pigment.

A second simple picture can be made by using hills, a middle distance of trees and a pond in the foreground. As before, you put the horizon in, and you can then put in the whole of the sky, even over the part where the hills will come (the hill colour will go over the sky colour). For relatively simple shapes, you may not need to pencil in the outlines, or you may prefer to put them in using some kind of neutral tint and a pointed brush. The darkest area of the picture will be the line of trees between hills and pond, and you can experiment with reflections, adding tiny dots of pure colour to suggest people. Remember that reflections are always absolutely vertical. For the hill part, you can apply further washes to suggest where the light is falling, or you can take out some of the first wash with blotting paper. You can also use blotting paper to take out clouds (and reflections of clouds). In the line of trees, try not to make them too green, adding brown or red to cool the colour down.

If you wish to try your hand at more detailed work, put in grasses and reeds in the immediate foreground, suggesting that this is the limit of the pond, and you can use fairly strong colour for such features. When you have got the basic picture down, and are reasonably happy with it, do not be afraid to experiment. If you do not quite know *what* to put in, look through some illustrations; there will certainly be something suitable, and if you do not feel sufficiently confident to put in a detailed object try a blocked-in silhouette, remarkably effective against a background. From the start cultivate a spirit of adventure.

Below: This charming scene has been created by first painting in the background hills, middle distance trees and foreground pond. *Right:* Try practising details that can be used in the foreground as shown here.

Right and below: A gradual build up of washes (notice that areas of paper have been left open) for sky and clouds, finished with small applications of thicker white paint.

Far right, top: Here, the cloud formations are painted with thicker white paint on an overall blue wash.

Far right, bottom: A light wash, with subtle washes of darker colour for clouds, creates a dramatic, but not overworked, sunset effect. Notice how the 'edges' of the clouds are highlighted with yellow. It is important to remember that clouds are not flat; they have a form and will therefore react to light.

116

117

Manganese Blue

Sap Green

Cobalt Green

Vandyke Brown

A simple seascape, using washes and flecks of white paint.

Raw Sienna

Manganese Blue/Vandyke Brown

Sap Green/Cobalt Green

Vandyke Brown/Sap Green

A dramatic moorland landscape.

118

Plenty of colour and washes have been used to produce a slightly abstract landscape.

DRAWING AND PERSPECTIVE

The amount of preliminary drawing that goes into a watercolour depends on the artist. There may be a few scribbles indicating the approximate placing of the design, perhaps a few horizontal or vertical strokes, or the drawing may be realistic and exact and if necessary stand up by itself without any colouring. If you wish to do this kind of work, and nothing is more satisfactory than seeing a black-and-white picture gradually take on colour, you will need to know something about drawing techniques. These are not difficult, and the basic thing to remember is to draw what is there and not what you think is there. That is, if you want to produce a realistic drawing. You are not obliged to. You can put in an outline and colour what is inside it, as children do. An outline does not exist in nature; it is a convention which people who are drawing are obliged to use because they are interpreting a three-dimensional subject in two dimensions. What is an outline? It is a dividing line between areas which are light and areas which are darker.

In drawing all we have is outline and tone. Success is not dependent on manual dexterity – you are not playing the piano. It depends on looking and assessing, seeing how some shapes relate to other shapes and how light and dark they are with regard to each other. The shapes can be simple, looked at once, and put down with reasonable accuracy. It can be a barn in a field, or an apple on a tablecloth. Sometimes shapes can be complex, such as a face, but no matter what it is no shape is too difficult to depict on paper.

We do not have to know how the barn was built. All we see is a rectangle with a sloping angular shape on top (the roof). Depending on our viewpoint we may see part of the side of the barn, and the shadows will depend on where the sun is. The rectangle may be broken up by inner rectangles and squares – windows and doors – but although we know that they are these shapes they may not appear so. If the front of the barn is in part shadow, a window may show as merely a small horizontal splash of light where the sun picks out the window sill, leaving the rest in darkness. Or the window may appear as a small shapeless blob, where light is reflected from the glass. A door, which we know is a rectangle and which a child or primitive artist would put in as a rectangle, may be recognized by a dark shadow at the top, where the upper part of the door, slightly inset, is shadowed by the brickwork above.

Once it is appreciated that the outline is only a means to an end and that the effect of solidity

is more important than a line surrounding a white shape then a barrier is crossed. The effect of solidity is achieved by placing an object in space. It cannot be real space because paper is by definition flat, so we use the device known as perspective. There is nothing complicated about perspective. It is there about us all the time. You only have to lift your eyes from this page and look around you. Perhaps the television is in the corner, and the top of it will almost certainly be below eye-level. You will see that the top does not appear to be a perfect rectangle (even if it actually is), and that the two sides appear to move in towards each other. If the television set was 200 metres long the two sides would most probably appear to meet, though we know full well that they do not.

If you look along a straight road in the direction of the horizon the road appears to narrow; a person walking down this road seems to get smaller, losing height at the same rate as the road narrows. If there are telegraph poles alongside it they will appear to shrink, and if you draw an imaginary line connecting the bases of the poles and another connecting the tops of the poles you will find that these meet on the horizon. The only time to see a true horizon is at sea, where the sky meets the water, for a horizon has nothing to do with the skyline. If you were in the Alps the skyline would be way above you. The horizon would be

Right: This diagram explains perspective visually. The road seems to disappear into infinity. The figures, houses and telegraph poles recede to the points of convergence, the vanishing point.

120

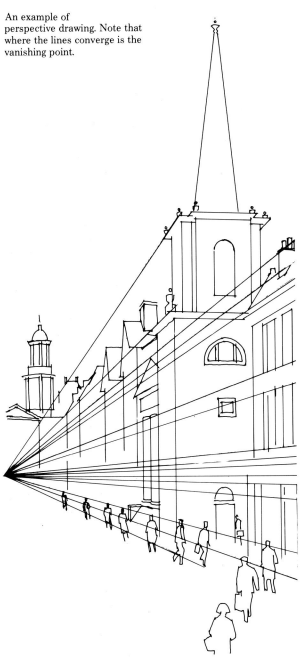

An example of
perspective drawing. Note that
where the lines converge is the
vanishing point.

behind the mountains, at eye-level. For that is
where the horizon is, at eye-level.

Objects above or partly above the eye-level
appear to go down towards the horizon and
those below appear to go up. If you look at the
roof of a house from any position except
straight on you will see it meekly obeying the
laws of perspective, and if you draw another
imaginary line it will lead to the horizon at what
is known as its vanishing point. If there is more
than one roof, and each is pointing in a
different direction, as in a higgledy-piggledy
village, you will see that every roof leads to the
horizon, but each roof has its own vanishing
point. There is only one horizon in a scene, but
any number of vanishing points.

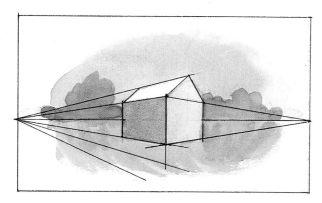

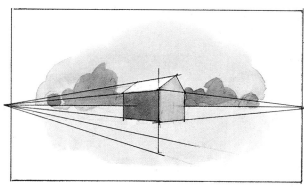

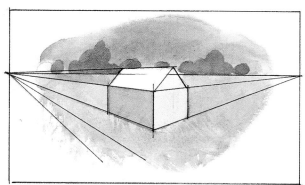

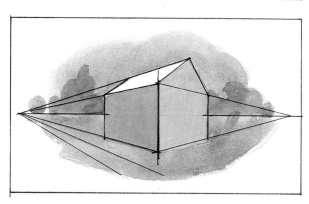

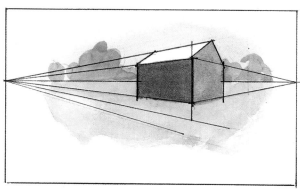

Without perspective a drawing or a painting will be flat, and by using perspective you obtain solidity and recession. Objects 'out there' will be laid out in their own kind of space. The horizon can be as high or as low in a drawing as you wish – it can even be off the top of the paper, but objects still recede towards it. Sometimes perspective can be tampered with to get dramatic effects (Salvador Dali was a master at this) and the experts at perspective are not artists but architects. Their perspective has to be right, whereas if an artist's perspective *looks* right that is all that matters. Playing with perspective can be fun and if you use two perspectives in the same picture it can be startling.

Although the ancient Romans knew about perspective, and used it in their murals, the secret seems to have been lost (or just ignored) and when it was rediscovered (or reissued) a few hundred years ago many artists painted pictures just to display their cleverness. And sometimes cleverness is needed, for all things, including human figures, have to obey the rules. If a person extends a clenched fist towards you it will appear enormous, sometimes larger than the rest of the person. And even objects which we do not associate with having solidity, such as clouds, have to follow the rules. That is why some clouds in pictures appear flat and uninteresting; they are merely put on as blotches with maybe a bit of shading beneath them. Of course you do not have to measure everything up; the main thing is to get the effect of perspective, not whether the interpretation is 100 per cent accurate. No one is going to award you a prize for being exceptionally good at perspective drawing; perspective is something to use, to manipulate.

Every law, of course, is made to be broken. And so we come to accidental vanishing points. Surfaces which are tilted sometimes converge on vanishing points which lie below or above the eye-level. If you hold a sheet of card at a slant you will see that its vanishing point alters as you move the card around. A good example is seen in a road going uphill, when the sides will appear to converge at a point above the horizon, or below the horizon if the road goes downhill.

You can gauge sizes by how objects appear in perspective. An object twice as far away from the viewer as another identical object appears to be half as tall; if it is three times as far away it seems one-third as tall; four times as far away a quarter as tall, and so on, and so on. This can be quite useful when putting in items to illustrate the scale of something.

Aerial perspective has nothing to do with what it might seem – perspective from above. It

Some examples of a few of the
many problems which can
arise in perspective drawing.

is about atmosphere. Dust and moisture are inclined to obscure the more distant objects, and the further away something is the less distinct and the lighter in tone it will appear. This is of more interest to watercolour painters than those who are making a drawing. The effect of distance can be reproduced in a drawing by very light or broken and dotted lines; in a watercolour by the use of bluish tints. This was used as a formula by 18th- and 19th-century watercolourists whether or not the distance appeared blue.

It is all very well reading about perspective, but does it work for you? It is a good idea to go out and look at a few buildings and begin sketching them. How do you start? The first thing to do is to put in your horizon. If you are not quite certain where this is, extend your fist with the thumb uppermost until it is on the level of your eye. You can then put in preliminary lines, casually, setting the scene, put in lightly, and then build up on these until you find a place on the paper which you think will be a good starting point. It may be the angle of a wall, it may be a doorway, it may be where the walls reach the roof, and once you have established one or two set points you can begin building up the drawing, altering the preliminary lines as you go along. There is no need to rub them out; just go over the top of them with a more determined and blacker line.

There is no necessity to complete the drawing if you do not wish to; concentrate on the parts that interest you, and if for example you find the windows and window surrounds particularly fascinating do these and forget the rest of the building or leave it incomplete. You may care to put in the individual bricks or stones, but there will probably be more of them than you think and a suggestion of brickwork is sufficient.

Landscape and Townscape

Landscape and townscape are the most popular forms of art, and in any exhibition of amateur work landscapes will outnumber everything else many times to one, with maybe flower paintings coming second.

There are several reasons for this popularity. Landscapes are there, and do not need to be arranged. You can pick your vantage point, and select only what you want to put in. There may be elements in the landscape which you may feel are too technically demanding; there may be a country scene with an old farm cart, and the open wheels may present a problem. You can ignore such objects either by omitting them from the view or looking elsewhere. Always draw or paint something which is of interest to you, and if landscapes bore you there are plenty of other subjects.

A further point about landscapes is that they are motionless, and you can spend as much or as little time on them as you wish. Naturally there are changes of light, and the shadows will alter, but at a fairly slow rate. Unless you are a very slow worker you are not likely to be caught on the hop by changing shadows, though weather changes are a different matter and what could be a charming scene with sharp lighting effects which pick out the detail can turn into a dull monotonous view with nothing much happening at all.

It is never fruitful to do anything just for practice. Some experts advise a newcomer to watercolour to make a series of small squares of different colour washes just to see what they look like and to get to know the contents of the paintboxes. It is difficult to imagine anything more tedious. The owner of the paintbox knows what the colours are; they are sometimes marked if there is any doubt. And it is much more interesting to see the colours in action. Sometimes there will be miscalculations, but what does that matter?

You may not be willing to hand out your early try-out efforts for others to see, but always keep your work even if it does not come up to expectations, for at some later stage you may fancy reworking it, using it as a base for a fictitious picture. And if you are making drawings with a view to turning them into watercolours, bear in mind that a relatively tame scene can be transformed with colour. Make written comments on the drawing about the colours you see if you do not have your paintbox with you, and as you do this you will find that you are analysing the scene afresh, looking at it in a new way. Maybe there is a yellow cornfield and you may think that the hedges which border it could be 'brought out' by making the colour and tones extra strong.

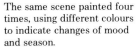

Far left: The buildings appear to recede into the distance because stronger colour has been used in the foreground.

Far left, below: An example of aerial perspective.

The same scene painted four times, using different colours to indicate changes of mood and season.

When choosing a landscape you should first decide what the main theme of the picture will be. The paintings on these two pages show (*far left*) where the foreground and, in the other, where the distance predominates.

125

Far left above: Lincoln by
Peter de Wint. Using only two
brushes, both large, one pointed,
the other stubby, de Wint was
able to achieve either a finesse
of detail or a sweeping bold
wash.

Far left below: Greta Bridge,
(1805), by J. S. Cotman.

Left: Wood Scene (1810) by
John Crome

127

128

Top left: Having decided upon his subject, the artist has carefully worked out his composition and has decided to place a large tree in the foreground to give depth to his painting.

Bottom left: The painting springs to life as simple areas of colour blocked in with flat washes are applied. It is at this stage that the tonal quality of the finished picture will become apparent.

Below: The painting has now reached an exciting stage. With accurate drawing and carefully thought out perspective, the artist can now confidently work into his picture in the knowledge that his problems have been solved in the first two stages.

Left: Detail.

Overleaf: At this advanced stage the artist is concerned solely with detail. Note carefully how he has used various techniques and effects, such as stippling, to create the shapes of the trees and how convincing the wooden cladding of the barn appears.

130

Figure and Pool
by John Singer Sargent, 1856–
1925.

A watercolour and pencil
sketch of clouds by John
Constable. The sky is the
keynote, the standard of scale,
and the chief organ of
sentiment.

Summer Day, New England by Maurice Prendergast, 1859–1924.

Woman Sewing by Winslow Homer, 1836–1910.

Painting a townscape
highlights all the problems of
perspective in the drawing of
buildings, cars and people.

When you are looking at a landscape it may be a problem deciding where the 'edges' come, where the picture should begin and end. An easy solution to this can be a homemade viewfinder which is nothing more than a piece of card with a rectangular hole cut in the middle. Alternatively the viewfinder of a camera can be used. And it is always worthwhile to bear in mind that pictures can be vertical (known as 'portrait' shape) instead of horizontal ('landscape' shape).

This will help not only in composition but also in relating the elements to each other, helping you to see in tones rather than shapes. Sometimes tones seem to be much of a muchness, and it is advantageous to half-close the eyes, so that although the detail is lost the broad masses are more easily differentiated.

When drawing landscape, and indeed anything else, put down what you can see and not what you know is there. If there is detail it should be in the foreground. Trees are most likely to be a stumbling block to the newcomer to landscape drawing and painting, and it is very easy to make them symmetrical, with the boughs and branches distributed in an even pattern. Mostly they are not. All artists have different ways of doing trees, and some of them try to put on every leaf, which can be a long laborious job. A suggestion of leafiness is better, with the awareness that leaves occur in clusters and masses. What might at first appear to be changes of colour are in fact changes of tone, due to the fact that some leaves are in the light and some in the dark, and some are in the

shadow of other leaves. In drawing this can be expressed in shading and in watercolour painting by adding a 'shadow colour' to the basic 'local' colour. So if you are using a medium green for leafage you would add a darker colour to the mix (it is immaterial what it is as it depends on what general colour scheme you are using); you would not use a different kind of green for the darker parts. The trunks of trees are much easier to do than leafage, and it is important to make them seem solid by using shading. And often trunks are leaning slightly to one side, especially if they are single trees in an exposed place. Study how other painters do their trees; you will find incredible variety. A short cut to putting in leaves is to use a sponge doused in colour, not too wet, so that by applying the sponge lightly you can lay down an arrangement of little flecks. You can add shadow colours while the paint on the paper is still damp.

If you intend to use trees and tree parts in the foreground of the drawing or painting take some typical branches home and draw them there. You can then arrange where the light falls rather than by leaving it to nature.

Grass may present a slight problem. Except in the immediate foreground the blades of grass cannot be picked out individually and grass is best expressed by shading or in painting by using a 'shadow colour' in the mix. Tufts have a shaded side and cast shadows onto the ground. In the middle distance grass is best represented by graduating the tone as the ground rises and falls.

Below: Lines of perspective
have been worked out on this
initial townscape.

Much that applies to landscape applies to townscape too; never imagine details which you cannot see; observe and do not assume; always put your horizon in at an early stage; and do not necessarily count all the bricks. Townscape is unquestionably easier than landscape, though there are one or two extra things to remember such as always keeping your verticals absolutely upright. A building which is even slightly askew will look silly. If you have difficulty in drawing verticals use a setsquare, with the bottom of the paper as your horizontal.

In these days some people will think twice about venturing into a city armed with a sketchpad. So go in your car, and do your sketching from there, with the windows closed and the doors locked if necessary, preferably on a Sunday when you can park easily by the side of the road. If you feel like venturing out on foot the choice is yours.

Below: The painting begins to come alive with the use of some simple washes.

Bottom: The second stage before detail is added.

135

The finished painting. Note how each area has been simply blocked in with only the minimum of detail yet the overall impression is of precision and accuracy.

Townscapes can look unnatural without people, and often a few briefly sketched-in figures can bring life to city streets. They can also give scale to the buildings. If you want to put in a fairly large number of people, either singly or in groups, draw in 'perspective lines' so that the people will fit in, not too small, not too large. If there are no people in the sketch at all, take an object in the foreground of known size, perhaps a doorway, or maybe a parked car. Place a figure there and see if it looks right. Then take a rule, place the edge at the top of the head of the inserted figure and draw a line to a vanishing point, perhaps the one you have used for the principal buildings. Then do the same with the feet, so you have two converging

lines to the horizon. At any point along this route you can place a person of the appropriate size relative to the rest of the picture. Naturally you do not want the people in the same line as if they were standing in a queue; so you fit in people across the paper, making certain that they are in scale, which is easily done by looking directly across at the distance between the upper converging line and the lower and seeing that the people fit between them. The figures need not be specific; they can be suggested with a well-placed slash of paint, lightening the top to suggest a face (faces do not have to be put in in pink, as novices often do).

When putting optional extras in, such as a

137

Similar and even greater
problems of perspective,
inherent in the townscape of
the previous pages, are
experienced here.

few extra people, remember that they too have shadows which must run the same way as the shadows of the other objects. Groups of people can often be represented by a rough rectangle with blobs (the heads) on. Legs are often not seen when there are strong shadows. Townscapes can also be made realistic by including cars and other vehicles, parked and moving; and when using watercolour they can be used as accents of pure colour (just as artists of yesteryear used post boxes). If you draw a car from memory you may find it an odd experience. You will perhaps overemphasize the upper part of the car, and will almost certainly overestimate its height. In a street scene with pedestrians and traffic, heads will always be well above the roofs of cars. When next out, take a look at the windows of cars. Are they opaque? Can you see

through them? These factors depend on what lighting there is and from what direction it comes. The same applies to other solid scene-fillers – the bus and the coach. If the wheels of cars and other vehicles seem to present a problem remember that a good part of them is in deep shadow and a suggestion of 'wheeliness' is often all that is necessary. If you cannot draw any kind of curvature try using the side of a coin; the aim is to indicate the presence of a wheel, not to draw up a set of blueprints for a motor manufacturer.

Of course both landscapes and townscapes can be tackled directly, using the point of the brush as a drawing instrument to lay in the basic design. But without some kind of framework, even just a squiggle or two in pencil, the straight-in approach using brush and paint can

A complete contrast to the city scene of the previous pages; only a minimal amount of detail has been employed in this landscape.

Far left, middle and bottom: A continuous progression of tonal washes will bring the picture to its finished state.

be hazardous without experience and the result can be a mess, with splodges of colour merging into each other. When you are using water-colour directly, think before you apply the paint. Have some idea what you are going to put down.

Landscapes can be approached using pencil and paint together, building the picture up little by little. The watercolour can be applied in sectional washes, and the pencil work can be

put in on top of this, with more watercolour used to finish it off. Pen and ink can also be used, with the ink blending in with the wash. If pencil is used it can be erased when all the watercolour has been applied, though the eraser may remove a little of the paint surface, usually without any detrimental effect. If you propose to carry out this method always use good quality watercolour paper; it is very easy to take the top off inferior paper.

Above: Final washes and a little more detail complete the picture.

The photograph *(top left)* was used as a reference for the above picture.

Basic shapes are sketched in lightly in pencil *(centre left)*.

The artist has used masking fluid to indicate the stonework detail *(bottom left)*. After the initial washes have been applied and have dried the masking fluid has been removed.

142

In the final stages *(above)* the white lines of the stonework have been lightly washed over to give a more realistic effect and the picture is now finished.

143

Working from a colour transparency. Notice how the artist has altered the 'wide angle' look of the original and made the perspective more realistic.

Far right: A chart of colours which have been used to make this interesting study.

Manganese Blue

Manganese Blue/Vandyke
Brown

Vandyke Brown

Vandyke Brown/Purple
Lake/Cadmium Red

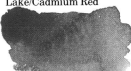

Cadmium Red

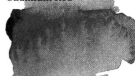

Purple Lake

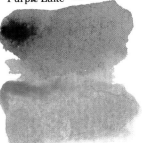

Sap Green/Cobalt Green

Raw Sienna/White

145

The colour chart for this study.

Manganese Blue

Windsor Blue

Olive Green

Gamboge Yellow

Hooker's Green

Permanent Mauve

Burnt Sienna

Neutral Tint

The wax-resist method was used on the tree trunks in this watercolour; it clearly helps to demonstrate the effect of strong sunlight in a tropical setting.

Figure Studies and Portraits

If you want to improve your drawing the classic way is to draw – and paint – the human figure. Most of the great artists of the past have done so, for the human figure is the most challenging of all subjects. No two people are the same; no two poses are the same. As, by and large, people are unwilling to take their clothes off to be drawn – and those who are willing probably cannot stay still – it will probably be necessary to enrol at an art school or join an art group (many art groups employ their own models). Fees are low, especially at evening classes run by the local community. The classes usually last two hours; much of the time is devoted to one or at the most two poses, but most teachers towards the end of the period go in for 'quickies'; five or ten minute poses in which there is just enough time to sketch in the basics.

Some people who have just started drawing and painting fight shy of going to life classes, feeling that they will be embarrassed, or, worse, make a fool of themselves by incompetence. There is no need to be diffident, of course, as nearly everyone feels nervous at first. Many people who go find that they can learn from fellow students as well as from the teachers. These teachers are tactful and helpful and the stuffy, autocratic art teacher, usually found not in art colleges but in second-rate schools is a comic figure from the past.

All styles and methods, all kinds of medium, straightforward and weird, are common at life classes. As an art student in the early 1950s the author was once asked in perfect seriousness if he was drawing the figure in 'the Egyptian style'. He was not, he was just experimenting with the new wonder of the age, coloured pencils in three million different shades. The emphasis of this book is on fun and pleasure, but please think seriously about life classes as they offer great opportunities of widening your artistic experience.

It is easiest to start off with drawing rather than painting. The drawings can be a base for watercolours when you get home, but until you get some experience in reproducing a person in two dimensions a pencil, pen, or length of charcoal are the best to begin with. You will be standing up to draw, so you will need a drawing-board (easels are usually supplied by the art college). It is a good idea to use a large sheet of paper, for you will find that if you are working on a small sheet legs and arms most probably will not fit in.

There are numerous ways of beginning a drawing of the nude, but it must always be remembered, as with landscape, that you are drawing what you see, not what you know is

This effective study has been painted directly from life with no preliminary work.

When drawing faces in watercolour it is always a good idea to practise the individual features first. Try to use form rather than lines to build up your shapes.

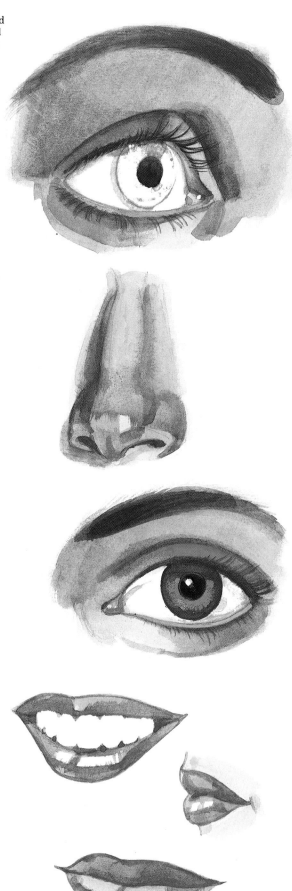

there. For example, anyone can draw a mouth freehand. But when actually looked at, a mouth may be seen as a shadow beneath the lower lip. Similarly with a nose. In certain light, a nose can only be detected by the shadow of it on the cheek. Old style books on drawing the nude spend half the time on anatomy, and why certain bones are there and why others are not. Muscles were regarded as important though they look no more interesting than elastic bands. You are not a surgeon about to cut somebody up. We are not about to draw skeletons so we can take it that they influence the shape and movements of the body. The proportions of the body are much more useful: a man is about eight heads tall, a woman six heads, a one-year-old child four heads; the halfway point down a man is the crutch. Fashion designers have their women eight-and-a-half heads tall, mainly to emphasize the legs, so physical facts can be manipulated if it suits the purpose. The shape of a man's torso is an equilateral (equal sided) triangle on one of the points.

An especially tricky point for newcomers is putting the head on the shoulders in a convincing manner. The neck does not sit on top of the shoulders, but is slightly below. A man's neck slopes slightly outwards (reading from the top), a woman's neck slopes slightly inwards. Hands and feet may present problems (even to important artists – look at Turner's figures and have a quiet chuckle). The hand is not all in one plane; the thumb lies below if the hand is held casually and not outstretched. In the foot, the ankle has to be exactly placed otherwise it looks like a frogman's flipper.

Where do you start? It is up to you. You can begin by putting in a rough outline, amending as you go along, putting in some guiding shadows; shadows are shapes which have no meaning and do not have to be interpreted. Some artists prefer to start by putting in the background shadows, 'bringing out' the figure against them. Or you can start with the head, working down from it; the eyes are a favourite place, as once in it is easy to begin sketching out the other features, and the eyes have the advantage of being set halfway down the head. Once the eyes are in, the ears can be put on. If the head is straight on without being bowed or tilted, the tops of the ears are on the same level as the eyes.

Build up with a mixture of line and tone, lightly pencilling in possible shapes and then going over them later when you are certain that they are reasonably accurate. Compare different shapes. Put out tentative scribbles where they may be. If there is a solid piece of torso such as the buttocks and thighs seen at an odd angle,

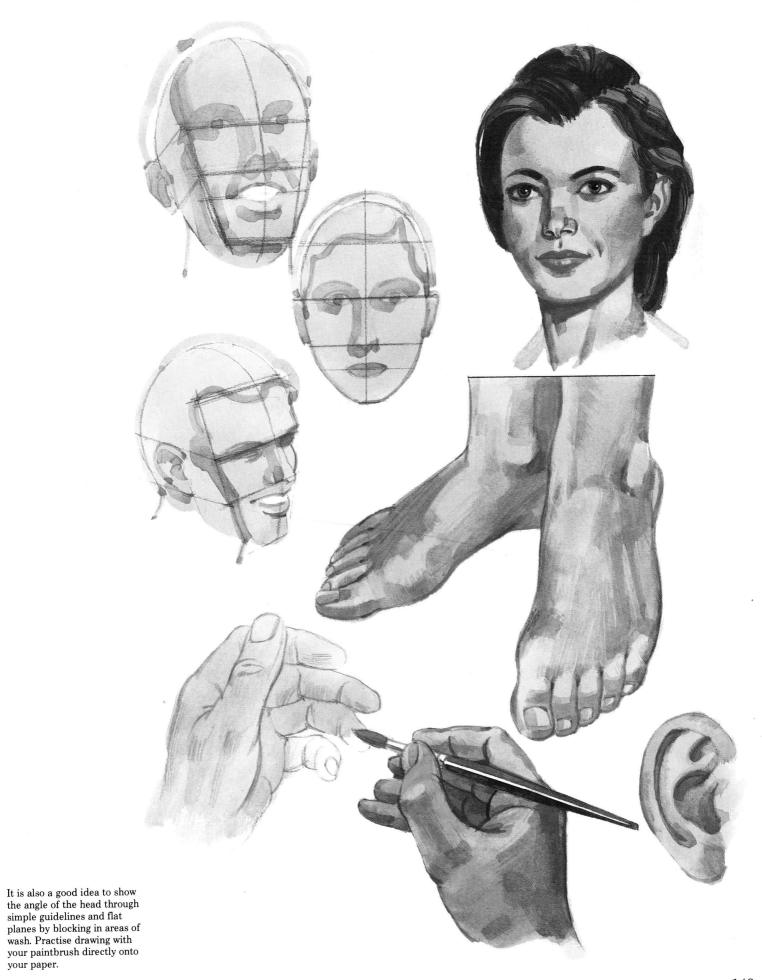

It is also a good idea to show the angle of the head through simple guidelines and flat planes by blocking in areas of wash. Practise drawing with your paintbrush directly onto your paper.

do that before tackling the subleties of the arms and legs. The only thing which is not advised is to start at the hands and feet and work inwards.

The effect of solidity is more important than physical accuracy. Do the legs look as though they are made of plywood? Look at the shadows. Look at the shadow below the knee and the slight protruberance of the knee bone. The ankle may only be indicated by the semi-circular shadow beneath it. And what is the drawing-pin in the middle of the stomach? Ah, the navel. It has been put in because the artist knows it is there, though all that can be seen of it is the merest shadow.

Once you have made progress with pencil or charcoal, bring in the paints. Watercolour is ideal for nudes, because the white paper coming through a pale orange or pale brown can evoke a marvellous skin colour. You can use the paint in washes over the pencil sketch; there is no need to stop the wash where the pencil line stops. You are not a child filling in a drawing in a colouring book. Outlines, as we have seen, are a convenience. Build up more washes if you wish, adding 'shadow colour' where necessary. Or you can use pencil and watercolour at the same time, a few suggestive lines here, a splash of paint there, a little grey to indicate back-ground shadow; there is no end to the possi-bilities. Or you can go straight in with colour, sketching the figure in outline in a very light colour, and amending it as you go along, building up flesh tints, adding shadows when appropriate, providing a background when you feel that you are on the right track (if you are wrong you can use a sponge and take the back-ground out). Another way is to put the back-ground in first, and then, using a brush loaded with water, 'fix in' the figure before beginning to apply colour. If the background colour is beginning to seep too much into the figure, take it out with a small piece of blotting paper, sponge, or a cotton bud. If the picture, although reasonably 'like', is turning out wishy-washy or faded, add more colour, or perhaps bring in coloured pencils, inks, or pastels.

There is no best 'one way' to draw the figure or paint it. There are dozens of approaches. It may need a good deal of concentration, but if you can apply a wash, if you can handle a pencil, if you can differentiate between high tones, low tones, and middle tones and can draw a distinction between what you see and what you think you see, there is nothing more satisfying. And if you can draw or paint a figure you can paint almost anything.

These delightful wash
drawings owe their freshness
and spontaneity to the fact
that very little preparation has
been made beforehand. Note
that any guidelines can be
erased once the watercolour
has dried.

Experience in drawing the nude is a great help in drawing clothed figures. Folds in clothing fall into four categories – in hanging, pulled, heaped, and crushed materials. Folds are expressed by shading, but only put in those which are important. Clothing can be painted in one tone, and the shadows added afterwards in two tones, one for background shadows, one (stronger) for cast shadows. Pattern and texture should be put in discreetly as otherwise they will dominate the picture to the detriment of the figure.

The ability to draw and paint portraits is one of the most envied of talents. As with drawing the nude, it is important to observe and draw and paint what you see, not what you know is there. The outline of the face can be put in first, but it is more sensible to start with a fixed feature such as the eyes, or to put in the background shadows first. The great advantage of doing a portrait is that you have a model on the spot – yourself – and that you have an ace critic near at hand – your nearest and dearest. The eye is halfway down the head, for instance, and other useful dimensions are: the distance between the top of the forehead and the top of the nose is about the same as that between the top of the nose and the bottom of the nose. The distance between the top of the upper lip and the bottom of the chin is about the same as that between the top of the ear and the bottom of the ear. A good rendering of the eye is a key to a successful portrait; it is often forgotten that it is in three parts – the eye itself, the eyebrows, and the eyelids. When doing the eye, always put in a highlight, but make certain that it appears in the same place in both eyes.

The easiest pose is three-quarter, perhaps the most difficult is the profile. Up-tilted and down-tilted heads do not present problems if you remember about perspective and foreshortening. Even non-professional models can usually keep their heads still, but if you are doing a fully worked out portrait it is sometimes wise to take a Polaroid photograph to establish the pose if a coffee break is taken.

If you have become skilled in drawing and painting nudes and faces, you will have few problems with drawing animals, except that at any time an animal can suddenly move and will rarely go back to its original position. Many professional wildlife artists keep a collection of stuffed animals and birds. Quick sketches are often more satisfactory than fully worked out pictures, whether they are done in pencil, charcoal, pastel, or paints. Animals with the same all-over texture in their coats and fur are easier to do than those where there is a mix. Textures can be depicted in many ways: by using the point of the brush and making a

A selection of watercolour portraits. It is essential when painting portraits in watercolour to ensure that one does not muddy the colour but places washes that are not disturbed.

series of close dots; by hatching; by using a sponge; by using overlapping washes; and by representing hairs with lines drawn side by side with a thin nib. Changes of tone are more important than changes of colour. It is useful to remember that the torso and legs of many animals are contained in a perfect square.

The simplest kinds of creature to draw are those which can be taken in at a single glance, such as rodents, where the texture of the fur is consistent. Because of their bright colouring, birds are often the subject of watercolour artists, but it must be remembered that the feathers are in groups, each overlapping other feathers and throwing shadows, and the practice of adding single feathers with a short dab of the brush may not be convincing.

Still Life

The kind of painting which allows delicate gradations of tone is typified by the still life. This can be imaginary – it is no difficult matter to visualize bottles, jars, and the odd apple or lemon – or from life. Bottles are useful as they have highlights, which appear on the same side as the light source.

The simplest kind of still-life painting is carried out by covering the whole paper with a tint, then sketching objects in roughly with a pencil, charcoal, or the point of a brush. The paper will still be slightly moist, so do not worry if the outline design (if done with the brush) bleeds into the background. Then, using a medium wash for each object, making certain that the colours do not clash too much, fill in the objects, defining the bottle shapes, jars and fruit. This should not take long, and before the paint is too dry take out the highlights of the various items with a damp brush, again not worrying if the colour slops over. For darker objects, apply further washes, either of the same colour or some other, skirting round the highlights you have put in. If the paper is still moist, this helps merge the colours.

You now have four tones, including the highlights, and you provide a fifth, with shadow, which need not necessarily be black. Brown plus blue makes an excellent shadow mix. You can leave the outlines fairly loose if you wish, or you can tidy them up, either by applying further washes on the objects, applying a further wash on the background, using a small brush to run along the edge of the bottles, or you can tidy up by using a wet brush and taking off the wash where it has leaked over into an adjacent area. You can use white for the highlights rather than the white of the paper. This, of course, is the traditional light-to-dark method.

Rather than start off again, you can take off the paint with a wet sponge, or put the paper under a tap, so that you have the merest skeleton of your original watercolour painting. You can then go from dark-to-light, putting in your shadows first, your next darkest tints, and so on back to the background, putting in highlights with white paint last of all. If you are used to oil painting this method will come easily. For the whole of the painting you can make do with one brush, a medium about number three, pointed.

After inanimate objects, it is tempting to be more ambitious and try flowers. These are more difficult than bottles and jars, but you can bluff your way through by giving impressions of flowers rather than portraits, using dabs of muted colour on a slightly moist paper. If you are anxious to do justice to the flowers, look at them closely; what might at first glance appear

The initial stage of a still-life painting. In this type of picture you are able to arrange your subject matter exactly as you wish. Make sure that the objects overlap each other and thus present a unified composition.

The still-life arrangement carefully sketched out. In a watercolour it is most important to leave all highlights as blank paper. This is particularly difficult in a still life.

The finished painting.

155

Watercolour lends itself particularly to flower painting. Start by sketching in the basic composition.

Remembering to leave highlights, continue to lay your washes from light to dark. More precise detail can be added in the final stages to bring the picture to life.

156

to be a colour change may turn out on closer examination to be the shadow of one petal on another, so you do not modify the colour you are using, but add a slightly darker colour to the wash or try taking off part of the wash with a damp brush. It is sometimes worthwhile analysing certain flowers, seeing how a rose is in the form of a spiral, and how even a flower such as a pansy is not merely a symmetrical group of petals around a centre. The spontaneous approach really does pay off in flower pictures; if you do flower paintings too tightly you are in unwitting competition with the professional botanical artists, and you (and most professional painters) will soon realize your shortcomings. Roughing in flowers with a pencil can often be more of a hindrance than a help; you may well find yourself running out of space when you have miscalculated the distance between bloom A and bloom B, while if you are drawing with the point of a brush or just putting in blotches of likely colour you amend and adjust as you go along. You can let the flower colours run into each other, but it can be very tiresome if the greens infiltrate the rose pinks or snapdragon yellows.

In flower arrangements some of the leaves will be in deep shadow, and it is often a good idea to emphasize these shadowed leaves, even exaggerating them, so that the main flower colours stand out. The actual painting of a flower group can be carried out either light-to-dark or dark-to-light.

Flower paintings are a good introduction to indoor scenes. These do not have to have every item picked out as if for an auctioneer's catalogue, and you can keep some objects in mysterious shadow. It is an interesting process, working out how much you can suggest with a square of colour or a couple of verticals. For those who regard their paintings as a visual diary there is something uniquely satisfying in having a portrait of the interior of a well-loved room, and although interiors do pose a challenge it is one well worth taking up.

Many of the characteristics associated with interiors are shared by life paintings, in particular getting the perspective and the foreshortening right. It is vital to get the eye-level set in accurately, and as you will have objects which straddle the eye-level you will have parts of these objects appearing to go up and others down. The vanishing points of the boundary line between walls and ceiling should be worked out; they will rarely fall within the scope of the picture. The same goes for the division between walls and floors, You will probably not get floor area and ceiling area in together, but even so it is useful to know what their vanishing points are. Getting these right will establish the correct

dimensions of the room. There is no need to accentuate the wall/ceiling wall/floor dividing line heavily as a preliminary step. Roughly sketching it in is sufficient.

It is often more satisfactory to paint direct without pencil outlines, using the point of the brush to establish where things are and getting the tones in, leaving any detail to a later stage. It is easier if there is just one light source, either a window or a light. With a standard lamp or table lamp you can establish where you want your light source – in other words you can pose your interior to suit yourself.

As with still life and flower arrangements, one advantage of the interior is that it does not move around, and you can spend as much time on it as you like – unless you are using natural light from a window, which of course will mean that the shadows are constantly altering. In doing interiors, you can explore to the full the possibilities of direct painting, and as you become more adept you can create more difficult problems, for example using additional

light sources or putting in a mirror.

If you are painting direct and are aiming for effect rather than an inventory, use a rough paper where detail is difficult to put down. With rough paper it is important to dampen it first, for otherwise you will find that the paint is adhering to only part of the surface. This creates a sparkling effect as there is a good deal of paper exposed, and if you want this by all means leave the paper dry.

If you go to an exhibition of amateur artists you will find very few interiors. They *are* more difficult than the ordinary open-air landscape, but they can be no less satisfying. You may find that you have a high ratio of failures in painting direct without pencil guide-lines. If you are in a sketching club and painting outdoors you may not want these failures exposed, while if you are painting interiors you can happily discard them (or wash them off and start again on the same sheet of paper, maybe leaving the vestiges of the previous attempt to show you where you went wrong).

When painting interiors it is essential to determine the light source as this area of the paper will be left white. Work away from the light source to the darkest areas of the picture.

Top: Having first made the design, trace down the image on stout paper or thin card.

Middle: Cut out the design with a sharp pointed knife or a designer's scalpel.

Bottom: Use a stipple brush to dab on paint, which should be thick.

Far right: Finished designs.

Watercolours are usually one-offs, but there may be occasions where you want repeats, perhaps for personalized Christmas cards. There is no way you can repeat a watercolour *exactly*, but you can get a close approximation by using homemade stencils. It is easy to make a stencil. The best kind of material is fairly thick polythene of the type used to make office folders or envelopes. Trace the subject with tracing-paper, and then place carbon paper between the tracing-paper and the polythene. You then go over the tracing with a ball-point pen or a hard pencil of at least 2H grade. Do not use subjects with interior spaces, as these pieces will drop out when you cut out your stencil. You can use either the cut-out part, or the empty space from which the cut-out comes.

To cut out the stencil you need a pair of small scissors or a scalpel (available from good art shops, and more suitable than craft knives as they are smaller). You can prepare the paper with a wash if you wish, wait for it to dry *thoroughly*, and then, firmly holding the stencil down on the paper, go *over* the polythene with your second wash so that the paint outlines your subject. This is when you are using the actual cut-out. If you are using the polythene from which the cut-out has been extracted, you will lay your wash over the space and over the adjacent area of stencil. Take care in lifting the stencil up, preferably leaving it there until the wash has dried. You should find that you have your design just as you traced it in.

There are many different ways you can use stencils. You can overlap the washes, you can add pure colour to the wash design, and, by not applying a first all-over wash, you can draw the subject in masking fluid. If you do this you can take off the stencil when the fluid has dried (not long) and apply an all-over wash to the paper. When this wash has thoroughly dried, you can peel off the masking fluid, and thus you have a white design to which you can do what you like. A smooth paper is preferable to rough when using stencils.

Stencils can be very intricate, and it is well worth spending time on the cutting-out process. If you enjoy experimenting, the use of stencils can be very stimulating. Overlapping stencils can create new shapes to fire the imagination.

159

GOUACHE

It is not a difficult transition from orthodox watercolour to gouache, and you can use the same equipment, plus bristle brushes and a palette knife. There is no need to change brushes if you are employing both gouache and watercolour in the same picture, and indeed gouache diluted is not far removed from ordinary watercolour, though perhaps a little grainier. You can therefore lay a wash in gouache exactly as you would do with watercolour. Indeed, almost everything that has been written about watercolour applies to gouache. Gouache lends itself to large designs, so larger brushes, including household decorating brushes, can be employed. You can use gouache by itself, or in association with any of the water-based mediums. It is perfect for fine and 'hard line' work, though if it is used thickly there *is* a tendency for subsequent detail to 'float' on top.

Gouache dries lighter than when first applied, but this affects mainly the pastel tints, and the blacks and dark colours are very solid when used at full strength. The caps of gouache tubes should always be kept on otherwise the paint will dry out; it dries out far more rapidly than the pigment in watercolour tubes. An absolutely solid tube of paint can be annoying, but it *can* be used by scraping out the paint and putting it in the depressions of a palette. You will never be able to recapture the full density of the stronger colours, but it will remain workable.

Watercolour paper takes gouache very well indeed, but mounting board and card are also excellent surfaces, as gouache does not need a tooth and if a smooth effect is wanted there is no better medium. Gouache in pans is not nearly so pleasant to use. Gouache is *not* such a powerful covering agent as acrylic, and for quick successive thick coats of paint acrylic is better. If you are using a thick creamy mix of gouache always start with enough, because its tendency to dry out lighter makes it very difficult to repeat the exact colour when mixing up a fresh quantity. For an all-over, absolutely even, matt surface, gouache is supreme, and it is ideal for decorative purposes, having the virtues of tempera. Gouache is a refined form of distemper, and for very large areas some artists use distemper and its various modern offshoots.

Tempera, which has only quite recently been commercially packaged, is a delightful medium, and most of what has been written about watercolour and gouache apply to it. Tempera dries more rapidly and is more delicate without quite the covering capacity of gouache and is best

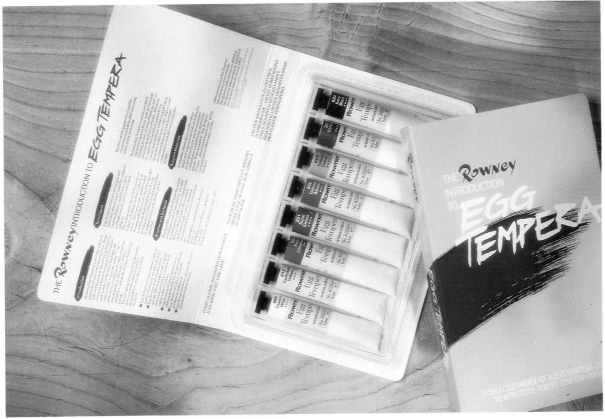

The *Adoration* (above), a painting by Botticelli, who used the method called tempera in which the pigment is ground with egg yolk to give an adhesive and binding quality to the paint. The artists of the Renaissance built up their paintings with a succession of wash glazes. *The Adoration* is one of the finest examples of the use of tempera.

Far left: A selection of gouaches and tempera which can be bought commercially in pots or tubes.

161

applied in strokes.

As a preliminary exercise, the sea scene mentioned is an ideal starting-off point. Put in all the components firmly in pencil, and fill in the areas with flat colour, ignoring light and shade, and making a pattern of the subject. You can use a large flat soft brush of sable or nylon for the larger areas, a smaller flat one for the boat and the land, and make certain that there is no overlap of colour by drawing the brush sideways along the outlines. If there is a mast on the ship this can be put in with a small sable. To get a really crisp horizon, lay a strip of masking tape along the horizon line and apply the paint so that it overlaps the tape. If you do a still-life study in gouache you can begin by laying a wash of much diluted gouache over the entire paper surface, rough in your design (better at this stage as diluted gouache is a better covering agent than watercolour), and build up, gradually reducing the amount of water in your mix so that at the end you are using the gouache straight from the tube. Do not leave paper peeping through for your highlights, but use white paint.

Watercolour and gouache can be mixed together, and so of course can other mediums, such as pastel and ink, in fact anything which is compatible with water. If things go impossibly wrong but there is a skeleton there somewhere which is worth working on, use a sponge and take off the top surface, or even soak the painting under a tap. If you have provided a pencil drawing as a basis this will eventually reveal itself, and if you have used pen-and-ink on top of gouache, when the gouache is removed the pen-and-ink will also disappear.

In this picture the artist has used a variety of mediums – gouache, pen-and-ink and pastel.

Gouache is an ideal medium for applying areas of flat colour such as in the background of this street scene. Pen-and-ink work has then been added to give the painting an 'illustrative' effect.

164

165

Gouache and watercolour as washes can be successfully combined with pen and waterproof ink to add colour and depth to a drawing.

Winter scenes containing snow can be something of a challenge, and it often helps to counteract the sheer intense white of the snow with off-white.

Far right: An impressionistic watercolour study. There were seven stages in its genesis: (1) a charcoal sketch; (2) a wash of Payne's grey and ultramarine for the sky, the clouds being taken out with blotting paper; (3) the first shadows were added to the land-based objects, in Payne's grey and raw umber; (4) the sea was put in with washes of viridian with blue and raw umber, much diluted, blending in with an orange wash which became the sandy foreground. Payne's grey was added at the foot of the picture. The orange and grey washes were allowed to overlap the shadows; (5) the local colour was put in with crimson, burnt sienna, and yellow ochre, and some detail was added; (6) the shadows were reinforced, and the horizon was affirmed with ultramarine; (7) the picture was tidied up (but not too much so) and the outlines of the objects were strengthened with vandyke brown. Foreground detail was applied in burnt sienna, yellow ochre, and Payne's grey. Throughout the painting process, no colour was used at anything like full strength. The paper used was a heavyweight watercolour paper, slightly rough and therefore was a discouragement to pettifogging detail. Two soft brushes were used, a half-inch flat, and a medium (number three) pointed.

Right: A wartime 'home front' scene carried out in a series of self-contained flat washes in a colour scheme restricted to browns and greens. There was no improvisation in this watercolour and the whole was laid down in pencil, with the exception of the sky. The white everywhere is the white of the paper showing through, and some of the textures are produced by rubbing off the wash with an eraser, which gives a pleasant mottled effect (useful also for mist effects).

168

169

170

Watercolour washes are
perfect for sketching animals
and pets.

Facing page, top: The projection of slides onto a wall or canvas is another method used by artists to enlarge photographs.

Facing page, right: In the Middle Ages, the camera lucida was used to project images.

Facing page, left: A pantograph is an excellent instrument for enlarging (or reducing) an original on to paper. The size is varied simply by changing the radius of the pencil arm.

SHORT CUTS

Someone who is very good at painting can be hopeless at drawing, but there are a number of short cuts. You can trace your design, and get it down onto the paper by using black carbon paper and a sharp-pointed pencil. You can use a slide projector to project transparencies onto a sheet of paper fixed to a screen and then paint the image. With watercolour the brush has to be kept moist rather than loaded, otherwise the paint will drip down the paper; the same applies if an episcope is used. This problem does not arise with gouache, tempera, or pen-and-ink. If you are using pen-and-ink try to hold the pen slightly downwards so that the ink runs down the nib and not up it and onto the pen-holder and the fingers.

An episcope is a box-like device with a lens similar to that of a camera (which is pushed in and out depending on the size of the image wanted), a bright interior light, and a system of mirrors. An illustration of any kind, black-and-white or coloured, is placed on a kind of window and the image is reflected onto a screen.

Then there is freehand copying, and part-freehand copying where the main features but not the detail can be put in by tracing and carbon paper. Many professional artists use, for reference, portfolios of photographs and illustrations cut from newspapers, magazines, periodicals and books, and these are not only useful to jog the memory but can also spark off ideas for pictures only remotely concerned with the particular illustration being looked at.

Below: Drawing a grid on any print or photograph is an excellent method of enlarging it accurately.

172

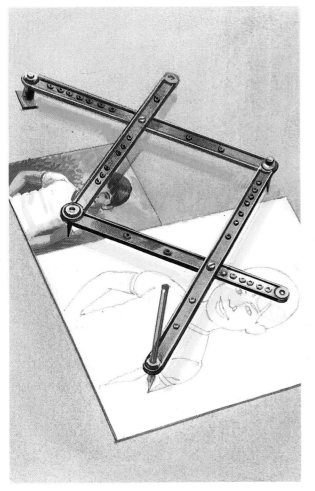

Artillery Officer
by Théodore Géricault.

INTRODUCTION TO
Pastel and acrylic

Above: Grazing Goats by Ken Jackson. This interesting composition uses sophisticated pastel techniques.

CONTENTS

Introduction

Why, it might be asked, are acrylics and pastels coupled together? There is a very logical answer. The use of both these wonderful mediums can create instant pictures. You don't have to spend time waiting for the paint to dry, and you can go over what you have done time and time again until you feel that you have it right.

And bringing acrylics and pastels together serves to emphasize that painting methods can be combined. You can use pastels with watercolor, you can use acrylic with pastels. There are only two divisions – mediums to use with water and mediums to use with oil.

Acrylic paints are newcomers to the art scene, a product of modern technology. Their scope is virtually unlimited. In a recent art scandal a number of fake early Picassos were sold at vast sums, but how were they finally recognized as fakes? They were painted in acrylics and were dated forty years before acrylics were discovered!

Those who have not discovered the delights of pastel have a treat in store for them. As with acrylics, pastels can do almost anything. You can use them as drawing tools, you can use them flat, that is on their side, and thus create masses of color, you can go over a pastel drawing with a watercolor brush, and you can use pastel dust dropped onto watercolors or acrylics to create a magical effect. Read on...

Left: This very simple acrylic of oranges by Denis Barker is brought to life by a lemon interestingly placed.

179

WHAT ARE ACRYLICS?

Acrylics are the only new paint to have come onto the market for centuries. Introduced in about 1962, they are as versatile as it is possible to imagine. They can be used thickly like oil paints, or in transparent washes like watercolours. They can be applied to almost any surface whether it be paper, panel, cardboard or canvas. Their main attribute is that they dry *very* quickly and are ideal for those who work at top speed and like to see a finished picture in half an hour. They dry too quickly for some, but the drying speed can be slowed down with a retarder, and there are all kinds of additives such as mediums and texture pastes to suit every taste, though normally water is used as the painting agent. Van Gogh would have loved acrylics. Some established painters are suspicious of them despite the many claims (justified) made for them.

It may seem unusual to share a book between pastels and acrylic, but they have many resemblances, obvious and less obvious. The main one is ease of working and the possibility of doing a picture very rapidly indeed, in a few seconds if need be. Pastel, being dry, can be worked over with subsequent layers immediately; and so can acrylic, being very quick drying. With both, there is a temptation to regard a quick flashy picture as a good picture; it is almost impossible to avoid making a picture by putting on colour at speed. Both pastel and acrylic can be mixed with other mediums to create something wholly new, and both pastel and acrylic are virtually permanent. Unlike oil paints, where asterisks on the tube denote the degree of permanence, you can be pretty sure that acrylics last, and we know that pastels from the eighteenth century have come down to us with their colours and their bloom absolutely intact.

Much of the advice and recommendations regarding pastels are applicable to acrylic, and rather than repeat information about perspective, about the necessity of looking, assessing, and painting what you see, not what you know is there – all of which can be read in the section on pastels – the advice on acrylic will tend towards the practical application.

WHAT MATERIALS ARE NEEDED?

Paints These come in fairly large tubes, as acrylic paint is often used in bulk, and there is a very large range. Because acrylic dries very rapidly the top should always be kept on.

Mediums and Glosses These can be used at will, and impart a lustrous texture. Used with water, acrylic is slightly matt.

Retarder This slows down the drying process, but never to the same extent as one normally gets with oil paints. To dedicated users of acrylic the adding of a retarder defeats what to many is the medium's great asset – rapid drying and the consequent ability to apply coat after coat within a few minutes. Acrylic paint is opaque when used thickly, and obliterates what has gone before, except when diluted and used as a glaze.

Texture Paste An optional extra, as you can build up texture anyway, and using thick pigment you can get what textures you want.

Primer This is a thick white paint rather like household undercoat and is used to paint on an absorbent surface, though size is better (and cheaper).

Varnish Acrylic varnish is a curious milky substance, and when used has the effect of completely obliterating the picture surface until it starts drying, when it is quite transparent. There is no reason why the traditional varnishes as used in oil painting cannot be used.

Brushes Nylon brushes *only* should be used. More people have discarded acrylic because of clogged brushes than for any other reason. Acrylic paint dries not only on the picture, but on the brushes, and only methylated spirits will clean them and only then if caught in time. The remedy is simple. *Always* keep the brushes in water, *not* point down but fairly flat in a brush tray. Nylon brushes will last for years if this practice is adopted. Do not be put off by nylon brushes; they are superb, even the smallest ones marked 00. If you really want a rough paint texture, you can use bristle, but the same advice applies – always keep them in water. Some artists still prefer to use sable for fine work, but these will suffer if kept in water continuously. Use the complete range of brush sizes from very large to very small.

Far right: A comprehensive range of acrylic materials by a major manufacturer.

180

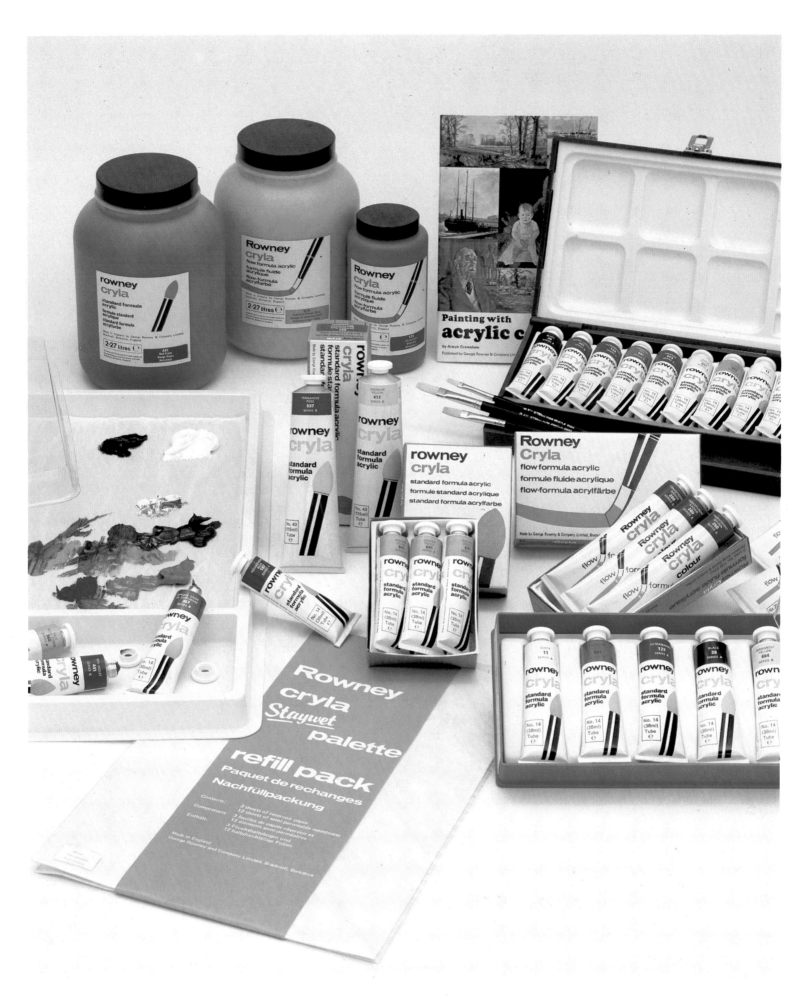

181

182

Palette Knives Palette knives come in several sizes, and are useful in acrylics. Do not let the paint dry on the steel of the knife, for although it can be scraped off there is always a danger of damaging the thin steel of the smaller palette knives. Acrylic is ideally suited to palette-knife work, as it is not messy and does not ooze oil all over the place.

Palettes and Mixing Trays There is something on the market called a Staywet Palette, perfect for acrylics for as the name implies it stays wet and stops the paint coagulating. It is worth noting that the bigger a blob of paint in the tray or on an ordinary palette the longer it will take to dry out. In normal use, acrylic paint will *not* dry out on the palette before it can be used, and if in doubt add water to keep it moist. When acrylic paints start to dry on the palette, a crust forms. The paint can still be used if this crust is prised off gently with the tip of a palette knife.

Paper Almost any type can be used, but cartridge paper is as good as anything and, for those who like to use their paint smooth, mounting board or white card is suitable. If you are using acrylic paint fairly thickly, water-colour paper is rather an expensive option. Because of the heaviness of the paint, thin paper is not really advisable. Canvas is excellent, but no better than card unless you are keen on using the natural texture of the canvas without overlaying it with too much paint.

Easel Acrylic lends itself to broad handling, and consequently an easel is essential if you like a bold style with lots of bravura

Pencils and Charcoal Because of the great covering ability of acrylic, any medium you use to lay down your design will be obliterated by the paint (unless you are using it in thin water-colour style). If you are painting in several layers, making use of acrylic's drying rapidity, remember that you may need something to apply a design or an outline on to the *earliest* layers. In this event, bear in mind pastels or a felt-pen, something that will carry a line over paint ridges better than pencil.

Water Containers No less than three, one for clean water, one for less clean water, and one to splash the brushes around in between changes of colour. The brush tray *should* hold the brushes not at that moment being used, but if you are working at top speed it is more convenient to pop the brushes into the medium-clean water and trust that the points won't be damaged.

Masking Tape A very useful material, suitable for fixing paper to a drawing-board instead of drawing-pins, and also of great help in painting straight edges (the tape is laid alongside the area to be covered, and is then taken up when the paint has been applied, taking with it the ragged edge of paint and leaving an absolutely straight edge). For irregular areas, including circles, the masking tape can be stuck around the area to be covered. Of course, as masking tape comes in rolls of varying thickness, the tape will be buckled, but that does not matter.

Drawing Board As always, this is an optional extra depending on what you are painting on (technically known as the ground), but essential if you are using an easel and paper.

In addition you will add all kinds of odds and ends to your working material from time to time, and do not be afraid to improvise. A pair of dividers may come in useful if you want to compare one line or area of paintwork with another or to calculate distances between point A and point B. You may find that you want to 'work up' your textures, and that the usual range of brushes do not give quite the effect you want. Two handy stand-bys are old tooth-brushes and old shaving brushes, which give a texture of their own, unrepeatable with ordinary custom-made paint brushes. You can achieve interesting textures in acrylic by scoring the paint surface while still wet, and the point of a pair of dividers will do this, as will a knitting-needle or one of the blades of a pair of scissors.

Far left: This Ron Brown acrylic landscape painting uses all the materials and principles described in this book, including aerial perspective and over-painting.

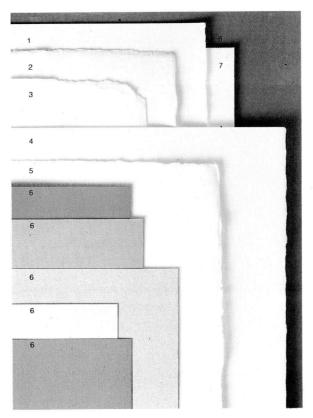

Left: A selection of papers: 1. RWS 90; 2. Green's Pasteless; 3. Whatman's Rough 200; 4. Fabriano NOT 90; 5. Whatman's HP 140; 6. Ingres; 7. Bockingford.

183

HOW DO I START?

You can pick up acrylics as and when you like. There is little mess, though, if you are working on the flat, you should use sheets of newspaper to protect the working surfaces adjacent to your paper or canvas from any splashes of paint. This newspaper is also useful to try out colours you have mixed. Go through your brushes, and check that they are not clogged up. Make certain that you have plenty of water and always keep brushes-in-action in water, ideally not on their points or bristles. A Staywet Palette is really not a luxury, but a necessity if venturing into acrylics with any kind of commitment. It consists of a flat plastic tray divided into two sections, one large, one small. The small is partly filled with water and it holds the brushes. The large section has two sheets of paper on the bottom, blotting-paper and a type of paper which lets water through but remains taut and unbroken. The paint is applied on top of this paper. When these paper sheets have become plastered with paint or are otherwise unusable, refills can be purchased at any art shop. Both the palette and these refills are very reasonably priced. On top of the plastic tray is a close-fitting polythene cover; this makes the tray airtight when not in use.

Water from the tap is gently poured into the tray until the two sheets of paper are soaked through. The blotting paper is always at the bottom. Surplus water is then poured off. Now lay out your colours, remembering to replace the tops of the tubes immediately the paint has been squeezed out. You may prefer the colours in a set order, from light to dark, or higgledy-piggledy. There is no need to clear the paint off after each session; in doing so you may tear the paper and make it useless, though it will stand a good deal of ordinary wear and tear. If you are using a medium or a retarder keep it near at hand, and in a small tin or receptacle rather than in the original bottles or jars, and dole it out as you need it.

If you are working standing up, make certain that the easel is at a convenient height and that the tripod legs are not too splayed out. Of course, you can sit at the easel; a stool or wind-up office chair is better than a chair with arms. Position the easel so that you get good light, even if artificial, which is sometimes better as it does not change during the course of a painting session.

As always, get something down before you get transfixed by the blank paper, but if you are exceptionally modest and feel that blank paper is wasted on you, get something down on a sheet of newspaper or some old wrapping paper. Acrylic is an ideal medium for newcomers to painting, because whatever you put down can almost immediately be obliterated by more paint.

You may like to get the feel of acrylics and work out for yourself how much water you need on the brush, whether you prefer to use a medium with the paint rather than water, and how the paint goes down compared with other sorts of paint you have used. You can do this whether making a picture or merely doodling; making some kind of picture is certainly more interesting.

When you take up acrylic, you may not want to do it with an audience, so you will not want to try it out in a life class or outdoors. If you are indoors, perhaps a still life, either imaginary or created from the objects near at hand – a loaf of bread, some fruit, maybe a jug. You can draw these in pencil fairly roughly, just sufficient to place the shapes on your working surface, and then put in your patches of colour. If you are not as yet too certain about your handling of colour, use a few colours, or perhaps just black and white, which gives you all the tone you want. Get the shapes more or less right, and then put in the edges as loosely or tightly as you wish. Try to make the picture hang together, and try not to make it too bright. Sometimes it is an effort to keep the painting low in tone (lower than it is in real life), but muddy colours have their own appeal and in the 1950s and 1960s they were the favourites among contemporary artists of the new realist school.

Perhaps you would prefer to kick off with a landscape, either imaginary sparked off by a photograph or one of your own drawings. If you have already tried watercolour and have found that you can get along with it, do a watercolour first, and use acrylic on top of that. Or use watercolour washes to put in the feel of a landscape without being precise, and then build upon this, using transparent acrylic washes as if you were continuing to paint in watercolour. Then you may, or may not, use opaque acrylic on top of that.

There is no *best* way, in any medium, to paint a picture; there are *convenient* ways, there are ways that suit you and you alone, and to find out whether acrylic is a medium you need to persist with – after spending the money to buy the equipment and materials – you want to be *aware* of the techniques, even if you do not use them. Many of the techniques associated with acrylic painting have been lifted from oil-painting methods. One of these is the 'wet on wet' technique, which means exactly what it says, applying wet paint on to wet paint, which helps

The versatility of acrylic techniques is shown below.

Acrylics can be used like oil paints after just a short period of time for drying. One colour can then be painted on top of another without 'showthrough'.

This shows the effect when colour is used fairly dry and a stippling is employed.

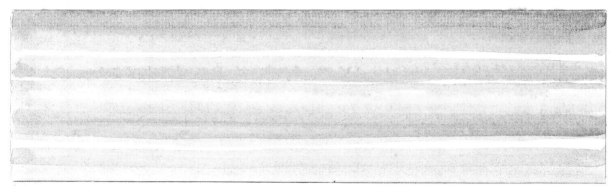

Acrylics can be used as a wash as with watercolours.

A simple example of what can be achieved by using the above methods.

to merge colours, and is very useful for skies. You can use the acrylic very wet, or you can add retarder. The reverse of transparent acrylic paint is the use of texture paste. You may wish to build up areas of pigment so that the painting is almost like a relief, and the effect can be quite impressive, especially in the foreground of a picture. Being white, texture paste when mixed with paint tends to weaken the colour, and if you want darks it is best to lay down the texture paste first and add the dark colour when the texture paste is dry.

When the surface of the ground is porous, such as an untreated canvas, acrylic paint can be used thinly as a stain, but for general purposes this has only a limited appeal. In the first instance, you will probably want to use the full body of acrylic, either rough finish or smooth. When this surface is dry, there are a number of subsequent techniques to use. You can scumble, meaning drawing a dry brush loaded with paint across the dry surface, so that some adheres and some does not. It is no good trying to do fine work using this technique, but it adds texture to a painting and is good for doing water ripples. Scumbling using a dry brush and very little paint is ideal for mist and fog effects, and also to obscure partially a distant scene which may have become too prominent.

Another worthwhile technique is glazing, which is putting a transparent or semi-transparent wash over the existing picture. The colour should be heavily diluted with water or medium (which will make the glaze more shiny) and it is perhaps best applied with a soft brush, whereas scumbling is most effectively done with bristle or nylon. There is no limit to the number of glazes you can apply, and by a shrewd medley of glazes you can alter the whole character of a picture. You can experiment with taking some of the glaze out of certain areas using a piece of rag, and you must not think that glazes are necessarily light in colour. There is no reason, for dramatic effect, why black should not be used as a glazing colour.

When you are putting on a glaze or using acrylics in a diluted form do not expect quite the same feel as using watercolour wash. As I have said, acrylic is not a subtle medium, so do not expect the same kind of effect. Be prepared for a little annoyance when the colour dries out more quickly than you had anticipated. However, this is more than compensated by its covering properties; you can put white on black and confidently predict that the black will not show through.

All subjects can be tackled the same way. It does not matter what they are, whether land-

186

scape, seascape, still life, or figure work. You do not have to change the approach because there is something different – maybe something unfamiliar – in front of you. And any subject can be made as easy or as difficult as you wish.

One of the simplest kinds of picture is a straightforward seascape. No complicated shadows or intricate drawing are involved. It can be done on any surface, and we'll assume that you are using inexpensive card. But this is a deceptive project, for though it will be kept basic and straightforward it will illustrate the capabilities of acrylic and the possibility of

transforming one kind of picture into something entirely different. Naturally this can be done with any kind of painting medium, but not so conveniently with others.

Pin or tape the card onto the drawing board and, using a T-square or a ruler, draw a straight line across in pencil two-thirds of the way down. This is the sky-line. Mix blue and white, not much blue, plenty of white, using sufficient water to make the mixture run, but not too much to make it translucent. There is no need to make a bland mixture; let bits of white remain untouched by the blue. With a medium

187

or large brush, depending on the size of the card, begin applying the colour from the top down, left to right, not too fast, letting the mixture slide but controlling it. Take it to the sky-line; if you drift past the line it does not matter.

While the top of the sky is still damp, try to put more blue into it, fusing it with the original colour. Add clouds, not absolutely white but muted with perhaps a touch of yellow ochre or raw sienna. At the bottom of the clouds add shading, a touch of burnt umber or similar.

Mix a sea colour. Select your own blend – blue plus green, perhaps with added browns and yellows, perhaps a touch of red, which tones down all greens. Paint the bottom third of the card, making a neat join with the sky colour. If you have overlapped the line with sky colour, go over it with the sea colour. You can empha-size the sky-line by tracking across with the edge of a flat soft brush before the paint dries. Add further darkish colour in the foreground. You can suggest waves with flecks of white, with a hint of shading below.

Put in a land feature on the sky-line, dark colour, perhaps with added blue to give the feeling of distance. Do this with a small pointed hair brush, outlining the shape and filling in. The sky will be dry by this time so the over-painting will be crystal clear without fudging.

In the centre of the picture, or near the centre, put your ship. Depending on ability it can be a sailing ship, a ship with funnels, or (as there is nothing in the picture to suggest scale) a rowing boat. This serves as an accent. It can be any colour that differentiates it from the sea. Using the softest brush (even 0000 which is tiny) put in highlights on the deck of the ship, or bow, or on the waves at the base of the ship. Add birds (flat Vs) at will.

Thus a simple picture, unpretentious, but neat and recognizable. We will now add to it, by providing interest in the foreground. If you have mixed a good quantity of sea colour you will have some over, so add to it a reddish colour, perhaps vermilion, perhaps burnt sienna; if too bright, add a touch of black. These are for rocks. With the tip of a soft brush outline a structure of rocks in the foreground, and begin filling them in, with some parts medium strong, others darker. Keep aside a little dark paint to add separately. Decide which way you would like the light to come from; if from left, paint in shadows on the rocks away from the light source. These can be as simple or as compli-cated as you wish. If there are sharp edges, you can assume that the light will catch these with full force, so with a small brush put in delicate highlights.

You can then put in dashing waves, basically

188

The text and illustrations on the previous pages describe the step-by-step build-up of these exercises.

whitish, but not absolutely white as otherwise it will nullify your highlights. Remember that waves have shadows, so darken the waves at the bottom; waves nearer the foreground can have light crests so that they are silhouetted against those behind. You can have a series of waves, each painted on top of the previous set, wet-on-wet, or on dry. You have rocks but no absolute scale; the rocks can be any size, so you specify what size they are by putting in a lighthouse. This can be a vertical shape, slightly tapering, outlined in pencil maybe by the use of a ruler or drawn in with the point of the brush. The shading on the side of the lighthouse must match the direction of the shading on the waves. As lighthouses are usually in cylindrical section, grade the shading, so that the tones come in various vertical densities. Near the top will be the lamp. You can light the lamp. But first of all you have to turn a daytime scene into a night-time scene. Mix a thinnish blue-black so that it is close to the density of a watercolour wash, and from the top left of the card cover the whole area with the possible exception of the lighthouse. Add a small muted yellow circle in the sky to indicate the moon, remembering that this will cast shadows. Paint in the lamp with a glowing yellow, adding a flick of white, then mix a yellow wash.

This can be laid around the top of the lighthouse in a halo fashion, or it can be put in a segment through the sky and over the dimly lit waves. If the underlying dark overall tint recently applied is too strong, reinforce the yellow wash with another one, and maybe another one until you have got the strength right. Bring up the lighter side of the rocks where they are in the moonlight, darken the shadow side still more, for the shadows of moonlight can be very crisp.

What time of the night is it?

Perhaps it is approaching dawn, so we concentrate on the sky-line, adding a pale wash with a trace of crimson, reinforcing it if it is not powerful enough. We tone down the moon, and add a tinge of pink to the undersides of the clouds. To further the idea that this is our new source of light, the yellow beacon can easily be toned down or taken out by passing over it another dark wash. The top of the sky can be darkened even more, as can the immediate foreground. With the light coming from a different direction – straight ahead – the shadows of the rocks need to be drastically altered. The shadows are now face on. The land mass on the horizon is now a focal point, being so near the light source, and this can be built on, with detail put in so that some of this island is in shadow, some in sunrise.

This demonstrates how easy it is to convert

an acrylic, and there is more to come. It is no longer a seascape but a landscape. The lighthouse is no longer that, but a trunk of a tree. The order of transformation need not be fixed, but we can alter the lighthouse by slimming it down, taking out the yellow of the lamp, and extending it right to the top of the picture where it disappears. Further trunks can be inserted across the picture, not too mathematically, in dark brown, just sufficiently toned to be seen against the black background of what was water and sky. The rocks can be converted into ground by softening the contours, altering the shadows, which, as we are at this stage still retaining the sunrise on the horizon, will be those of the trunks. These shadows, perhaps burnt umber with a trace of blue, will extend to the bottom picture edge, flaring out as perspective has to be taken into account. The edges of the trunks will be lighter, and these tones will merge with the really dark ones running up the centre of the trunk.

The sea and the waves are no longer wanted, and neither is the ship, so they can be overlaid with rich pigment in greeny-grey, darker near the foreground, getting lighter towards the skyline. As the ground colour approaches the horizon, contours can be picked out against the pink, and to break up the ground colour trees can be inserted as vague shapes in a dark green, together with hedgerows, always a good feature in a landscape. This will form a great contrast to the sea picture, but it will not be a good picture, however the transition is dealt with, because the frieze of trees running across the picture plane will destroy any notion of composition, even if branches are added to alleviate the effect of all the verticals.

As the tree trunks are occupying too much attention it is necessary to reduce their importance by creating a more interesting foreground. This can be done by suggesting plants or flowers. They will necessarily be subdued in tone because they will be in the shadows of the tree trunks, but nevertheless the tones can be rich, by using oranges and reds with added neutral colours. These foreground features can be enlarged so that they occupy most of the bottom third of the card, and 'spot-lit', reducing all other tones in the picture, so that the tree trunks merge into the background and are no longer intrusive.

The next adventure can be to take out the trees completely, together with the top two-thirds of the picture, and convert the whole thing into a flower picture, adding detail to flowers, inserting blades of grass (remembering that each blade of grass has a bright side and a shadowed side and that individual blades can only be seen in the foreground). Blades of grass

Left: The final exercise of the finished night scene.

Left: The development of the above exercise into a landscape using the overpainting properties of acrylics to make a continuous painting exercise.

191

do not go in the same direction, and some cross over other grass. Behind the flowers there can be shrubland, not too highly differentiated, and in the middle distance grass, depicted in changes of tone, not colour, demonstrating the rise and fall of the land. At this stage, some of the picture will belong to a previous episode, and some of it can be kept. You may wish to retain a dark sky; a stormy sky can be dramatic against the greens of grassland. Behind the flowers and shrubs you may care to suggest cottages, in light greys with not too emphatic shadows, and even, with a few stabs of colour, indicate the presence of people.

At this stage you may like to change the centre of interest from the flowers to the cottages, blurring the foreground or throwing it into shadow. Pick out the main details of the cottages, the shadow thrown by the underside of the roof onto the walls, the windows, the doors, maybe indicated by just the shadow of the overhanging bricks or stone above the door or window. The glazing bars of the window may

be seen as the shadows beneath the bars, not the bars themselves. If the cottages are going well, you can spotlight them, perhaps using the palette knife when adding highlights, and blurring everything else, even the sky-line. The blurring can be done by melting compatible tones into each other so that nothing is specific, and if you find it easier use the finger tip instead of a brush.

Continuous art may be a new concept. It is certainly fun, whatever your degree of proficiency. You can change your techniques throughout, using both bristle and hair brushes, applying the paint with the flat of the brush in squares, dabbing it on in stabs and strokes, applying glazes and scumbles at will. A pinky scumble would have worked well in the project when changing the picture from night to dawn.

And adventure and enjoyment are what it is all about. Painting in whatever medium opens a magic door. You may pick up a brush at seven o'clock in the evening. The next time you look at the clock it may be midnight.

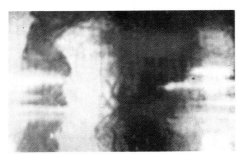

Left: This painting uses all the continuous methods explained in the previous pages.
Top: Figures in a landscape help to indicate scale and enliven the picture.
Above: Detail showing reflections in water.

Far left: The continuous painting exercise is described in the text.

Cobalt blue

Permanent green deep

Burnt sienna

Yellow orange

Raw sienna

Ivory black

Titanium white

Acrylic can be used as a very dense medium, with good covering power. Notice how the preliminary outline, taken from a drawing, is totally covered by the final painting. Much detail, including shading, can be drawn and painted over, without fear of showthrough.

195

Top: This charming beach scene has been painted from a photograph. Acrylics can be handled, as here, like oil paints.

In this painting of a Spanish
sunset the artist, rather than
trying to re-create the original
photograph, has chosen to
simplify the shapes and
colours, while still retaining
the heat and atmosphere.

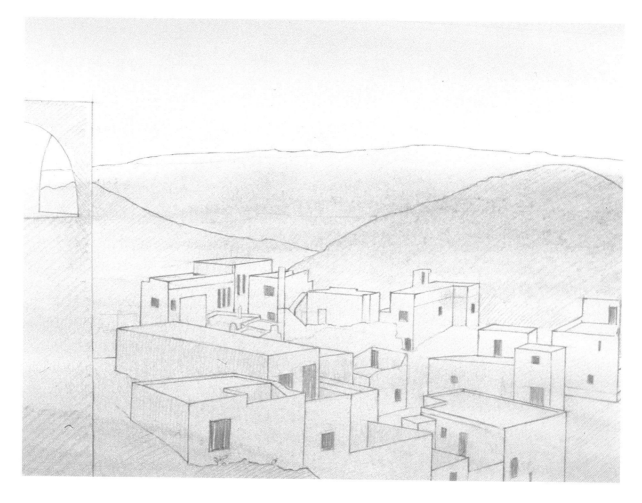

Medium yellow

Yellow orange

Orange red

Medium magenta

Prism violet

Burnt sienna

Titanium white

Black

199

Winter Landscape by Denis Barker is brought to life by its very interesting composition.

PASTELS

A selection of pastels and accessories shows some of the vast range available.

203

WHAT ARE PASTELS?

Pastels are powdered colours mixed with water and chalk or oil and chalk, and made into sticks. Some manufacturers put in a binder to stop the pastels crumbling; the softer the pastel, the less binding is used. Water-based pastels are more often used than oil pastels.

WHAT MATERIALS ARE NEEDED?

A Selection of Pastels Pastels are sold in boxes, with a compartment for each pastel, and to stop the sticks rattling about they are protected by a layer of cotton-wool or tissue. There are at least 200 distinct tints, and boxes usually contain 12, 24, 36, 72 or 144 pastels, plus specialized selections for landscape and portrait work. Pastels are also sold singly and, where expensive ingredients are used, prices of some individual sticks are higher than others. There are hard pastels and soft pastels; the soft pastels are usually cylindrical in section, the hard ones square or encased in wood (the extremely useful pastel pencils which can double as coloured pencils). Hard pastels, the most famous of which is Conté crayon, are chalk based. Because of their hardness they are mostly used for preliminary work and detail, and are often used at an early stage in the picture as it is sometimes difficult to apply hard on top of soft pastel if used loosely, though not if rubbed in with the finger tip. Soft pastel, far more frequently used, goes well on hard pastel.

Paper The most popular kind of paper is called Ingres, and it comes in various sizes and colours. It has a slight tooth, which is ideal for picking up the pastel powder. Any kind of paper can be used, such as watercolour paper, brown wrapping paper, cartridge paper, cardboard, and even sandpaper.

A Drawing Board Although not absolutely essential, a drawing board is very useful, as the paper can be fixed to it with drawings-pins or Scotch tape (or masking tape). Some artists prefer to work on a surface which has more 'give', in which case a pad of folded newspaper is placed under the pastel paper.

An Easel Again, this is a matter of choice. Some artists prefer to work on a flat surface, but when you are using an easel the surplus pastel powder falls off and makes the surface less messy. There are many kinds of easels, large studio easels, fold-up easels, and table-top easels. They have to be modestly robust as a good deal of pressure is applied to the paper when pastels are being used, and an easel which slides away as it is being used can be annoying, as well as bewildering to the sitter if you are doing a portrait.

Charcoal Charcoal comes in thin sticks, and is very useful to sketch out the preliminary design. Charcoal does not have any real bite, and does not overwhelm the pastel. It also mixes very well with pastel, and can be taken out with an eraser or even the finger tip. A putty rubber and a piece of bread are two of the best forms of eraser, but a putty rubber does get very grubby when used with charcoal. You can also use a chamois leather. Charcoal is usually bought in made-up packs, so the buyer cannot really select the sticks he or she wants, but charcoal without a hard core is the better.

Pencils Pencils can be used to make preliminary sketches, and a softer rather than a harder pencil is better (2B or 4B though some prefer HB, which is neither hard nor soft and is the ordinary office pencil). Pencil in general should not be used in the final stages of a pastel picture, as it shows up shiny.

The effects which can be obtained from various grades of pencil.

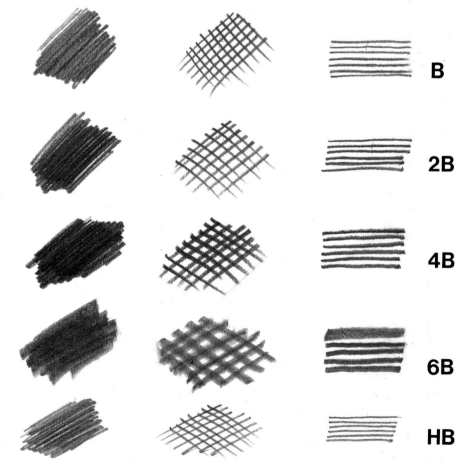

B

2B

4B

6B

HB

Pastel Pencils Pastel pencils are quite new, and are merely pastels in the form of a pencil, useful for fine work, but rather tiresome as the wood has to be constantly shaved away. **Coloured pencils** are also very useful and come in a great range of tints. Mostly they are compatible with pastel, especially those which dissolve in water, as pastel does.

Stumps or Torchons These are compressed 'pencils' of blotting-paper or a similar substance, used for blending the pastel colours on the paper.

Tissues Tissues can also be used to blend the pastel colours on the paper, but they are useful to have about as when using pastels the hands tend to get powdery.

Cotton Buds Again these are very suitable for blending pastel colours, especially for fine work. They can also be used to apply pastel powder where the pastel itself is too clumsy.

Erasers The best kind of erasers are putty rubbers; ordinary pencil erasers are too harsh, and can mess up the tooth of the paper. The use of any kind of eraser should be kept to a minimum, except for preliminary sketches. When pastels are applied layer on layer, an eraser can ruin the whole thing.

Fixative Some artists prefer not to use a fixative, as they think it takes some of the freshness away, but the risks of smudging a pastel picture are great enough to make a fixative very useful. Fixatives are sold in liquid form, and used with a mouth-spray (two narrow metal tubes on a hinge, and used with the tubes at right angles), or in aerosol cans (more convenient). Full instructions go with the cans. When the fixative is used, the pastel picture goes very dark, which can be alarming the first time, but it dries out in a few minutes without any great colour change taking place.

Brushes Both soft and bristle brushes can be used in association with pastel, to blend the dry pastel, or used with water to turn the powder into a paste (the word pastel comes from the word paste). This paste can be drawn over with dry pastel. Bristle brushes can impart interesting textures to the picture surface. Some artists do not use brushes at all, and it is entirely up to you.

This is the basic equipment for painting in pastels, but there are extras which you can add at will. If you wish to do a detailed underpainting on which you will put your pastels later, you may want to do this in watercolour, acrylic, pen and ink, or felt pen. All these go well with pastels, simply because they go with water. The thing is to experiment, to find out what suits you. It may be that the sight of a clean sheet of paper is daunting. In that case, get something down on it right away, anything, even a splash of colour by using a sponge (which can spark off an idea for a picture, just as looking at a fire does).

Pastel techniques. The *left column* shows direct application by rendering for maximum density. *Centre column:* The effect of cross-hatching. *Right column:* the subtle use of pastels by blending in and spreading with a finger.

205

The ingredient essential to the success of this pastel painting by Denis Barker is correct perspective, with the bales of wheat straw in the foreground, the barn in the middle distance, and the horizon giving a natural feeling of depth.

HOW DO I START?

One of the most exciting things about pastels is that the artist can exercise ingenuity to the full, and there are absolutely no rules. Some people prefer to start their painting with only the haziest idea of what it is to be about, while others prefer a detailed drawing. These drawings can be outline drawings only, or they can be finished drawings in their own right, with colour, and light and shade. The pastels can then be used to fill in the colour.

The colour of the paper used contributes much to the finished product, and pastels are unique in this respect. The paper colour is, in fact, another colour. Pastellists, especially portraitists, often leave part of the paper blank, with maybe two or three lines across it to suggest what would have happened had colour been used overall. This is not laziness; by merely indicating, for example, the top of the dress or clothing, attention is not drawn away from the focal point of the picture, the portrait itself.

Before putting pastel to paper, it is worthwhile going through the various subjects of paintings, in descending order of suitability for pastel: Portrait and Figure, Still Life, Nature, Landscape, Abstract. Naturally all these subjects *can* be done with pastel. The kind of picture you are going to do is bound to influence in some way or other the kind of technique you are going to employ. Another important factor is whether you are doing a picture from life, with the subject before you, doing a picture from a photograph, postcard, or other illustration, or if you are doing a picture from imagination. Illustrations are often a good taking-off point, stimulating a memory, or suggesting a line of approach. There is something to be said for trying to copy a famous pastel painting from a colour photograph.

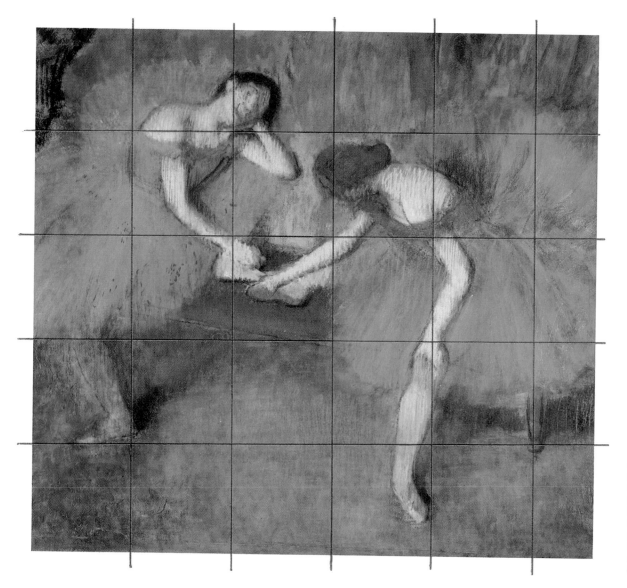

A good way of learning all about the use of pastel is to copy a master, as in the delightful *Two Dancers Resting* by Degas. It can be squared-up by drawing a grid on a photograph or print and using the lines as positional reference as in the exercise *(far right)*.

The Very First Steps

Decide what kind of paper you are going to use, pin it or Scotch-tape it to a drawing board, or place it on a flat surface, with or without a pad of newspaper beneath the paper. Place your materials within easy reach – if you are right-handed keep the pastels by the right of the paper. It may seem obvious, but sometimes the obvious is overlooked. When the pastels are new, they have neat labels on transparent wraps; these labels soon go as the pastels become used, so it is no bad idea to keep the pastels on a labelled tray – a piece of corrugated paper is ideal. The sticks of pastel soon break anyway, so if it is more convenient break them beforehand into one-inch lengths. Pastels being used will soon get dusty, with specks of other colours adhering to them, but there are ways of cleaning them.

The best is to place the grubby pieces of pastel in ground rice, and to shake the container about. This simple operation will clean off the unwanted dust, which is absorbed by the rice. When the rice gets dirty, replace it. No matter how you use the pastels you will eventually have tiny fragments, too small to pick up with tweezers, which seem to be useless. Get all these odds and ends together and pound them with a mortar and pestle (household ones are not expensive). Having done this, add water, and let the mixture set. When this has occurred, cut the mixture into lengths, and you have new pastels, maybe an odd colour, but very useful. If you have a lot of bits, sort them into dark and light colours and make two different hues.

Beginning the Picture

The first marks do not have to be important. As suggested earlier, you can give the paper a few splashes of colour with a sponge or perhaps a soft brush. You may care to develop this in watercolour if the first signs are promising. If you have a definite object before you, then you may wish to put down your first impressions in charcoal, which rubs out easily with an eraser or the finger tip. It can be held like a pencil, or loosely by the far end. Do not press too hard or it will snap.

If you are painting with a subject in front of you, the still life can be most satisfying. Ordinary kitchen equipment is a good starter, maybe combined with a loaf of bread and some china. There is nothing better than an assortment of fruit as a still-life subject – far easier to paint, in any medium, than flowers.

There is always a temptation to draw in outline, but remember that a line does not exist in nature – it is merely the edge of a shape. So if you can think in shapes rather than outlines it is a big advance; and shapes are easier to do

than outlines. Of course, you need to define the edges of the shapes, but a good way to get the shape down is to use the *side* of a piece of charcoal, so you are working with a flat piece.

These first marks can be tentative, as you try to get the feel of it. They can be squiggles, they can be lines exploring the way the shapes go, they can be little blotches setting down the shadows. No matter what medium you are working in, remember that light and shade are vitally important, far more important than colour in making a picture which is 'like'. It is a good idea when setting up a still life (or for that matter when doing a figure painting or a portrait) to have strong light coming in from one source (easier from the sides, more difficult from the front, more difficult still from the back). Light and shade *define* the forms or shapes.

It cannot be stressed too often that the way you work is determined by you and you alone. If you feel that you want to put in the outlines first, and fill in from there, go ahead.

Your preliminary sketches may seem meaningless to everyone except you, but you may know exactly what is going to come out. The main object should be to get the articles you are painting coming together on the paper as a coherent group, not odd things scattered around by themselves. This is more important than accuracy; no one is going to award you a prize if the bump on an apple is absolutely right or if the curve of a banana is too pronounced. Unless your aim is to be purely decorative, try to get the feeling of the solidity of the objects you are painting. You do this simply by finding out where the light is falling, and darkening those areas which are shadowed.

There are two kinds of shadows. There is the shadow which occurs away from the light, and there is cast shadow, in which an object already in the shade throws a shadow over something else. Cast shadows are darker than ordinary shadows. Ignoring light and shade is the reason why so many amateurs' pictures in all mediums are flat, no matter how well they are coloured.

The preliminaries can naturally be done in pastel without the use of charcoal. It is best to use a neutral colour, though tempting to use black (neutral means a colour such as muted brown or grey). Black pastel is far more substantial a colour than charcoal, and not so easy to remove. Although pastels are opaque, some colours are more opaque than others. Again, however, it is a matter of personal choice, as you can build up a pastel picture layer upon layer until even the blackest underpainting is hidden. When you are using pastel for the preliminary sketch you can also use it on its side to give areas of colour rather than strokes.

1

3

210

2

4

1. A pointillist effect has been achieved by the careful blending of colours.

2. A sense of atmosphere can be carefully captured by using a limited range of colours, in this case greens, to give a cold effect.

3. As in *1*, colour has been built up by using two or three different pastels to create the overall colour.

4. A studious approach to colour selection can produce an advanced abstract painting.

Applying the Pastel

The natural way to use pastel is to hold the stick like a pencil and using the end to colour the paper. Held at a slant, the pastel will give a thin line; held upright, a thicker line. Held lightly, the pastel will deposit less colour on the paper, and the colour of the paper will show through. Sometimes the colour of the paper can be the background without anything more needing to be done to it.

There are numerous ways to apply the pastel. Short stabs of colour can be put down, giving a patchwork effect. Various colours can be set side by side in thin strips, or 'cross-hatching' can be used – making a network of strokes, like a crossword, either the same colour or different colours. Dots of colour can be used, areas of colour can be laid down by using the pastel on its side, applied thickly by pressing down, or thinly by a lighter touch. All these techniques can be combined.

It is best to experiment with these methods when painting a picture than to do meaningless exercises on a piece of paper. A picture of some sort will emerge – it may not be much but in all art the painter gets better. A technique acquired is a permanent acquisition.

Unlike watercolours and oils, pastel colours are not mixed or blended beforehand but are mingled on the paper, using contrasting dots or patches of colour, cross-hatching, or, the favourite way and the one most used by the great pastel painters of the past, blending the colours together with the finger-tip a stump or torchon, tissue, a cotton-bud, or a brush. Some art teachers frown on finger-blending, as they say it destroys the 'bloom' of pastel.

What is this bloom? It is the effect arising from the reflection of light on the tiny granules of pigment. It can be destroyed by too much rubbing, but the remedy is to apply more pastel after the colours have been suitably blended. You have to use some discretion when finger-blending, for it is easy to make a muddy mess when too many colours merge.

Sometimes the immense variety of the tints available encourages colour mess, and if there is a risk of being overwhelmed by the sheer quantity of colour it is not a bad idea to try using a limited range of black, white, and some intermediate greys (green-grey, blue-grey, etc.).

Finger-blending can produce a perfectly even colour surface, to which shading can be added by a few granules of darker colour. This does not have to be black. Sometimes a subtle shading is wanted, where the light area merges into a darker, as around an apple or orange. The colour can then be a darker tint of the same colour, or maybe a blue.

In the early stages of painting a pastel, the

211

subject can be gently covered with a light single colour, to set the tone of the picture, and the shadows set out on this, with a touch of white to pick out the lightest parts. The 'real' colour can then be added. It is a matter of choice whether you do the picture bit by bit or tackle the whole picture in stages, so that it all comes together at the end. If you think that the picture is becoming flat and boring, you can enliven the textures, either by using pastel in a different way or roughing up the surface with a dry bristle brush. The 'highlights', those vivid small patches of white which can make a picture live, should be reserved to the very end.

At some stage in a picture you will look at the blunt end of a worn-down pastel and wonder how you are going to get any kind of detail. This problem will occur particularly in portrait painting and landscape. Do you break off a short length of pastel so that you have another sharp edge? Do you grind the blunt end down with sandpaper? You can waste a lot of pastel, and in fact a worn stick of pastel is clumsy, so that you have to resort to smaller fragments, too small to hold in the fingers. The answer is to hold a fragment of pastel with a pair of eyebrow tweezers, and use this to get fine detail, or make use of a pastel pencil. But do not expect pastels to give you the degree of precision you would get with watercolours or oils. Nor can you expect the kind of coverage you get from oils. On the other hand, it is very easy to be impressionistic or 'suggestive' with pastels, and once you are experienced it is the ideal medium for extremely quick on-the-spot sketches – you can cover a sheet of paper in two seconds flat.

One of the great advantages of pastel is that correction can be carried out quickly and decisively, either by applying a further coat of pastel or by removing some, either with a putty rubber or the dry bristle brush. It is also easy to correct or transform tones, and alter any shapes, very important in portraiture where the proportions *must* be right. An excellent way to check accuracy is to hold a work-in-progress up to a mirror, where any faults will stand out immediately. The speed with which you can work with pastel is a real asset when it comes to painting portraits; still life and landscape do not move. People, with the best will in the world, do.

There is always a temptation in pastel to make the colours too bright and, it must be said, insipid. If a picture is turning out tamely, a remedy is to mute *all* the pure colours with a neutral tint and add more colour very sparsely. If the greens of a landscape are too garish, blend in greys or some red. There is also a temptation to be satisfied with pastels that are

over-bright; pastels can be rich and subdued, as the great masters of the 18th century have shown.

With the possibilities of instant art, the ability to get an immediate effect without any kind of preliminaries, there is a temptation to apply pastel without prior thought. Without any need for preparation, the appeal of the various coloured papers, which look so agreeable in the pads of mixed colours, is often irresistible. So colours are put down; a picture is completed; from a distance it may look all right, even impressive. But perhaps it is merely flashy. Perhaps the artist can mute the garish colours, but should they have been garish to start with? And is the blaze of colour just that, colour without drawing or tone? Look at the pastel work by the great masters such as Degas and Manet. There was preparation here, as much preparation as these artists put into an oil painting. They were not interested in an immediate effect, they were not bemused by the easiness of it all, and there is no doubt that the act of putting a pastel to paper is the simplest of all actions, whether it is a child playing with its first box of wax crayons or the newcomer to pastels finding that an impression of the sea can be obtained in five seconds by drawing a flat length of dark blue pastel horizontally across a piece of light blue paper.

A simplified pastel technique can effectively suggest trees or foliage in contrast to that used by Degas in *Dancers Preparing for an Audition.*

Eight drawings of apples, each one having a different tonal background to enhance the colour. It is worth noting that the drawings in which the colours are most enhanced are those where the backgrounds are dark. This demonstrates the luminosity which can be achieved by using dark coloured papers.

214

215

Drawing with Pastels

The first thing is to choose the right tint of paper for the picture you have in mind. This can be a very personal choice; it may not be everybody's. You have to visualize what sort of impact certain colours will have on certain backgrounds. If the paper is very light, a lot of work will need to be done with dark pastels; if the paper is very dark, you will be busy with the light pastels. This may be what you want, but if you are undecided it is perhaps better to choose a paper halfway between black and white. It is possible that you have a landscape in mind, perhaps a sunset, in which case a pink paper may prove the appropriate one; the pink can be used, it does not have to use the artist.

Unless you are just interested in creating a flat pattern or a picture with the various elements running parallel with the picture surface – in other words nothing recedes and nothing is placed in space – it is necessary to know something about perspective and simple drawing. Neither is difficult. Much of it is common sense. The amount of preliminary drawing that goes into a pastel is determined by the artist; there may be very preliminary scribbles in charcoal or pencil to indicate the approximate placing of the elements in the picture, perhaps a few vertical and horizontal strokes to determine proportions. If you want a realistic picture it is important to draw what is there not what you think is there. And remember that although you will use outlines, an outline does not really exist 'out there'. It is a convention. You are drawing three-dimensional objects in two dimensions.

What is an outline? Nothing more than a dividing line between areas which are light and areas which are darker. Successful drawing, whether with a pencil, a paint brush, or pastels, depends on looking and assessing, seeing how some shapes relate to other shapes, and how light they are regarding each other. The shapes can be simple or they can be complex, but all can be put down in a convincing manner. A good example of a simple shape is a single apple on the table. We are not interested in how it grows, what the arrangement of the pips is inside, or how it tastes. We are more concerned with its solidity, and how it sits there. The look of the apple is determined by the light shining on it; away from the light the apple will be darker, and this darkness becomes less as the light area is approached. The apple will throw a shadow, and the shadow – the cast shadow – will be darker than the shadows on the apple or the background shadows.

Where the lighting is very stark and dramatic you may not be able to detect the shape of the

apple at all. All you may see is a bright curve where the light strikes the side of the apple, with the rest of it in darkness. You will know what the apple looks like even if you cannot see it in full light. The same applies to another simple shape, a cottage in a field. We do not need to know how the cottage was built or how many rooms there are inside; all we see is a rectangle with a shape on top, the roof. Depending on where we are standing we may see part of the side of the cottage, and the shadows will depend on whereabouts the sun is. The rectangle will be broken up by inner rectangles – the doors and the windows – and we know they are there because we know about buildings and are interpreting what we see. If the front of the cottage is in part shadow, a window may show up as a small horizontal slash of light where the sun picks out the window sill. A door which a child would portray as a tall rectangle (with maybe a blob for the door knob) may be recognized by a dark shadow part-way up the cottage, where the upper part of the door, partly inset, is overshadowed by the brick work above.

The cottage may be built of brick, and some of these bricks, depending on the light, may show up more than others. So although you will know the bricks are there, and you may be tempted to begin putting them all in, you will not be able to pick them all out if you are standing some distance away from the cottage. You will just see changes of tone and, if the bricks are old and handmade, some changes of colour. If the lighting is from above, if the sun is high in the sky, the bricks may merely be detected by shadows beneath them (bricks slightly protruding casting their shadows on to the bricks below or the mortar).

The effect of solidity is achieved by placing an object in space, space of your own making, and this is done by using perspective. Perspective is with us all the time, and we take it for granted. If you lift your eyes from this page and look around at any angular surface such as the top of a chest-of-drawers you will see that the top does not appear to be a perfect rectangle, and that the two sides almost imperceptibly seem to move towards each other. If the chest-of-drawers was 200 metres long the sides would most probably appear to meet. If the top of the chest-of-drawers is just below eye-level the angle of the top will be sharper than if you are standing up and looking down on it. Perhaps perspective is more readily appreciated by going outdoors.

If you look along a straight road towards the horizon the road appears to narrow, and a person travelling up this road seems to become smaller, losing height at the same rate as the

Cornfield by Denis Barker. An
atmospheric study of harvest
time.

Detail above: Sharpened pastel has been carefully used to show tree details.

Detail right: The detail shows pastel technique

Water Meadows by Denis Barker. This interesting composition is enlivened by the dramatic winter light.

218

road narrows. Telegraph poles will seem to shrink in proportion, and if you draw an imaginary line which connects the bases of the poles and another which connects the tops of the poles and extend them you will find that they meet on the horizon. The only time to see a true horizon is at sea where sky meets water. The horizon has nothing to do with the sky-line. If you are in mountainous country the sky-line is way above you and the horizon is behind the hills and mountains at eye-level. For that is where the horizon is, always at eye-level.

Objects above or partly above eye-level seem to go down towards the horizon and those below seem to go up. If you stand at the top of a high-rise building and study the pattern of roofs you will see them all converging towards the distance, where the horizon is. They will not always be converging towards the same place on the horizon, for although there is only one horizon at one time, and in any one picture, there can be several vanishing points. If you go outside and look at the roof of a house you will see it obeying the laws of perspective. It will point towards its own vanishing point. If it is a terrace of houses of the same size and kind their roofs will all recede to the same point, unless they are in a crescent. But in a traditional old-world village with houses and cottages built anywhere, each roof (and each wall) will have its own vanishing point.

The horizon can be as high or as low as you wish, and can even be off the top of the paper if you are looking down on a subject. But it is there. Sometimes perspective can be tampered

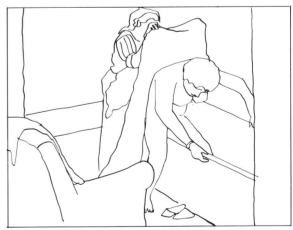

This small pastel study by Degas is brought to life by the clever use of perspective. The lines of convergence would, interestingly, meet behind the figure. *Woman Getting Out of her Bath.*

221

with to get an effect, and perspective can be fun. The painters of fantasy pictures sometimes use two perspectives in the same picture to achieve a kind of unreality. Perspective is a tool of the artist; it does not have to be exact; that can be left to architects.

One of the obvious facts about perspective is that objects 'in the front' of the picture are much larger than those behind. A way to illustrate this is not in drawings but in photography. If you photograph a figure in bathing costume on a beach, a favourite subject, and the legs are extended towards the camera, these legs can appear ridiculously long and malformed. When we are looking without a camera we make mental adjustments; the legs are so long, and that is the end of it. But the camera does not make such adjustments. It records. If a person extends a clenched fist towards you it appears enormous, and can appear larger than the rest of the person. This 'device' is much used in advertising and in posters.

Some of the least obvious subjects are governed by perspective. Failing to take account of it can result in pictures being flat and uninteresting, white blobs against the sky. Clouds are objects in space, just as everything else is.

Perspective is not so much a law as a convenience; it is certainly not a hard-and-fast law like the law of gravity, because there is an exception which goes under the name of accidental vanishing points. Surfaces which are tilted sometimes – and the key word is sometimes – converge on vanishing points which are above and below eye-level. The best way to illustrate this is to hold a sheet of card at a slant. A good example is to look at a road going uphill where the sides will appear to converge at a point above the horizon; below the horizon if the road is going downhill. This of course is useful if you want to depict a road going uphill or downhill from memory.

A working knowledge of perspective is a help if you are inserting extra features into a 'real' landscape. If it is a person you work out how tall he or she would be in the foreground, perhaps getting the dimensions by reference to a tree or a door in a building. You then draw perspective lines to the horizon from the top of the figure and the bottom, and you use these as a reference to fit in the extra characters wherever you like. They do not have to be within the lines of course. They do not have to look as though they are waiting in a queue. You can set them anywhere parallel with their projected position.

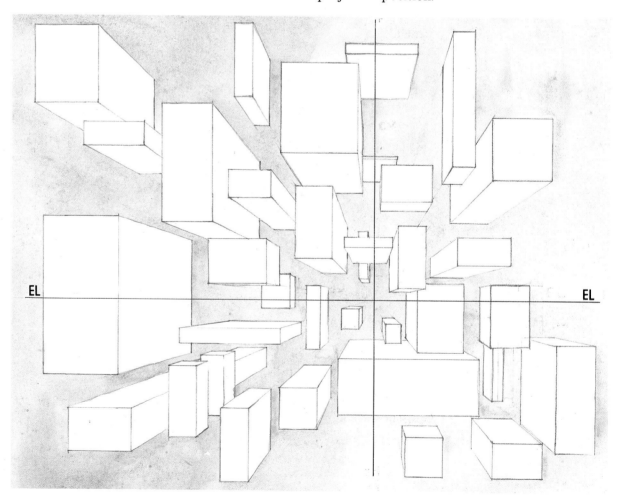

A student's drawing showing a perspective exercise.

222

Aerial perspective has nothing to do with the kind of perspective we have been looking at. It is all about atmosphere. Dust and moisture obscure more distant objects, and the further away something is the lighter in tone and the less distinct it will appear. In pastel this can be indicated by lighter colours, a broken line, absence of detail, and the use of bluish tints, perhaps overlying the 'local' colours by using the flat of the pastel very lightly, just brushing the paper surface. Detail in the distance can be blurred by gently going over the pastel with the tip of a finger, a stump, or a cotton bud.

Does perspective work for you? The easiest way to find out is to go out and sketch a building, where perspective can most easily be seen in action. How do you start? First put in a horizon. If you have difficulty deciding where this is, extend your fist with the thumb uppermost until it is on the level with the eye. This is your horizon. If you stoop, the horizon will change. You can then put in preliminary casual lines, perhaps in charcoal or a neutral tint such as mid-grey, not worrying if they are accurate but setting the scene. As you become more certain you can press a little harder on the charcoal or pastel, finding a good starting-off point, maybe an angle of the wall where there are sharp, easily depicted shadows, perhaps a window or window surround. Concentrate on the parts which are most interesting; maybe an elaborate doorway, with interesting shadows inside. There is no need to go on to complete the drawing.

Cottage and Stream, an exquisite pastel by Ken Jackson, uses advanced perspective techniques.

Landscape and Townscape

Landscape is unquestionably the most popular form of art amongst non-professionals. It always has been and always will be. And it is equally suitable for pencil, pen-and-ink, watercolour, oil, acrylic, and pastels. The reasons are many: landscape is there and does not have to be arranged; you can pick the vantage point that suits you, avoiding difficult subjects if you wish; landscapes are motionless, and although there will be changes of light they proceed mostly at a leisurely pace. And doing a landscape on the spot can be an enjoyable day out. Pastels are very convenient for outdoor work as there is no water to spill, you do not have to wait until the paper is dry before carrying on, and if there are sudden climatic changes you can take advantage of them simply by virtue of the speed with which you can put something down on paper. The main thing to remember is to keep your pastels in a secure box or tray so that they do not roll or get blown away. Always take a variety of different colour pastel papers with you, and use the appropriate colour for the weather conditions. If the weather is brooding and it is all set for a storm, use a grey. If it is brilliant sunshine, and there are promising cornfields, use a yellowish tint which will give a sunny feel to the picture and can also be used to depict the cornfields without much added pastel (except to add tone and shadow).

Only depict what you personally find interesting. If you find the view dull you will produce a dull picture. It is never much fun to do things for practice; you are not being paid after all. Some advisers recommend pastel-users to do little squares of colour to see what they look like. But you know what the colours look like. If you miscalculate, what does it matter? Trial and error will teach you more than a series of little squares of pastel colour.

When you are looking at a landscape you may wonder where the 'edges' of your picture should be, and where you should start off. Where should the picture begin and end? An easy way out is to make a home-made viewfinder, a piece of card with a rectangular hole in it which you hold against a likely view, either horizontally or vertically. Not only will you be able to pick a good composition (in which the interest is held in the picture rather than drifting out the sides) but it will help to relate the elements to each other, working out which shapes are darker than others, when half-closing the eyes helps. When you start, it is better to start at the focal point of the composition (a barn, a tree, a stream) and work outwards rather than start at the left of the picture and fill in methodically across the paper (or right to left if you are left-handed).

224

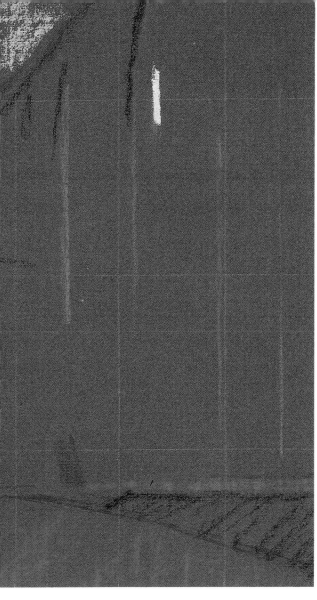

Left, above: The first step in the making of the pastel overleaf. The artist has quickly sketched in the basic shapes, using the sky for definition.

If you are doing a realistic pastel, put down what you can see, not what you know is there. If there is detail it is in the foreground only (you are not a predatory bird which can see a mouse at 200 metres). If there are trees look how the shadows fall, how groups of leaves throw shadows on those below, and those below that, and discover that you cannot really see the individual leaves in a cluster but only varying tones. What might seem changes of colour may be changes of tone.

Trunks should be made to appear solid, by shading, and varying the degree of shading to indicate roundness. Try not to put in a symbol of a tree, rather than a real tree, and trees by themselves often have trunks which are not absolutely vertical. Do not forget the shadows beneath the tree, which may well prevent the trunk being seen, and study how the trunk goes into the ground and does not stick up on top of it. When doing a landscape, all the objects are in it, not on it. Individual blades of grass are in the foreground, not the middle distance, and in pastel they can be expressed by putting in a background colour and adding discreet strokes, remembering that even individual blades of grass have their shaded side. Except in the foreground, grass can best be expressed by shading. Tufts have a shaded side and cast shadows onto the ground just as something more solid, such as a boulder, does. In the middle distance grass is best represented by graduating the tones as the ground rises and falls.

Bushes should be observed very closely, for the changes of tone need not be dramatic, and there is nothing easier than making a bush look like a crumpled dishcloth. Half close the eyes, and try to get the feel of 'bushiness', observing how the clumps of leaves near the top of the bush throw shadows on those below, and how the bottom of the bush, often in deep shadow, can be enlivened by foreground grass and plants which are in the light and therefore silhouette themselves against the shadow. Hedgerows are marvellous props in the distance, helping to define fields and establishing relative sizes of other objects, such as far-off buildings.

Much that applies to landscapes applies to townscape. Never anticipate detail which you cannot see; always place in the horizon at an early stage, and use perspective lines as a help in drawing objects to scale. Of course there are more pure verticals in townscape, easy to put in with lightly applied pastel on its side (what the verticals represent can be added later). If you are nervous about venturing into town armed only with a pad of paper do your work from your car. This helps, too, if you are embarrassed by people looking over your shoulder. Townscapes can sometimes look odd without people,

Left, below: The atmosphere of the picture is beginning to come alive through the dramatic use of light and shade.

225

The finished painting. A limited range of colours has enhanced the dramatic quality.

so add them in. There is no need to do more than indicate them with a stab of the pastel, perhaps adding a little light pastel on the top to indicate the presence of a face. Use perspective lines to establish their relative size, and remember the shadows and that they fall the same way as other objects in the picture. It is also worth noting that groups of figures appear in a blob with smaller blobs (the heads) on top and that legs may not be seen if the light source is high.

Cars and other vehicles also contribute to the liveliness of a townscape. They can be indicated roughly, and act as focal points to direct the attention towards a certain part of the picture. If you do a car from memory you may get it wrong, overemphasizing the top and making the car too high. In a street scene the heads of the pedestrians are over the tops of the cars. You may make the windows clear, where in certain lights they may be opaque. The wheels may be almost completely in shadow, which may be a plus as you can suggest the curvature of wheels rather than patiently put in arcs (use the side of a coin if you cannot do curves freehand).

If you find pastel too broad for intricate landscapes and townscapes use sharper tools for detail – coloured pencil, pastel pencils, felt pens, and if the pastel surface is thick and fluffy go over it with an aerosol fixative which gives a crisp surface to further work, whether in pastel or some other medium.

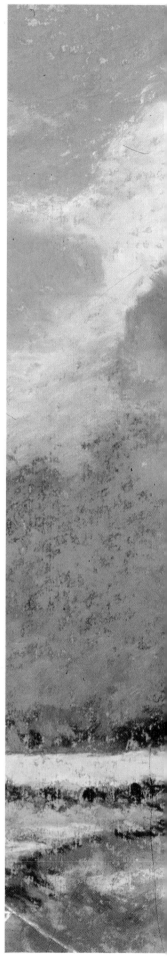

Barn in a Field by Denis Barker: All the drama of aerial perspective and linear perspective are brought to bear in this atmospheric pastel painting.

Detail above: Note how the artist has used the reflected sunlight on top of the telegraph poles to reverse what would normally be dark against light as distinct from light against dark at the bottom of the poles.

As a general rule, as in this picture, warm colours suggest nearness and cold colours distance. The artist has managed to bring the picture to life by the suggestion of the yellow roof which is reflected light from the wheatfields.

In this sequence of
illustrations we show how easy
it is to make a picture which
uses the simplest design.

Step 1: The artist has chosen a
blue-grey background and
with soft pencil has drawn in
his rough composition.

Step 2: With a broad rendering
of the basic colours the
picture has already
established itself.

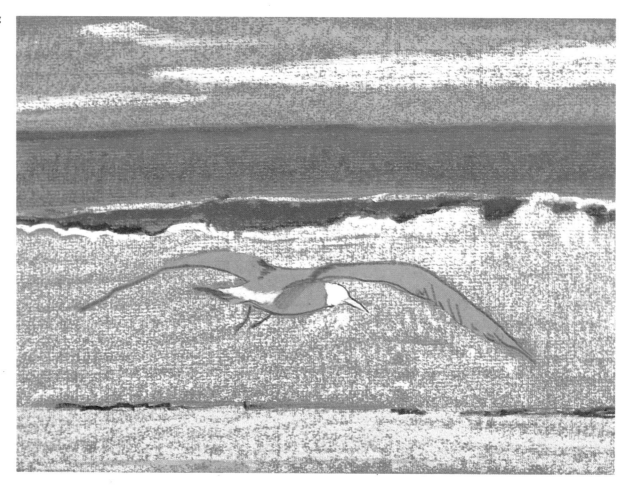

Step 3: Vigorous use of pastel has been applied to give more contrast.

Step 4: The finished picture. (One thing a student of pastels must learn is to know when a picture is finished. Many a painting has been ruined by an attempt to render too much detail. One could argue that *Step 3* is in fact a better picture than *Step 4.)*

231

232

Tugs on the River by Denis Barker. The artist uses a broad technique to capture the atmospheric quality of the scene.

Left: A good example of aerial perspective. A painting in which a coarse technique has been used.

233

Lupins in the Landscape by Denis Barker. This charming landscape has been brought to life by the intelligent use of colour in the shadow detail which gives an Impressionistic quality of light. The lupins in the foreground hold your eye as the warmth of the flower causes the landscape to recede.

(a) Below: The clever use of aerial perspective is shown in this detail.

(b) Bottom: The whole picture has the feeling of moving to the left, thus uncovering the delightful rabbits which are brought to our attention.

Any landscape provides interesting subject matter. The ditch flowing through the centre of the picture is enhanced by the telegraph poles reaching upwards to the storm-laden sky. Denis Barker's picture brilliantly records the atmosphere of this late autumn scene.

A New Orleans street scene offers an example of dramatic perspective. One of the important techniques used in any painting is not to draw the shapes but to draw the spaces in between the shapes. Details of the telegraph poles have been shown not by drawing them but by filling in the areas around them.

The same thing applies to the artist's method of rendering a car.

238

Oil Pastels Oil pastels are less versatile than water-based pastels, and are really a substitute for painting in oils. They can be softened and applied to the surface with a palette knife, and, like ordinary oil paints, thinned with turpentine. Perhaps they are most useful as an oil-painting accessory, though some people might find that they take to them better than ordinary pastels, as they are denser in texture. They can be used on paper if they are employed in purely stick form, but if they are thinned with turpentine the paper will stain through, leaving the pastel surface dull. If paper is used, and the oil pastels are softened or diluted, it will need to be sized.

Oil pastels are excellent for capturing movement and for drawing animals as they do not smudge easily when the hand is moving rapidly over the surface. They also have the potential value of being used as a basis for oil painting later.

239

Figure Studies and Portraits

There is no better medium for figure work and portraits than pastels. In France in the 18th century portraits in pastel were brought to a peak of excellence, with beautiful skin tones and a luminosity and a freshness that persist to this day. Pastels do not deteriorate with age. If you want to improve your drawing the best way is to draw or paint the nude human figure; if you can do this you can tackle any subject, and the best way is to join a life class, perhaps at a night school. Do not be embarrassed or alarmed in case your standard of work is too low; no-one else is. Many people who go to art classes go as a hobby, some have been going for several years, have never been or may never be much good, but no-one bothers. Art classes usually last about two hours; the first part of the session will be devoted to one or two rigid poses, but towards the end many art teachers organize five-minute poses for quick sketches, ideal for pastel work. And sometimes the need to finish off a pastel drawing in a few minutes brings out a hitherto unrevealed talent.

It is best to use a large sheet of paper, for if you are working on a small sheet arms and legs have a tendency not to fit in. There are many ways of tackling the nude figure: sketching in a brief charcoal outline and building on that; putting in with the flat of the pastel the background shadows, and depicting the figure against these; blocking in the main masses of the figure with a medium tint, then toning in the darks and then the lights: using a dark paper and starting with the highlights, working up to the mid-tones and the dark-tones. It is up to the individual. As in landscapes, only put in what you see, not what you know. Anyone can draw a mouth freehand and have it recognized as a mouth. But when looked at in a certain light the mouth may only be discernible as a shadow beneath the lower lip; the nose may be detected as a shadow shape on the cheek.

Again, it is up to the individual artist where to start. Some begin at the head, some a solid torso, building this up with tones and then adding the legs and arms, indicating them *en route* with tentative lines and patches of tone and colour. Proportions are more important than anatomy; a man is eight heads tall, a woman six heads, a one-year-old child four heads; the halfway point down of a man is the crutch. There are one or two tricky points – the neck does not rest on top of the shoulders but is inset slightly below. A man's neck slopes outwards, a woman's inwards. When drawing a hand, remember that unless it is extended the thumb droops. Watch where you put in the ankle; it can make all the difference between a convincing foot and one that falls short. Getting

the proportions right is helped by holding the fist at arm's length and measuring up with the thumb. For instance, the body may be a three-quarter thumb length; the legs a thumb length. If you prefer, use a wooden ruler instead.

Solidity is more important than accuracy. If the body looks as though it is made of cardboard the shading is wrong. The shading can be altered in a few seconds in pastel either by adding tone, or, if it is a dark paper, by taking off some of the pastel and letting the paper show through more. The shading can be 'moulded' by gently merging the pastel tones into each other with the finger tip. If you are more experienced with landscape than life drawing, look on the human body as a tree trunk in which the shadows vary according to the direction of the light (the French artist Leger interpreted human beings as a collection of cylinders, which may be going too far!)

If you have begun the pastel with a charcoal outline and are beginning to apply colour, it is worth remembering that you do not have to stop at the lines; you are not a child filling in a colouring book. Outlines, as we have seen, are a convenience. You use them when you want them. When they have served their purpose, as a preliminary basis, they are disposable,

In this portrait the artist has used a variety of pastel techniques such as the subtle combination of colour explained in the abstract diagrams on page 43.

Victor Ambrus's study *Seated Girl with Hat* is a splendid example of the use of a quick outline drawing with a broad, flat rendering obtained by using the side of the pastel stick to allow the background colour to show through.

240

doomed to languish under their pastel covering.

Many artists who do costume work – clothed figures – often depict their subjects nude then add the clothes on later. This helps some, but there is no need for it. But it does emphasize that the pose of the figure determines the way the clothes lie or fall. Folds in clothing are of four kinds: in hanging, pulled, heaped, and crushed materials. Folds are not expressed in changes of colour but changes of tone. The 'real' colour can be laid in first in a broad spread and the 'shadow' colour can be pastelled in on top. It is tricky to try to reproduce patterns and textures as they are, but better to indicate them briefly unless the pattern is very aggressive.

Victor Ambrus's reclining
nude. A broad technique has
been employed to capture the
soft translucent quality of the
flesh. In this case the subject
matter is lighter than the
background as described in
the exercise on apples on page
46. The delightful 19th
century drawing (*inset*) gives
the feeling of full colour in
spite of only two colours being
used.

242

Of all the subjects, portraits are perhaps ideal for the pastellist, and it is easier to get models; all you need is a mirror and you have yourself, and you will probably not need to walk more than six feet to get expert advice as to where you went wrong (if you did). There are, as with figures, numerous ways to do a portrait, many ways to start. Many portraitists start with the eyes and, whether or not they are windows of the soul, a good eye can be a decided plus when the portrait is completed. The eye comes in three divisions – pupil, eyelid, eyelashes, not to forget the pouch beneath the eye. Always put a highlight into the pupil of the eye; it need not be dead centre, but make certain that it is in the same position in each eye.

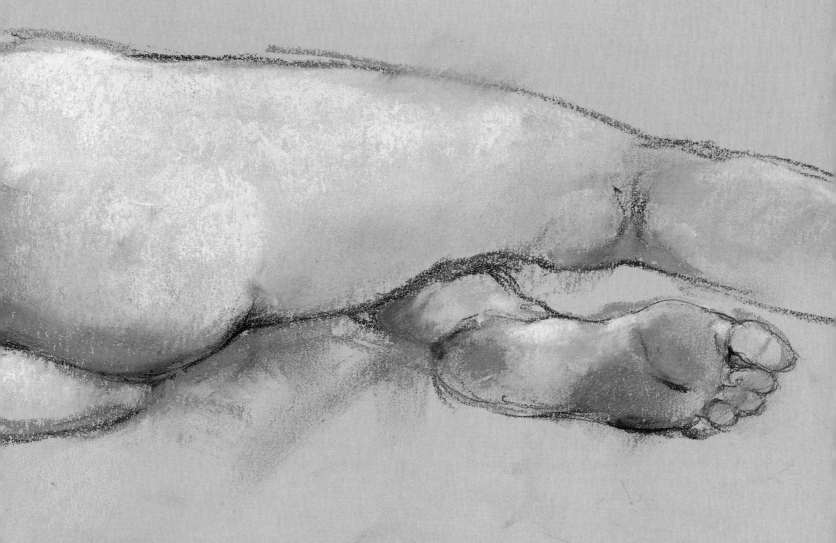

One experienced portraitist, W. H. Allcott, R.W.A., R.B.A., described his method of work. He first drew the outline of the head in charcoal or black Conté crayon, choosing a three-quarter view as this provided the best shadows. He then drew in the features lightly and fixed the shadows, which he toned in. Then with pale orange or yellow ochre pastel he drew lightly over the entire drawing, except the hair, using the pastel on its side and letting the paper show through. On this tinted surface he then used sepia to put in the eyes, nose, mouth, etc., and then filled in the mouth with vermilion or crimson. The shadows were then inserted, with definite edges, in brown. If the eyes were blue or grey he lightly tinted with those colours. The next stage was to indicate the lines of the neck, stressing the pit of the neck, very important for setting the head on the shoulders. Then the hair, first of all put in lightly, and built up. It was important to note the direction of the growth and the shape of the masses. That was the end of the sitting. He then took the drawing back to his studio and built it up from there, adding colour and tone, but he had the basics. The next day he would return, check his work, and make any alterations. He made the point that some newcomers to pastel find spectacles difficult; some artists add them later, but Allcott was not in favour of this, preferring to incorporate them in his first drawing, emphasizing the need to note the size of the lens and how far the bottom rim was from the wing of the nose. He found that the line of the frame from the lens to the ear was useful in estimating the proportion of face and head. Another method, equally commendable and used by practised artists, is to use a mid-toned paper, put in an oval shape in charcoal, and mark off the position of the features. There are various aids to this: the eye is halfway down the head, if the head is front on, the tops of the ears are level with the eyelid; the distance between the top of the forehead and the top of the nose is about the same as the distance between the top of the nose and the bottom of the nose. The distance between the top of the upper lip and the bottom of the chin is about the same as that between the top of the ear and the bottom of the ear. It is advisable to stress the word 'about' for the small variations – and they are small – is what distinguishes one person from another.

After the features have been set in, charcoal is rubbed in to establish light and shade, using a putty rubber to pick out highlights. Colour is put in from dark to light, keeping the pastel strokes loose and not putting in too much detail. Background tones are then put in, and where the figure abuts the background a light

The building-up of a head, using pastels. Here, the artist has worked from a sketch outline through to a very finished study.

colour is put around it, forming a discreet kind of halo. This helps to locate the subject in space, against the background. Warm tints are used for the face, using a grey of the same colour group to increase definition. Bluey greys are then worked into the hollows of the cheek, chin, and top of nose. Simple detail is introduced to the clothing, but the clothing 'tapers off' leaving a good deal of the paper blank.

The colours can also be applied first without preliminary drawing. The dark and warm colours are first loosely laid down, and then the lighter and colder colours are added, using the flat of the pastel and rubbing in with the finger tips if required. The work is carried out dark to light, and the outline is drawn in with a hard pastel. As the background is fairly thin in texture the hard pastel will take; there is no need to use black. Brown or red are sometimes preferred. Add colour to the parts, shadows and dark tones first, using the finger sparingly or not at all. The colour of the paper of course can be fully utilized. A good paper colour for a portrait is yellowish or warm brown; both impart a cheerful character to the picture. Grey is also good, giving a quiet effect, but blue is not recommended for portraits as when the first colours are put in they appear warmer than they do later when the whole of the painting is coloured in. To keep the face clear of the background, the tone immediately round the head should be darker than the half tones of the face but lighter than the shadows. A good way of applying one colour over another is to apply the first diagonally, letting the paper partly show through, and then apply the second colour, also diagonally but in the opposite direction. These tones can be blended with the finger tip.

245

This series takes the student step by step through the development of a portrait.

The picture is beginning to develop. The artist has paid more attention to his colouring and tone rather than to the sketching of the detail.

Choosing a background colour (as previously described) darker than the subject matter enables the pastel to illuminate from the negative colour background. The artist has broadly, with a brown colour, sketched in the darker areas and has suggested the shape and position of the subject with other colours.

The portrait is very near its completion. The colour has been built up not by one but by several applications of colours and the finger is used to merge in the soft tone.

The final picture is brought to life by the application of darker and lighter tones. Note that the only white used is on the highlights of the nose and eye.

In these two studies by Victor Ambrus, there is a contrast in styles. In the one on the *left*, pastel is used extremely subtly, with the colours softly merging and the detail suggested by a black line which is all that remains of his preliminary sketch. The *right-hand* figure, in complete contrast, is drawn with vigorous application of pastel end-on, thus producing a spontaneous effect. Note that the artist used a number of colours to make up the whole despite his vigorous technique.

250

251

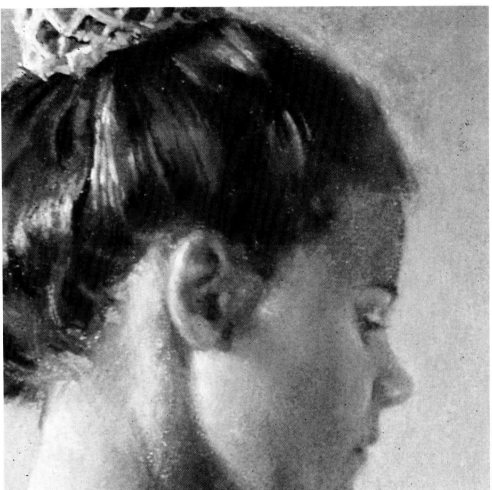

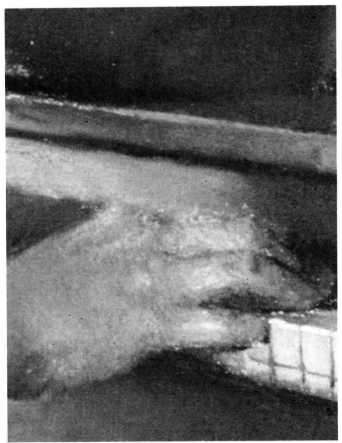

Girl at the Piano by Ken Jackson. All the techniques previously described have been used to make this delightful composition. Interestingly, the artist has chosen to draw the figure pointing away from the light source.

Above: In this detail you can see that the softness of the face has been achieved by massaging the colours with the finger and using darker colours to suggest the detail.

Left detail: Although hands are said to be difficult to draw, the artist has suggested the detail of fingers by his subtle use of lightness of tone and colour.

253

Finger painting is another option. The head is sketched in in charcoal on smoothish, fairly dark paper, and flesh colours such as yellow ochre and vermilion are put down on a separate piece of paper. These are taken up on the finger and applied to the light parts of the face such as the cheeks, forehead and chin. A brown or black pastel (brown is warmer) is then used in the orthodox way as a drawing instrument to emphasize the shadows, but the features are only suggested, and the paper is left for the half tones. Then, using the finger again, a little white is added to the flesh colour and the highlights are put in. This can be carried to any degree of completion. When doing portraits it is wise to stand back from the picture from time to time, assessing how it is going, and the same is true of figure studies and still life.

If you can do a good portrait in pastel you will never have any lack of sitters; and some of them will eagerly pay to have their likenesses done. The artist William Rothenstein wrote many wise things about the art of pastel portraiture:

'The success of a portrait drawing depends on many fortuitous things, as the quality of the paper and chalk; on the artist's mood at the time; but mostly on the sitter, for the sitter helps to make or mar his own portrait: some the moment they pose excite one's pencil, others paralyse the will, one cannot keep a pose; others, especially old people, must be kept interested. Men, equally with women, wish to appear other than they are – the mirror will not lie, but the artist must be persuaded; yet if he compromises over form,

his drawing will suffer.'

Of course the various pastel techniques can be used on other subjects, such as still life and animal pictures, which offer enormous scope to the pastellist. Fur and coat is ideal, and there is no better way to reproduce rabbit hair than a mixture of grey and white blended together with the finger tips, and then overlaid with strokes drawn with the corner of a pastel stick. Easy creatures to draw are rodents, which can be taken in at a glance and can be blocked in immediately with pastel used on its side without the need to do a preliminary charcoal sketch. A useful tip is that the torso and legs of many animals such as a dog and a cow fit into a perfect square. When drawing animals remember that they have necks! The right proportions are vital for good animal studies, so use photographs and other illustrations to ensure that you get them right, if necessary using a pair of dividers to compare dimensions. The legs are important. When drawing a dog remember the peculiar shape of the back leg. But once you get it right you will always know in future where you have gone wrong.

Because of their bright colouring birds are delightful subjects for pastels, but it must always be remembered that what might seem a change of colour is a change of tone. Feathers are rarely effective put on one by one; it is better to insert them in batches, aware that these sections of feathers shade those below them. Bright colours are not sacrosanct, and often they must be amended to make them hang together in all types of picture and in all mediums.

Pastel is an excellent medium to use for drawing animals. A few broad strokes is all that is required to suggest fur.

Even though this is a drawing
of a kitten, all the pastel
techniques previously
described have been used to
create this delightful study of
the artist's pet.

Still Life and Flowers

The above also applies to still life and flower pictures, where the hues may need to be altered, sometimes drastically, sometimes subtly, to create a picture which is all of a piece. More even than in landscape still life pictures need a focal point to which the eye is drawn; it is sometimes known as an anchor, and colour and tone help. Various techniques can be used to set down a still life – charcoal outline, broad masses with the tones added later, putting in the shadows first and laying the objects against it. If a still life picture remains a collection of objects without rhyme or reason it can be very boring. So how do we bring all the objects together to make the picture work?

By manipulating colour. Suppose you have a group of objects including a white cup. How do you depict the gleaming highlight on this cup? If you paint the cup its real colour, where is the highlight? Nowhere, for it cannot be seen. White against white does not go. So white must be reserved for the highest note in the picture, the highlight, and the cup must be painted grey. There is no other way. And with this highlight in, it must be protected. This may mean muting the yellows to greens, the reds become browns and purples, and the blues are put down as dark greys or blue-blacks. Because articles in the picture have to be toned down, so will the background, which will be undifferentiated so that it will not detract from the low tone elements in the picture.

Altering colour in this manner exercises not only observation but taste, and the great advantage with pastel is that experiments can be carried out without pausing, as would be the case with watercolours and oils where you may sometimes have to take into account the damp paint surface and wait for it to dry.

Many flower painters endeavour to represent every flower, stalk, and leaf as an identifiable botanical specimen, and this is all right if it is your favourite approach. But the accumulation of detail can be counter-productive, and can result in lack of atmosphere, colour clashes, and an absence of harmony. The background should be that, and not intrusive; blooms or leaves at the edge of the field of vision should be allowed to take second place by using muted colour and by softened edges. Some pastellists advise that the focal point should be painted in full colour and the passages of secondary interest should be pastelled in in quieter tones.

To get three-dimension roundness not only in flower paintings but in still life, figures, and portraits, you may need to tone down those surfaces which are receding. For example, in a face lit in front, the cheeks are seen as receding planes and so their edges must be subdued in tone otherwise the face will seem flat and uninteresting. This toning down can be done by smoothing with the finger tip or by using intermediate colours to bridge the gap. In flower painting, a yellow flower receding against a blue background would need a narrow band of yellow-green or a very muted purple adjacent to the yellow and a band of blue-green next to the blue background. Regarding the proportion of strong colours to neutral colours, an old recipe was to allot two-thirds of the paper to neutral colours, one third to full colours.

Closing Stages

Having reached the stage where the painting is coming along nicely, you should check that the picture hangs together well, and that the colour combination is right. The objects should look real and solid, and the light and shade realistic.

The shadows should not be too harsh; if they are too black add in a lighter colour. If you want to focus attention on just one part of the picture (for example a face in a portrait) gently blur the edges of features you want to demote. If you want to highlight something, add a fleck

of white. If you consider the picture finished hold it upright and gently tap it on a table to get rid of surplus pastel dust. Then apply the fixative. Fixative can be applied at *any* stage throughout the painting, and pastel used on top. It is not a varnish.

In this still life, the artist has chosen very brightly coloured objects with a bright background. He has used an outline, rather than the suggestion of shadow for shape, and has finger-blended the pastels.

259

MOUNTING AND FRAMING PASTELS

Some people draw a margin round their paper before they start doing a pastel, and keep their picture inside this inner area. Others use what area of paper they want, and consequently the subject matter is not necessarily in the middle. A number of mounts should be kept handy, so that when the picture is completed a mount can be placed over it to see what needs to be in and what is superfluous.

Pastels can be framed like water colours, with a cut cardboard mount to keep the picture surface off the glass. Large pastels tend to crinkle if mounted free, and should be pasted down on mounting board using wallpaper paste.

The pastel is placed face down on a pad of newspaper, the back moistened with a large soft brush, and then put on one side while the mount is pasted. The pastel is then placed snug against the mounting board, making certain that there are no air pockets. Suitable mounts can be cut using a scalpel or craft knife.

Pastels can also be framed without using a cardboard mount, in which case a fillet of wood or card (known as a 'slip') is fitted round the edge of the inner frame so that it separates the pastel from the glass. Even after the use of fixative, a certain pastel-powder loss must be expected if the picture is directly against the glass. Pastels do not fade, nor are they subject to mould. If pastel pictures are stored they should be interleaved with tissue paper; there is a slight powder loss, but of no great consequence.

INTRODUCTION TO
Oil painting

Poplars by Claude Monet. In this dramatic composition, the poplars follow the curve of the river bank, swing into the centre of the picture and back to the left and then down and away to the right. Cropping heightens the sense of rhythm and space.

CONTENTS

Introduction

For those who like a challenge there is no substitute for painting in oils. Many people believe that it needs three tons of equipment to set up. This is not so. All you need are a few brushes, paints, something on which to spread the paints for mixing, and something to paint on.

Oils have a quality of their own. The paint can be thick and luscious – some painters build up their paint until it is an inch thick – or it can be hardly more than a stain. There is nothing you cannot do with oils. You don't have to stand at a huge easel and splash about. Some of the best artists have done their work on tiny pieces of card three or four inches across.

There is no one best way of painting oil pictures. This book will name some of the methods, but you may very well evolve your own. Perhaps you like atmospheric landscapes but, when faced with thick pigment oozing from a tube, you wonder how you can do them. However much you try, you find that the paint is being built up on the picture surface. What do you do?

This was a problem faced more than sixty years ago. So what did an eminent art teacher do? He gently placed a sheet of tissue paper on the wet painting. This absorbed the surplus paint and left a misty film. Just what he wanted. And perhaps a trick that you can use.

Adventure, enjoyment, challenge – painting in oils has them all. Just take the first step.

Section of the still life study

WHAT ARE OIL PAINTS?

Most pigments are multi-purpose; oil paints are pigments blended with oil. They are put on a surface with a brush or a palette knife, either neat from the tube or mixed with something to make the paint run nicely. There is always learned dispute as to which is more difficult, oil or watercolour, and there is no answer. Neither is very difficult if you do not panic. Mistakes are easier to take out in oils, and you can use a canvas over and over again.

WHAT MATERIALS ARE NEEDED?

Paints These come in tubes, and there is an immense range. So-called 'students' colours are now labelled differently, and are much cheaper than 'artists' colours. Buying expensive ranges offers no real advantage as most paints will outlast you and your children. Until the last century artists made their own pigments from powdered colours, and as this was often a hit-or-miss system, especially when the artist was drunk, some of these hand-made colours were so fugitive that they could disappear from the canvas within a few years. Buy big tubes rather than little tubes; if you take the trouble to keep the top on, the paint will stay moist for years and years. I use paints which I bought in the 1950s and they are as good as new. Tubes are always well labelled, and these labels are marked with asterisks to indicate the degree of permanence. This is not very important. To all intents and purposes the colours will stay the same.

However, if you are concerned about the lasting properties of certain pigments, here is a run-down by R. Myerscough-Walker, A.R.I.B.A., who studied the question:

Lead whites: good in oils, not so good in watercolour. Avoid using with vermilion, pale madders, or cadmiums. When Myerscough-Walker was writing it was not realized how dangerous lead-based paints were and, although this danger is minimal to adults who are not going to eat paint or inhale any fumes, there are so many substitutes for lead white that it can safely be regarded as an unnecessary colour.

Zinc and Chinese white: good in watercolour or tempera, liable to crack in oil.

Titanium white: then a new colour, now known to be reliable.

Cadmiums: not to be mixed with lead white or emerald green.

266

Black

Chrome Green

Black

White

Yellow Ochre

White

Burnt Sienna

Alizarin Crimson

Burnt Umber

Cadmium Yellow

Cadmium Red

Chrome Green

Cadmium Yellow

Monastral Blue

Cobalt Blue

Violet

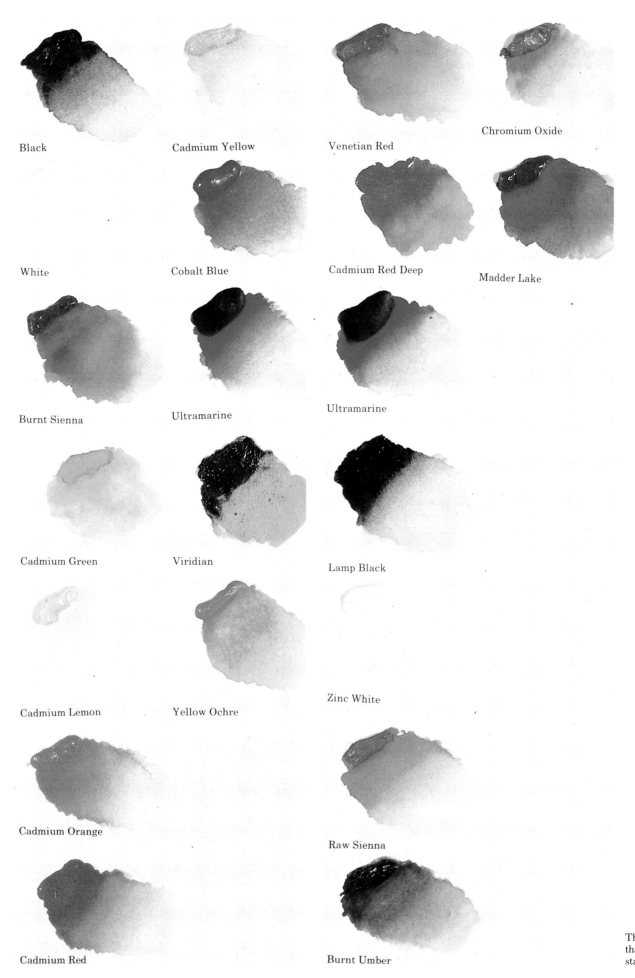

Black

Cadmium Yellow

Venetian Red

Chromium Oxide

White

Cobalt Blue

Cadmium Red Deep

Madder Lake

Burnt Sienna

Ultramarine

Ultramarine

Cadmium Green

Viridian

Lamp Black

Cadmium Lemon

Yellow Ochre

Zinc White

Cadmium Orange

Raw Sienna

Cadmium Red

Burnt Umber

The basic selection of colours
that you will need when you
start to paint in oils.

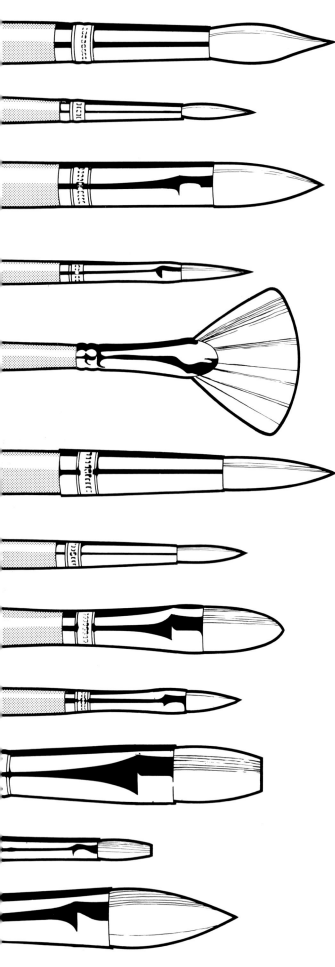

Chromes: uncertain unless of the best quality.

Raw sienna: very dangerous in oils.

Gamboge: not good in oils, fades in water-colours.

Cadmium red: must not be mixed with mala-chite, emerald green, or Prussian blue.

Vermilion: must not be mixed with lead white or emerald green. Tends to darken.

Spectrum red: good in watercolours, but may stain a superimposed colour in oils.

Alazarins: must not be mixed with ultramarine.

Crimson lake: unusable in any medium.

Ultramarine: must not be used in tempera or mixed with emerald green, chrome yellow, alazarins, or lead white.

Cerulean: difficult to use in watercolour.

Prussian blue (associated with Paris blue, Berlin blue, cyanide, and Antwerp blue): fades in light, must not be mixed with vermilion.

Indigo: a colour which should be rejected.

Emerald green: brilliant, but should be use alone.

Cobalt green: sensitive to moisture.

Terre verte: has a large oil content which may darken it.

Cobalt violet: will not mix with ochres.

Umbers: tend to darken in oil.

Prussian brown: no good in oils, and not durable in watercolours.

Vandyke brown: can be made from anything, difficult to classify, and may be regarded as dangerous.

All very interesting no doubt, but most of these strictures can be ignored. If you read too much about colour durability and fading you will find yourself devoting all your time to grinding your own colours or catching bugs such as cochineal, used as a colouring agent in food and also for crimson lake.

Mediums and Glosses There are many of these but the most popular is turpentine, which imparts a matt finish and is very good for detailed work. Most other mediums give a slight gloss, and some of those put out by the large manufacturers include varnish as well as linseed oil. These ready-made mediums are very good, and really there is no need to look further. Poppy oil is a slow-drying medium, liquin is a fast dryer. Some painters do not use medium at all, but use the paint straight from the tube. Others use varnish. Ironmongers' turpentine is much cheaper and just as good as the turpentine sold in art shops. If you are sensitive to the smell of turpentine, use white spirit.

Varnish There is no need to use varnish at all, though you will find that if you use a medium other than turpentine the degree of gloss finish

A selection of brushes. You will find some more useful than others, but do not be afraid to experiment, using bristle and hair, as well as nylon, brushes for oil painting.

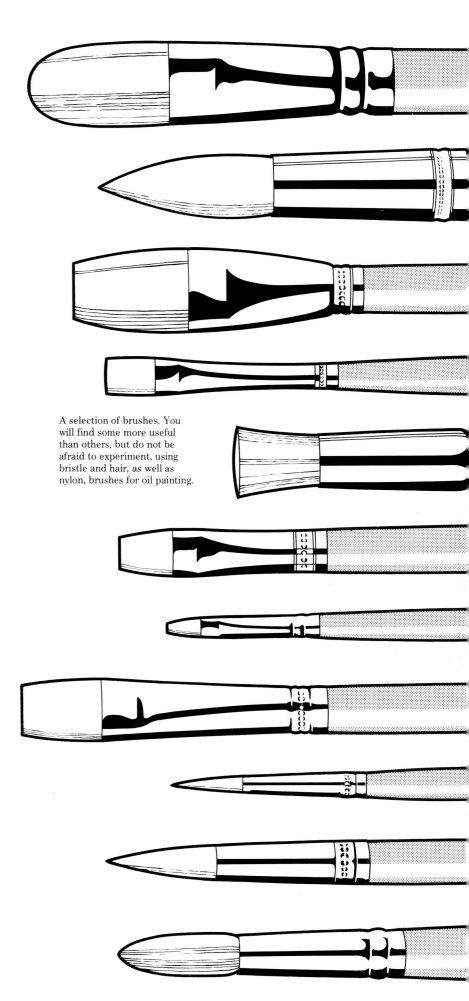

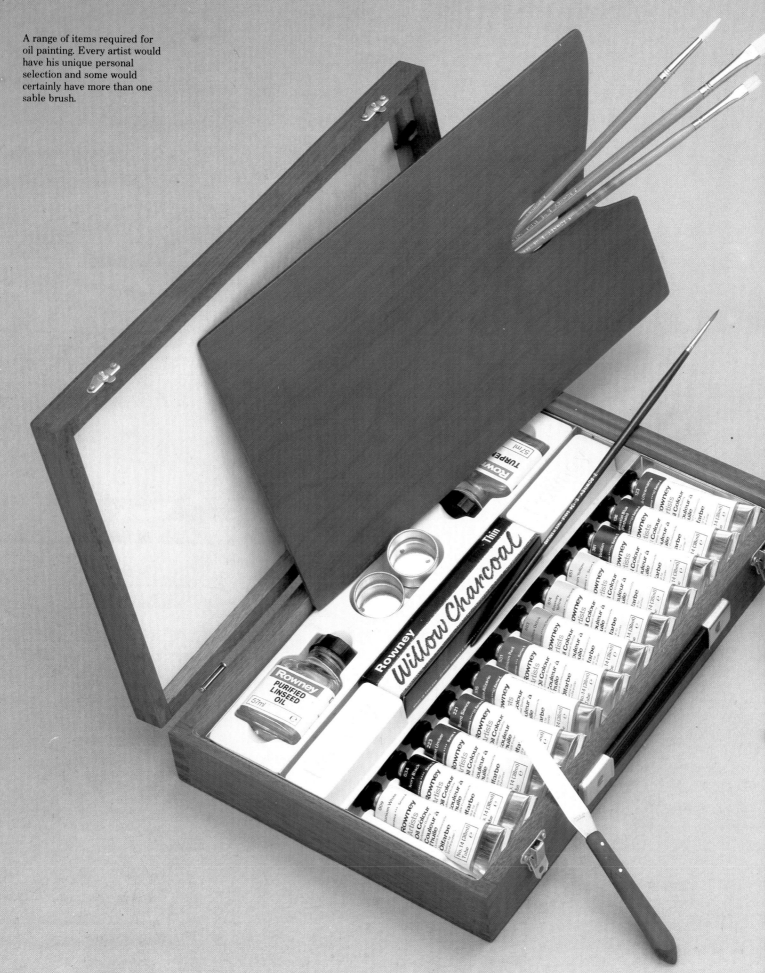

A range of items required for oil painting. Every artist would have his unique personal selection and some would certainly have more than one sable brush.

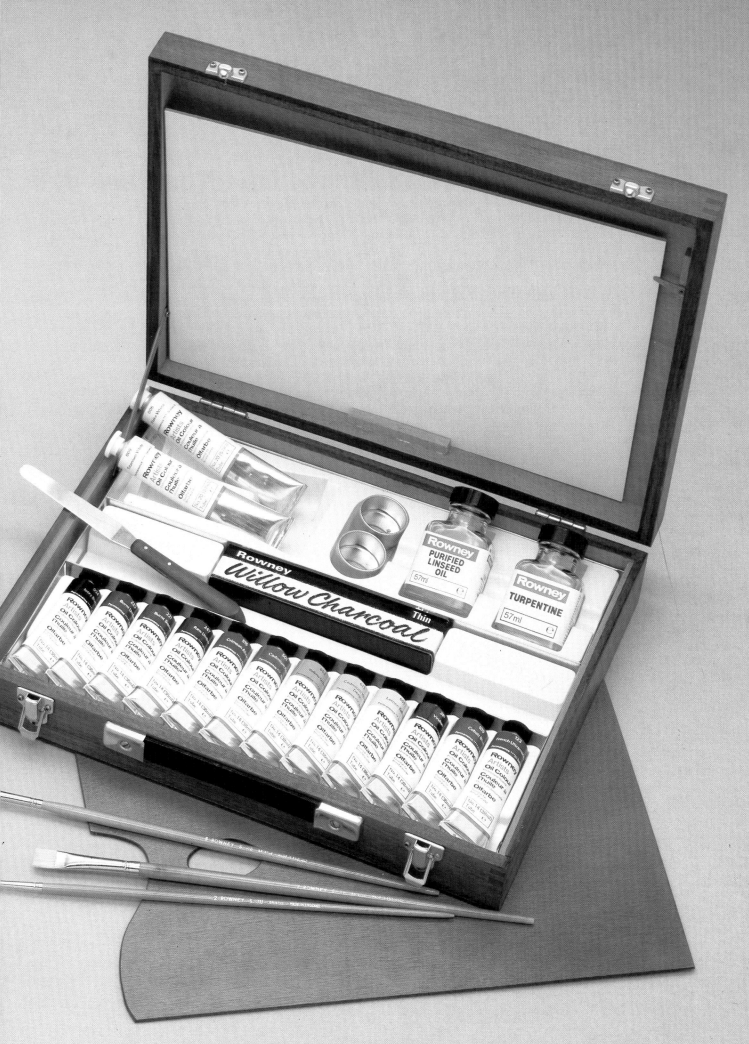

271

will be variable, and you will want to use a varnish to give an even appearance to the picture surface. Varnishes can be glossy or matt, and a retouching varnish is useful for areas that unaccountably have gone flat. Two coats of thin varnish are better than one coat of thick, and you do not have to wait too long for coats to dry. Some people do not advise varnishing a picture until it has been painted for weeks or months, but you will find that you can do this job as soon as the paint is dry. The thicker the paint layer (or 'impasto') the slower it is to dry, and white is one of the slower dryers, probably because it is applied more thickly for highlights. Many artists find that a flat square-edged soft brush is the best to apply varnish; if you use a bristle, there is a chance of the varnish getting a scratchy look when it dries out.

Brushes Some people prefer a lot of brushes, some a few, and many have their favourite brushes which they have broken in and would not give up for the world. You can use hard brushes or soft brushes; even if you are working on a large scale you can use soft brushes throughout. You have a choice of natural bristle or hair, and nylon, which comes in soft and hard grades and lasts longer than natural products. Artists who work on a small scale or who are keen on detail use small soft brushes; however if you are using sable you can get through two or three (or more) brushes in the course of one picture. After painting, clean your brushes by taking off the surplus paint with tissues or rags and rinsing them in turpentine or white spirit. Every so often, say once a month, wash the brushes using household soap and hot water, drawing the brush handle first through the soap surface and then rinsing under a hot tap. Despite the best care, paint brushes can get clogged, and one of the commercial brush cleaners can come in handy. Paint always clogs at the end of the ferrule, and after a time it becomes hard, even if you scrupulously clean your brushes. Sometimes a proprietary cleaner is essential. After cleaning, brushes should be kept upright in a pot, handles down, with perhaps something like a jam jar for the smaller sable or nylon brushes so that they do not rub against the side of a larger pot.

A basic brush kit consists of: a small, medium and large round bristle; a small, medium and large flat bristle; a small, medium and large round sable (or nylon); a small, medium and large flat sable (or nylon); an ordinary household painting brush for applying a priming coat to a canvas or board; and, an added option, a 'fan' brush, in which the hairs are spread out like a fan, useful for blending. An old shaving brush can also come in handy for giving textures.

Palette Knives These come in various sizes, and a small, medium and large should be bought. They are used to clean paint from a palette, or to apply paint to a canvas. You can use palette knives to paint an entire picture, or you can merely use them to deposit the paint on the canvas and then employ brushes. Some artists prefer to keep a layer of old paint on the palette knife, others prefer them pristine. The metal of the smaller knives is very thin, and if encrusted paint needs to be removed do it gently as the blades are easily damaged. Always store your knives in a safe place, as otherwise the blades may be accidentally bent.

Palettes Palettes were once made of wood, probably for no better reason than that colours were basically muted and earthy, and wood seemed an appropriate surface. Palettes have a hole in them through which the thumb fits, and now come in plastic, tin, china, aluminium, wood and paper (throwaway palettes). You may not want to use a palette at all, finding it a nuisance, in which case a large plate is just as good. If you are sitting down to do your picture, it is better, as the dished sides prevent the paint from slopping over the top. If you are using a traditional palette, you can get small metal containers which fix to the side of the palette and contain your turpentine or other medium. If you are using a dinner plate, the tops of jars can serve as containers, and be thrown away when the medium begins to coagulate or get dirty. Plastic and tin palettes have circular depressions in them for the paint, but these are often more annoying than useful. If you wish to mix your paints thoroughly, cake-tins are far more convenient.

Canvases The traditional surface for oil paint is canvas, but although the 'give' of canvas, which is on a stretcher and therefore has no backing, is pleasant, there are many cheaper substitutes for canvas, some of which cost nothing, and can be rescued from the attic, from under the stairs, or from the garage. One of the best surfaces to work on is ordinary cardboard, which merely needs sizing and maybe priming. There is also oil-painting board, oil-painting paper (sold in blocks like sketch-pads), wood panels, hardboard (rough or smooth side), and, indeed, almost anything. Oil-painting boards come in a variety of textures, from very smooth to rough. Plywood is a delightful surface to work on, and just needs a coat of size. Much depends on whether you like a rough tooth (grain) or smooth; if you are using stiff brushes you will need a surface with a tooth.

Detail of one of the heads in
the picture, treated in a way
reminiscent of Cézanne's
portrayal of apples.

Newcomers should not feel
that they are bound to paint in
any prescribed manner but
should bring a fresh eye to
unusual subjects, as shown
here. This can result in
striking and novel pictures.

Below: A selection of palette
knives of various shapes and
sizes.

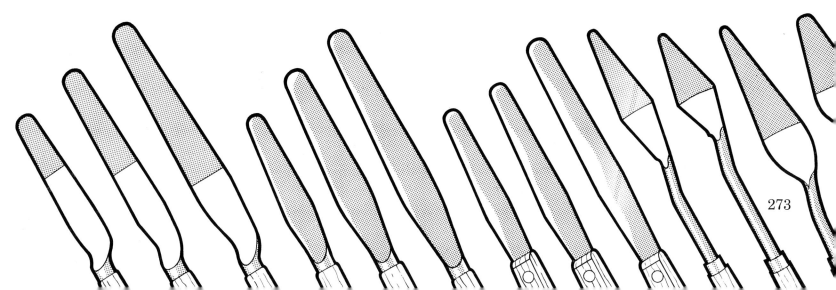

273

Easel Even if you prefer to work at a table with the canvas or board horizontal, an easel is very handy, if only as somewhere to prop up a picture to see how it is progressing. If you are working broadly or on a large scale, an easel is essential – or at least an easel-type object. A child's blackboard makes a substitute. Professional artists' easels can be huge contraptions, and a smaller travelling easel will serve most of us well enough.

Drawing Board If you use traditional canvases or canvas board you may not need a drawing board, but if you use oil-painting paper you will. Oil-painting paper is sold in sheets or in a block, but although the block has a thick cardboard backing it is often more convenient to take off each sheet as it is needed. When fixing oil-painting paper or anything which needs to be pinned to the drawing board, first cover the drawing board with a pad of newspaper. This provides a perfect working surface, and also the newspaper is very handy for trying your paint on, to see if you have the right colour, and for getting rid of any surplus medium on your brush. If you work fast and want to get the colours on right away, this is much more convenient than looking around for a piece of paper.

As you get into oil painting there are extra bits and pieces which you will want to add to your basic equipment, and many of these you will discover for yourself. A piece of *sponge* is one of these accessories. You may wonder why, as sponges naturally go with water, and oil clogs them. Sponges have as a matter of fact been used in painting for some considerable time, to give texture to paint already applied with a brush, and as a painting instrument. We have all seen those ready-made Victorian landscapes with a lake, trees, a bright blue sky, and a yacht in the water. The trees seem to be spattered in, with tiny globules of pigment; the leaves were put in with a piece of sponge and, although flashy, these trees can look very effective from a distance. These pictures, now in such demand by interior decorators, were hack work for the lower end of the market, and were turned out in less than half an hour to a simple formula. For newcomers to oil painting who want to get an easy effect – and no harm in that – a good look at some of these pictures can be helpful. The Victorian painters used natural sponges, because there were no synthetic substitues, but household and car sponges, at a fraction of the cost, serve almost as well if the sharp corners are cut off with a pair of scissors so that you have an irregularly shaped object. For sponge painting on a small scale, cut off a portion of sponge and hold it in a strong paperclip.

274

Another unlikely accessory is *tissue paper,* not household tissues which have a dimpled appearance, but ordinary tissue paper as used to wrap up articles in shops. This is to remove the surplus oil and paint off a painting while they are still wet, and it is a trick much employed by British painters of the earlier part of this century. It adds subtlety and atmosphere, and is placed over the moist painting and gently pressed, being taken up when you think that it has absorbed sufficient paint. It is known as 'tonking' after Professor Tonks, a teacher at the Slade School, who pioneered this extremely effective dodge. If you feel that your colouring is too strong and you have not succeeded in getting the picture to hang together, tonking is recommended – and if you find you do not like the effect you can always put the paint back on with a brush.

Sometimes you need a starting-off point for a painting. A few ambiguous dabs of a paint-soaked sponge can do this on the pictures-in-a-fire principle, but tissue paper from a successfully tonked picture can also do this, leaving enigmatic traces of paint on the new surface, ready to spark off the imagination. A surprising number of painters in the past, including Turner, have used random touches of paint to help them on their way, and oil paints, with their richness and variety, are ideal for adven-

ture and experiment. If it fails, all you do is to get a cloth soaked in turpentine and wipe it all off. It is a method well worth trying.

There is no doubt about it, oil paints can be very messy, and a painter's smock is not a quaint garment but very functional. Paint has a habit of dripping down the brush and getting on to the hands, and thus on to clothes, and it is always a good idea to be well provided with household tissues and lots of rag, to clean up the handles of brushes, to wipe surplus paint from the business end of brushes, to clear unwanted areas of paint off a canvas, and to wipe a palette clean when you feel that it has got altogether too congested.

Other items you may need are dividers, to get distances right between various sections of the picture, and a *mahlstick.* This is a wooden rod, often in three telescopic sections fitted together with brass ferrules, with a rounded tip. The stick is for resting your hand on while you are doing fine detailed work, the rounded end rests on the canvas or support, the right hand holds the brush resting on the stick itself, and the left hand holds its far end. A length of ordinary garden cane is a decent substitute for a mahlstick. Cotton buds come in very handy for removing surplus paint off a canvas, tidying up areas, or distributing paint more evenly on the canvas. It is sometimes easier to do this

Rough Sea with Wreckage by J. M. W. Turner: A good example of a free and random approach to painting, showing how you can build up detail as you go along.

A delightfully free oil painting.
If you happen to be painting in
a group with others, take the
opportunity to paint your
colleagues at their work and
they can do the same with you.
It is a good idea when starting
off to indicate quickly your
main areas of colour with paint
well diluted with turpentine.

with a cotton bud than a brush.

In addition there are the various items needed when setting down the outlines of an oil painting. Almost anything has been used for this purpose, with the favourite possibly charcoal. Pencils, pens, felt pens, ball-point pens, pastel, can all be pressed into service.

There is one piece of equipment which you will have to make yourself (if there is one on the market few have seen it). This is an aid to help you draw a straight line. The answer is to get a straight edge, preferably wood, and nail or glue together two blocks of wood on it, one at each end, far enough apart to reach dry canvas or, if using oil-painting paper, the drawing board. These blocks should not be more than half an inch high; if they are, the brush will be difficult to control, and if the blocks are not high enough the hairs of the brush will rub against the straight edge, thus damaging them. This do-it-yourself instrument can be very useful, not only in oil painting, but in acrylics and watercolour. Drawing a straight line freehand is *not* easy, and almost on the level of difficulty of drawing a perfect circle. If you are doing sea pictures and the ropes and tackle need to be taut and straight, this ruler-on-stilts can be indispensable.

HOW DO I START?

Some mediums such as pastels and watercolours can be taken up as and when it suits you, for as short a time as you want, but if you are going to paint in oils you do need a little preparation in order to avoid getting in a mess. If you are working on the flat, use pads of newspapers to cover the surfaces. These not only absorb blobs of paint or splashes of turpentine, but prevent them from going onto sensitive surfaces. Go through your brushes and check them to see that they are reasonably clean, and pick out the ones you are likely to use. Squeeze out the colours on your palette. Some artists have a set order, light to dark (white, yellow, orange, blue, green, brown, black), but others put them down in any order. If you like a specific range of colours (see **Colour Schemes** p. 91) you will no doubt get into the habit of placing the colours in some kind of order, but many painters put out the colours they feel they want to use in this particular picture.

There is no need to clean the palette after each painting session. When there is old paint on the palette, often in a mix, it can be used to evolve new colour blends. It is a question of personality. Some artists like to start with a pristine palette, and traces of previous paint

Left: Detail of a head showing simple glazes. When sketching in at the early stage, try to develop a simple shorthand technique, such as in the detail of the feet (*below*).

are a personal affront. If you are of this temperament it is worth while using paper throwaway palettes. Sometimes there comes a time when even the most reluctant palette-cleaner finds that the palette is completely clogged up. In this case, buy a strong household paint stripper and clear the old paint completely. Although oil paint takes a considerable time to dry out, it will acquire a thin shell after three or four days. This can be taken off by using the tip of a palette knife.

Mediums, especially the ready-made ones with an element of varnish, also film over after a time, and this crust can again be picked off with a palette knife. Turpentine evaporates slowly, therefore it is advisable to keep it in a jar with a screw-on lid. But do not be niggardly about turpentine; it is cheap, and if you are covering a large area you will find it convenient to use it from a small bowl, preferably a pottery and *not* plastic one. Some plastics melt when exposed to strong liquids.

If you are using an easel, make certain that it is at a convenient height and angle, and that the legs will not splay out as soon as you apply pressure to the canvas or working surface. If you prefer, sit down to the easel. Wind-up office chairs are better than ordinary dining or kitchen chairs, and a chair with arms can be infuriating. Make certain there is newspaper on the floor, or at least something which can be kept clean, and not carpet.

Keep the equipment you need within easy reach, and always have plenty of rags and tissues at hand. When you are setting up remember that if you are using natural light, and do not have a north window (where the light is constant), this will change in the course of a painting session.

'I have my equipment ready, and am working flat on a table. I have some smooth oil-painting paper. I have never touched a paint brush since I left school, I am by nature a meticulous sort of person, and I would like to do something simple and reasonably "like" and which does not look like something the dog walked over.'

One of the easiest kinds of picture to paint is a simple seascape. No complicated shadows are involved, and for the more ambitious there are extra options to make the picture more interesting.

Place the board vertically, and two-thirds of the way down draw a straight line across, using measurements and a ruler. This is your skyline. This is the only preliminary work you will need to do. Mix a blue with white, not too much blue, plenty of white, and do not mix it too thoroughly,

278

Step 1: Draw a straight line across the canvas two-thirds of the way down. This is your horizon line.

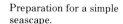

Step 2: Mix a blue with white and begin to apply the paint with a medium bristle brush, the darker blue at the top graduating to paler blue on the horizon.

Step 3: Mix the sea colour with blue and green and paint the bottom one-third of the canvas with this combination. Draw in the clouds using a little white mixed with a trace of yellow ochre.

and add a splash of turpentine so that the colour runs nicely. Begin applying the paint with a medium bristle from the top down, darker blue at the top, near white at the bottom, where the skyline comes. *Option:* Go over this area with a medium soft brush, fusing in the blue and the white, and getting a more enamel-like surface. *Further Option:* Draw in clouds, using a little white maybe mixed with a trace of raw sienna or yellow ochre. If you wish to have some shadow at the bottom of the clouds, use a very small amount of black or vandyke brown.

Mix a sea colour. Seas vary enormously, and you can select your own blend. Blue plus green is the traditional colour, but you can add browns and yellows. Paint the bottom third of the board with this mix, making certain that the paint at the top meets the sky perfectly horizontally. Use the side of a flat brush to make the meeting of the two colours clean. Make the bottom of the picture somewhat darker than the skyline area by adding a brown or a touch of black. *Option:* Go over this area with a medium soft brush.. *Further Option:* Suggest waves by touches of white. Beneath the white add darker colours (blue plus brown, or green plus brown) to indicate shadow. If you have difficulty indicating waves in this way, look at photographs of pictures with waves in them.

Put in some land feature on the horizon. Burnt sienna with a touch of blue is suitable. This feature can be quite small, and as the sky is light you can overpaint. If the sky paint is too rich and not dry, take out the area you want to cover with a small palette knife, and then paint over. *Option:* Indicate some kind of shadow on the land, by either applying a touch of white, or a touch of darker colour.

Paint a ship somewhere in the middle of the sea area, not too far from the horizon (otherwise you are looking *down* on the ship which makes the shape less comprehensible). You are painting the shape of a ship, and you have the choice of two simple forms, a ship with a funnel or funnels, and a ship with sails. Do not be too ambitious. The ship merely serves as an accent. You may care to wait for the sea to dry, but otherwise, with the point of a divider or similar pointed object such as the wrong end of a paint brush, pick out in the wet paint the outline of your ship, removing the paint enclosed in your outline with a small palette knife. Then fill in, using black. *Option:* Add highlights on the ship using the smallest soft brush with white. Highlights can occur on the funnel, on the superstructure, or on the deck where the black meets the sea. On sails, the highlights can occur on one side or on the hull. *Further Option:* Add a trace of white where the bottom of the ship

Right: The final seascape.
Step 4: Suggest a hint of land
on the horizon with a touch of
burnt sienna and blue and
then place a boat in the centre
of the sea area, with some
birds for added interest.

meets the waves. This white can be irregular, indicating the action of waves. Add birds at will (flat V-shapes in white against the sea, or black or grey against the sky).

Then you will have a simple picture. As such it will look neat and unpretentious. You can fill it in further if you wish, by adding foreground interest (a hemisphere in red, with the red darkened where it meets the sea – this is the traditional marine picture filler, a buoy). While the paint is still wet, you can modify the sky, by sunsetting it (a whisper of crimson in the blue/white), or adding a trace of yellow. You can make the clouds more specific. You can add a tiny ship on the horizon, using your smallest soft pointed brush, grading the colour down so that it is just visible against the sky. When the picture is dry, you can glaze it, putting on an overall coat of thin paint liberally diluted with either turpentine or medium. You can use almost any colour to transform the appearance of the picture, and you can apply further glazes as you wish. You can apply part glazes, covering one part of the picture. You may wish to darken the foreground with a glaze of dark brown or black. You may wish to brighten up an area of the sea with a glaze of white. When the glazes are dry, you can varnish if you wish (some pictures look better unvarnished and matt).

'I would like to try something a little more demanding, using traditional techniques.'

Try a landscape with hills in the background, a middle distance of trees, and a foreground of water. Mix your sky, blue and white, and keeping the top of the painting a darker tint apply the paint with a loaded bristle brush. If you have any sky colour left, add some red, and remix for the hills, laying in the colour with broad strokes, putting in your light and shade (darkening the mix with more blue or brown or lightening it with white or yellow). You can pick either side of the hills for your shadow area.

The trees in the middle distance are not too precise, yet not vague, and can be painted in either a mixed green (blue plus yellow) or a

Below: It is essential to remember from which side of the sky the light is coming. Try to vary the cloud formations in each picture, as an interesting sky will enhance any picture.

tube green such as chromium green with maybe a touch of Prussian blue. The bank on the far side of the water can be put in with yellow ochre with a dash of a green or blue. The water is put in with smooth horizontal strokes, blue, darkish green, with an added medium brown such as burnt sienna to cool the mix, and ripples added in white, using either the small bristle or the small soft brush. The reflections of the trees and the hills in the water are always vertically beneath the objects, a similar colour but darker. You can break the outlines of the reflection by ripple.

The overall impression of the foreground can be thick and warm, using the bristle brush fully loaded with paint. You can either thoroughly blend your colours (green and red), or can apply them wet on wet individually, adding maybe yellow ochre. Dabbing the colour on gives the impression of rough ground, and by adding shadows in the foreground you can specify the nature of the ground (grass, stones, add brown or black to your mix for shadows).

A three-step method of
building up a lake painting,
with the finished picture and
list of colours used.

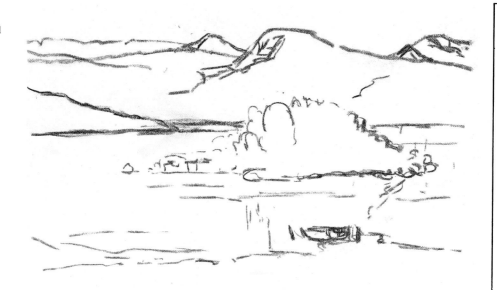

Step 1: Quickly sketch in the
scene, using charcoal or a
carpenter's pencil.

Step 2: Using a one-inch flat
brush, sketch in loosely the
colours, which are mixed with
plenty of turpentine. Make no
attempt at this stage to draw
in any detail.

Step 3: Using a long, size three
filbert brush start to build up
the thicker layers of oil paint.
Subtly indicate the cloud
formations to draw the eye
into the centre of the picture.

Colors used *(top to bottom):*
Titanium white
Yellow ochre
Chrome green
Sap green
Crimson
Prussian blue

If the final picture seems tame, add further hills behind those already there in a lighter tone with more emphasis on the blue, or in the middle distance add a touch or two of pure colour, suggesting the presence of cottages or buildings, or even figures. You can refine the whole picture by making the focal point the far bank, picking out the trees with more detail, and adding fairly precise figures (remembering to include them in your reflections).

For more subtlety, blur the hill outlines with a flat brush, and then blur the foreground, so that only the middle distance is in any kind of focus. When you are blurring distances or foregrounds, it is better to do it in light horizontal sweeps, and remember to amend any clouds you may have put in.

In many pictures pure white clouds can freeze a picture, and yellow ochre and a hint of red mixed in with the white can provide a warmer, less bracing, touch. Clouds are always sharper in outline at the top than the bottom, and also lighter. The sky need not necessarily be blue; yellow, pink, and even purple can be used for dramatic effect. A glaring sun in the sky is difficult to pull off, but worth trying.

'I would like to do a simple still life in a rather different technique.'
Bottles and jugs, with the odd apple or orange, can be used almost at a moment's notice. Place a thin wash of colour over the canvas to establish a general tone, and then roughly draw in the objects in charcoal. Then take a flat soft brush, half-inch or so, and using horizontal strokes *all the time* put in the shapes of the objects in their natural colour, or slightly subdued natural colour. Put in your background with rather thicker paint, not worrying if you are overlapping your objects, and then put in the darks of your principal items. You keep the same size brush throughout, though of course you can use two or three the same size if you wish to reserve one of the brushes for the lighter tones.

On top of the darks you put your half-tones, keeping the same *texture* of paint, and you can now use the brush vertically or diagonally, but keeping it flat and not overloading it with paint. Apply the highlights in white, still with the flat brush, but keep the whole composition muted. To increase the atmosphere you can gently add other colours – not necessarily those 'in life' –

Step 4: At this final stage, work in the overall detail using a smaller filbert brush until the painting appears to be finished. Stop then, before you overwork the subject and spoil it.

These illustrations, and those on the following pages, demonstrate the progress of a simple still life from the original photograph to the finished painting, showing the intermediate steps.

Composition and eye level are most important when sketching from still life. These sketches show some of the mistakes commonly made by beginners.

Objects are arranged too formally.

The eye level is too low and the objects too centralized.

but these additional colours are blended in to the basic colour. The whole surface of the painting will be regular, but avoid an egg-shell finish and allow the object edges to be a little fuzzy and indistinct.

This square brush technique was brought to a peak of perfection by the Newlyn School of painters who flourished in Cornwall just before the turn of the century, and it became a staple technique for art colleges throughout Britain. The practice of this method encourages sensitivity to tone. It is best practised with turpentine rather than one of the juicier mediums, and pictures painted in this way do not need to be varnished. If you feel that the colours are too strident, you can 'tonk' the pictures, by placing a sheet of tissue over the surface to absorb excess paint and moisture.

With oil paints there is no end to the possibilities and usable techniques, and it is the only medium where errors can be removed by the simple method of wiping them off with a cloth or scraping them off with a palette knife. If you wish to spend a fair amount of time on a painting use the methods employed by the great painters of the past (see chapter on Advanced Techniques). They painted in a series of transparent glazes, laying one on top of the other, building the picture up gradually. Another method is to carry out an underpainting in much diluted paint, staining rather than painting. The underpainting is not concerned with detail, but in establishing the areas of tone, and covering the white of the canvas. Whatever you are doing, it is often – even usually – better to tint the canvas. In an underpainting white is not used, and the dark and light colours are obtained by the amount of turpentine in the wash, and no more than four colours are needed – a blue, a couple of browns, and yellow ochre or raw sienna.

Once the tone of the picture has been set by the underpainting, the overpainting can be as thick as you like. It is often advisable to put the paint on in direct abrupt touches rather than stroking it on, without worrying too much about overlapping adjacent areas. Surplus paint can be scraped off or overpainted. But do not imagine that you have to be rough and ready to make a 'real' oil painting. The worst amateur paintings *are* these rough and ready paintings, in which the brush strokes come through as if they were made with a rake, and the edges are untidy and wispy, as if the artist was unable to come to grips with the task of getting colours to meet on a canvas.

If you want to work on a tiny scale, do so, but avoid canvas and use cardboard or a smooth surface (not oil-painting paper as that has a marked tooth). Be as precise as you like with your initial design, if necessary using a fine nib (always finer than the sharpest pencil point). Use small soft brushes (00 and 01) throughout, and if you wish make use of a magnifying glass (the type on a heavy stand is the most helpful). It is an odd fact that by using a magnifying glass, the hand seems to acquire the ability to carry out the most minute work.

All techniques can be used in miniature painting. The flat brush method can be employed by working with the smallest flat brushes. You can use successive glazes, and you can underpaint. There are some people who find it difficult to paint on a small scale, and if you are talented in this respect make the most of it. There is nothing that takes the eye more than an exquisite miniature.

The *usual* method of oil painting is to paint in the darks first, and superimpose the half-tones and the lights, and many painters in watercolours also do this, though you will find many writers on watercolour painting not keen on this idea. By putting in the darks first, you immediately get some idea of the shape the picture is taking, and it will give you freedom when you put in the lighter colours, freedom to intrude on the dark areas with your light colours, even mixing in the lights with the darks.

You can apply the paint onto the canvas in many ways. You can take the paint with your palette knife, spread it on the appropriate part of the canvas, and then get to work with your brush. You can load the brush with paint from the palette, and mix on the palette with your medium before going to the canvas. You can apply the paint from the palette onto the canvas, and add the medium to the paint already down. In this case, you will lay the paint down fairly roughly, keeping well within your outlines, only getting your edges in with the arrival of the medium. You can also apply the paint directly from the tube, and indeed some artists use the nozzle of the tube to spread the paint. You have to be very sure of yourself to do this, as it can result in an unholy mess.

If not using brushes at all but only palette knives, be sparing of the medium. You can mix paint on the palette, taking it off with a smooth sweep of the palette knife, or you can squeeze the pure colour on to the palette knife, spread it on the canvas, and do the mixing there. Do not try to do palette-knife work with too little paint, but if you want to work up a rich impasto while economizing on paint you can add wax to the mix, a technique used by van Gogh.

If you are using a palette knife or any method involving thick paint any outline drawing you have made will soon disappear, so do not panic if your guide lines suddenly disappear. You can

Here the composition begins to gain interest.

The complete composition with interesting placement of objects.

A rough sketch for 'abstraction' of shapes of the objects.

285

Making a still life poses an interesting problem for the oil painter as he can arrange his subject matter as he pleases. The paintings on these two pages show the progression and details painted from life as in the photograph *(right)*.

Far right: List of colours used to paint this picture.

Zinc White

Lemon Yellow

Cadmium Yellow

Yellow Ochre

Scarlet Lake

Bright Red

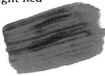

Alizarin Crimson

Cerulean Blue

Prussian Blue

Burnt Sienna

287

put them back using thin brush strokes, if your paint surface will take them, or you can 'draw' on the paint with the point of a pair of dividers or the wrong end of your brush. Always remember that a painting involves outline and shapes, at least in the initial stages. Adjoining shapes are not sacrosanct; you can 'bite' into them with neighbouring colours. For example, in a landscape one of your trees may seem lifeless and need pepping up with more interesting leafage. There is no necessity to add foliage in foliage colour; you can alter the look of the tree by bringing in sky colour on top of the green, taking out the superfluous green with a small palette knife if the paint is not yet dry.

The versatility of oil paint can never be emphasized enough. There is *nothing* you cannot do with it. You can work over and over again on some passage you do not feel happy about, though in watercolour overworking can show, resulting in a tired picture. Although the Victorian painter Burne-Jones was exceptional in spending five years or more on a single picture, give yourself plenty of time when painting an oil, and if you feel slightly uncertain about the progress of a picture put it to one side for a month or so and then return to it.

The palette knife can be variously used to apply a thin coating of paint or to work up to a rich impasto. It is traditionally used for building up thick layers of paint.

Scumbling. The paint is scrubbed sparingly onto the canvas with a stiff brush.

Glazing. This consists of successive applications of thinned-down paint. Ensure that each coat is dry before applying the next.

Left: A palette knife has been used for this simple still life, using limited colours and mixing the paint directly onto the canvas.

Below: This delightful van Gogh landscape depends a great deal on brush technique for its success.

289

PERSPECTIVE AND DRAWING

Oil painting can be as easy or as difficult as you wish, and you can make a good-looking picture without knowing anything about drawing or perspective. But if you want to do a realistic picture, in which the components are set in space – even if it is a space of your own making – it is advisable to know something about perspective. It does not have to be a lot; you are not going to be asked to do architectural drawings, and nothing about perspective is very complicated.

If you lift your eyes from this page and look around, you will no doubt see objects with flat rectangular surfaces, such as the top of a television set or the top of a table, both below eye level. Even if the top of the table is a perfect rectangle you will see that the two sides appear to move in toward each other. If these lines are extended they will meet. If you bend down slightly, so that the surfaces are only just below eye-level, the converging lines will seem to move toward each other at a sharper angle. This is perspective in action.

Of course all objects in the room will do the same, and if you are going to draw or paint them you will have to be aware of perspective, even if you just make a token gesture toward it to make the picture look right. For perspective is an instrument, nothing more, nothing less.

If you look down a straight road in the direction of the horizon the road appears to narrow, and a person walking along this road seems to get smaller, losing height at the same rate as the road narrows. If there are telegraph poles spaced along the road they will seem to diminish in size until they appear in the distance like matchsticks. If you draw an imaginary line between the bases of the poles and between the tops of the poles you will find that they meet on the horizon. The only time a true horizon is seen is at sea, where the sky meets the water, for the horizon has nothing to do with the sky-line. If you were in the Alps the sky-line, where the tops of the mountains meet the sky, would be high above you, and the horizon would be behind the mountains, at eye-level. That is where the horizon always is, at eye-level.

Surfaces on objects above the horizon appear to go down toward the horizon, those below appear to go up. If you look at the roof of a house from any aspect except straight in front you will see it leading down toward eye-level in the distance. The top of the roof will lead down at a sharper angle than the bottom of the roof. If you extend a line following the roof it will reach the horizon at a vanishing point. If there is more than one roof and each is pointing a

290

different way, as in a country village built around the village green, you will note that every roof leads to the horizon but each roof has its own vanishing point. There is only one horizon in a scene, but any number of vanishing points. If you stoop, the horizon will change, and the direction of the roofs – or walls, or anything in the view – will tilt further, not significantly but enough to notice. If you look up at a church tower, which you know is square-topped, the angle will be much sharper, and if you did not know better you would say that it was triangular.

Without the use of perspective a painting will be flat; you will be making a pattern on the surface. One part of the painting will be the same distance from the eyes as any other. Once perspective is introduced you achieve solidity and recession, and the objects 'out there' will be displayed in their own kind of space. If you have done a simple picture of a ship at sea you will have used perspective; you have made the ship smaller in relation to waves or anything else in the foreground, and if you have put in a land mass on the horizon you will have placed it behind the ship. And by examining the positions of these objects on the sea there is no doubt about it. As there is only one ship, there are no problems about size and whether it is exactly where it should be on the sea. If more ships are

added, and there are more objects relating to each other, you will need to fit them in with more circumspection. If you put a rowing boat in you may put it in front of the bigger vessel, so it is occupying its own space, but it may be in the wrong place; it may be too near the ship and look too large; it may be in the foreground and look like a toy. Using perspective will help to keep different subjects in a picture in proportion.

Still keeping to the marine theme, visualize a picture in which a ship is in the foreground. If the horizon is low, you may not see the top of the deck. If it is high, you may be looking down on the ship, as if you are standing on a cliff above a harbour or on a pier. Suppose you want to add other ships of a similar size to the one in the picture; do you just put them in, hoping for the best, and if they look out of proportion take the paint off and start again? Perhaps, but it is easier to draw a line from the bow of the ship where it meets the water, and a line from the top of the funnel or mast, and extend them to the same point on the horizon. It does not matter where it is. It can be very close to the ship, in which case the angle of the line will be acute, or it can be at the far edge of the canvas or board; it can even be off the canvas, and if you have the vanishing point a long way off the canvas the lines will be almost parallel.

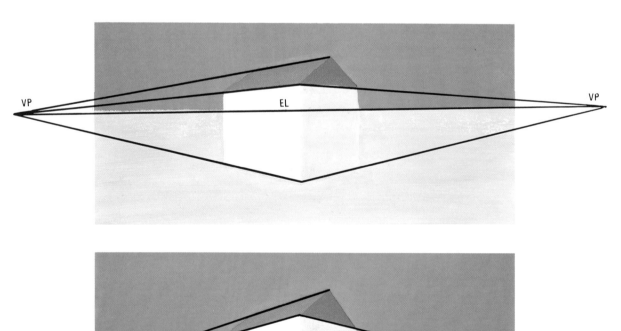

These two sketches of a building illustrate the way in which perspective alters according to the eye level (EL) and viewpoint. When the viewpoint is far away, the angle of perspective is very shallow and the vanishing points (VP) from both walls fall some distance away. As the viewpoint becomes nearer, the vanishing points close up, and the angle of perspective becomes much sharper.

292

The slot between these converging lines is where you place the vessel. This will give you the correct dimensions anywhere on the canvas – just behind the foreground ship, in the middle distance, near the horizon. Of course, you do not have to place the extra ships within the lines as if they were in a convoy. You can position them across the canvas, if they remain the right size to fit the slot. Naturally you do not want to keep these lines of recession, so if the sea and sky colours are dry, put them in thinly with turpentine and a dull colour, wiping them off when the extra elements have been added. If the background colours are wet, put the lines in with the side of a knife or the point of a pair of compasses or dividers, or the handle end of the brush, biting into the wet paint and smoothing the lines out when you have finished with them.

By using these convergence or perspective lines you can add extras to paintings which need livening up, such as people in a townscape, cows in a landscape, so that they fit in. They are not too big, not too small.

Sometimes perspective can be tinkered with to get dramatic effects, and playing with perspective can have startling results, but if you anticipate doing realistic pictures it cannot be ignored. It is a tool just as much as brushes and paints. All things come into the reckoning,

including human figures. If a person extends a clenched fist towards you it will appear enormous, often obliterating the rest of the person. Even objects we do not usually associate with having solidity, such as clouds, are in perspective; some clouds in pictures seem flat and uninteresting. That is because they are put in just as white blotches with perhaps a trace of shading beneath them, and they are placed parallel with the picture plane – in other words, all parts of the cloud are the same distance from the viewer. But they are not. They have shape and body and therefore have to fit in against the sky, to appear to float.

Perspective is not so much a law as a convenience; it is certainly not a hard and fast law like the law of gravity, because there is an exception which goes under the name of accidental vanishing points. Surfaces which are tilted sometimes converge on vanishing points which are above or below eye-level. The best way to see this is to pick up a piece of card and hold it at a slant, watching how the vanishing point changes as you move it around (half-close the eyes when doing this – it is more obvious then). Another example is to look at a road going uphill; the sides will appear to converge at a point above the horizon. If the road is going downhill, the sides will converge below the horizon.

Perspective is a simple matter. If you look at a straight road going towards the horizon it appears to narrow; a person walking along this road appears to get smaller as the distance increases between you and the other person, who loses height at the same rate as the road narrows.

293

Aerial perspective is to do with atmosphere. Dust and moisture obscure distant objects and views, and the further away something is the less distinct and the lighter in tone it will seem. This is indicated in painting by absence of detail and an all-over bluish tint (this can be done in oils by gently rubbing the background and getting rid of the detail and then applying a light blue glaze over that portion of the picture).

Does perspective work for you? It is a good idea to go out and look at buildings, perhaps taking a pencil with you. How do you start? First of all you put in your horizon. If you are not certain where this lies clench your fist with the thumb uppermost until it is on the level of your eye. This is your horizon. You can put in a few lines setting the scene, lightly, casually, finding your way about, and when you have found a good starting off point you can begin pencilling in with more determination, taking roof lines, the lines of window sills, the tops of doors, the lines which form the division between the walls and the ground, to their vanishing points on the horizon, extending them past the building if you find it easier. If you tackle more than one building you will find that other features intrude with their own particular vanishing points, so that if you are extending all lines of recession you will find quite a busy network of lines appearing on your paper.

There is no need to make a fully fledged drawing; there never is; if there is a window that interests – perhaps there is a fascinating pediment, perhaps you wish to try your hand at putting in the individual panes of glass so that the window does not look like a noughts-and-crosses grid – do this to your satisfaction and then forget the rest of the building. The more you draw the more practised you will be. Even if you are more keen on painting in oils, drawing techniques are a valuable back up, teaching you to observe and assess, and to realize that what you know is not necessarily what you see!

For that is one of the requirements for realistic paintings, to be aware that outlines do not exist 'out there' and are simply a practical means of putting on paper or canvas a division between one tone and another. This division may be sharp – such as the corner of a building where the sun catches one side and the other is in deepest shadow; or it may be so subtle that you can only just detect it, perhaps the merest hollow in the snow. Naturally you may not want to be realistic. It is up to you completely. You can put in an outline and then colour what is inside it, as children do automatically without thinking about it. They are not worried about comparing shapes; if they want to draw a house they make no bones about it – a square, some rectangles on it for doors and windows, and a

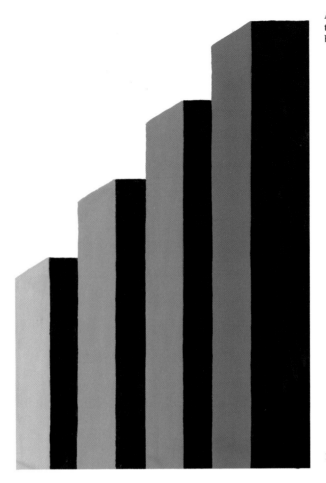

As the buildings recede into the distance, they take on a blue-grey tone.

Aerial perspective of New York.

294

chimney pot puffing forth smoke. Even if they live in high-rise flats and have hardly ever seen a chimney pot, that is the traditional way of doing things – and that's that!

In drawing all you have is outline and tone. In painting, of whatever kind – watercolour, oils, pastels, acrylic – you have colour. Tone is more important than colour, for colour by itself does not give an effect of solidity. You can depict an apple as a red circle; it is just that, a red circle, until you introduce some shading on the side and put some shading on the surface where the apple is resting. It is very easy for novices to be dominated by colour, to let it rule them. But colour must be managed, to perform the role you want it to.

Accurate drawing, whether for its own sake or as a basis for a painting, depends not on manual cleverness but on looking and assessing shapes and the way they relate to each other. All shapes can be drawn accurately, even if they are complex. Some shapes are simple and can be put down with reasonable precision. It can be a barn in the middle of a field.

We do not have to know how the barn was built, and how many rooms it has inside, and whether it is ripe for conversion. All we see is a rectangle with a sloping shape on top (the roof). From certain viewpoints we can see the side of the barn, and observe the shadows, the shadows on the side of the barn, and the shadows cast onto the ground, which are darker. The rectangle which is the body of the building may be broken up by inner rectangles and squares – the windows and doors – but they may not appear as rectangles even though we know that they are there, for we have spotted the telltale clues – the small horizontal splash of light in the front of the barn (if it is in part shadow) where the overhead sun has picked out the sill of the window leaving the rest in darkness.

The door is recognized by a dark shadow about seven feet up from the ground where the upper part of the door, slightly inset, is shadowed by the brickwork above. This is what you see, and if you are trying to portray the barn as it is this is what you draw or paint. If you think it is not going to make a good picture, go round to the other side of the barn on which the sun is shining. Always draw or paint something which is of interest to you, and if landscapes bore you select other subjects. Landscapes have always been the most popular sort of subject for a variety of reasons. Landscape is there and does not have to be arranged; you can pick any vantage point that suits you; if there are difficult objects to draw you can ignore them or move somewhere else; and landscapes do not move. There are changes of light, but mostly at a fairly leisurely pace.

This atmospheric painting of a barn set in a bleak landscape demonstrates all the problems one is likely to meet in both aerial and linear perspective.

Landscapes

How much preliminary work do you put in on a landscape? It depends entirely on you. Are you making notes with the object of finishing the picture at home? Or are you going to complete the picture on the spot?

You may care to put in a few tentative lines, locating the main points of interest. This can be done in pencil, charcoal, the point of a soft brush, or anything. Or you may take a square bristle brush and dab in a few muted shapes, perhaps squarish blobs, establishing where shapes are likely to come, but putting them in a neutral and unobtrusive colour because you may be wrong.

If you are working directly on to canvas one of your first actions is to put something down on the canvas, even if it is merely an all-over tint to take away the blankness of the white, which can be unnerving even to experienced artists. This preliminary tint can help to set the scene. If the sky is brooding and there is a storm threatening use a grey. This grey can even be applied thickly, and the features of the landscape can be inserted while the paint is wet or tacky, either with a brush or with a pointed instrument such as the handle of the brush. If it is bright sunshine and there are promising cornfields, a yellowish tint can be employed which will give a happy feeling to the picture and can be partly used to depict the cornfield.

When you are viewing a landscape you may wonder where the 'edges' of your picture should be. Should you start with something in the middle which will be the main focal point of the picture, and then fill in around it until you fill the whole of the canvas, or should you map it out beforehand? An easy way to decide where the picture will begin and end is to use a home-made viewfinder, a piece of card with a rectangular hole cut out in the middle which you will hold against a likely view, either horizontally or vertically. Not only will you be able to pick out a good composition in which the interest is held in, rather than seeping out at the sides, but by using a viewfinder you will find it easier to relate shapes and tones to each other. Half-closing the eyes helps.

When you start it is advisable to do so at the focal point of your picture (also known as an anchor) and work outwards. But as you have reviewed the scene through the viewfinder you will have a fair idea what will be included and what not. If there is detail it is in the foreground only. Do not imagine it is there in the middle-distance if you cannot see it and are only guessing. If there are trees look to see how the shadows fall, and work out whether these are going to change very much as you work. Notice how groups and clusters of leaves throw shadows on those below, and that individual leaves are not often seen unless it is winter and they are clinging bleakly to isolated branches. What might seem to be changes of colour in the leaf masses may be changes of tone, though the colour of the underside of the leaf is different from that of the top of the leaf, undetectable unless the leaf is a few feet in front of your eyes.

Trunks should be made to appear solid, by shading, and this shading should be graduated to indicate roundness. The trunks of trees in isolation are not absolutely vertical. Try not to put in a symbolic tree which will be recognized as such but will not fit in realistically. Don't forget the shadows beneath the bottom leaf cluster, which may prevent the trunk being seen, or may just allow glimpses of it through the foliage, and study how the trunk goes into the ground and is not stuck on top of it.

When doing a landscape, all the objects are in it, not on it. Individual blades of grass are in the foreground, not the middle distance, and each blade of grass has its shaded side and is not just a flick of green with a soft pointed brush. Many artists put their grass shadows in first, then insert their blades of grass. Grass further away can best be expressed by shading. Tufts of grass have a shaded side and cast shadows onto the ground just as something more solid, such as a fallen trunk, does. In the middle distance grass can be depicted by graduating the tones as the ground rises and falls. This should be done subtly, altering the basic colour with a series of added tints rather than switching to another colour such as from medium green to a yellow.

Bushes should be observed carefully, for it is very easy to make them appear like cardboard cut-outs. The changes of tone in a bush may not be dramatic, but they are there nevertheless. See how the clumps of leaves at the top of the bush throw shadows on those below, and how the base of the bush, often in deep shadow, can be enlivened by foreground plants and grass which are in the light and stand out against the shade. The tops of bushes fairly near may be around eye-level, so you may be looking down at much of the leafage, looking through clusters of leaves at the shadows below. Hedgerows are splendid accents of interest to have in a landscape and when they are in the distance they can help establish the sizes of other objects such as cottages.

The presence of water in a landscape can bring a picture to life, so look for the clues which tell you – and the person who is going to look at your picture – that it is water and not a path. It is no good painting a bit of light blue with a few tentative reflections in it and hoping

Top right: Step 1: When painting on location it is essential to paint in the entire picture as rapidly as possible, using thinned-down color.

Bottom right: Step 2: Paint can now be built up using a broad brush to give overall tonal value.

297

298

Step 3: The effect of the final stage is one of a more detailed picture which still retains the freshness and spontaneity of the original scene.

A selection of landscapes using a combination of oil pastels and oil paints. It is often a good plan to make the preliminary sketch with pastels and to finish off the details with oil paints.

Facing page: Four step-by-step palette knife paintings, with the finished townscape on page 50.

Step 1: For this street scene draw in guidelines with a stick of charcoal.

Step 2: First lay on broad layers of colour, keeping the paint texture quite thin. As soon as you apply the paint your guidelines will start to disappear.

Step 3: Gradually build up more surface detail.

Step 4: Start to indicate the figures and generally put in more detail.

for the best. Look and assess. It may be a brook in deep shadow, overhung perhaps by trees and foliage, and the only evidence may be a few highlights, establishing that it is water. Reflections in water vary enormously, and it is vital to spend a bit of time observing them, not assuming that you know the theory. Reflections are vertical; they do not slope away with water currents or vary according to where the light is coming from. Objects protruding from the water can seem to be behaving very oddly, due to the phenomenon of refraction.

All that applies to landscape is true of townscape, but in townscape there are more straight lines, more verticals, and it is simpler to see the effects of perspective, which makes it easier to set things correctly in space. But you cannot put in a vague shape and decide that it is a tree. Good drawing underpins a townscape, even if it is not obvious. The vertical lines and shapes must be absolutely upright and nothing is more annoying than to have sloping buildings. If there is any doubt about it use a set-square, but one of the advantages of oils over watercolours in townscape is that you can constantly correct before the paint dries.

Townscapes can look odd without people, and as you will probably be painting them when not many people are about, such as a Sunday, you may need to add them in, no difficult matter if you use perspective lines to insert them in the appropriate place, and you utilize guides, such as the doorways of buildings, to help you. Depending on the degree of detail in your painting, you can insert the figures either fully worked out or as a slash of paint with a lighter colour on top to represent the face. It is important that the shadows of inserted figures or objects of any kind go the same way as buildings and the fixed items in your picture. Groups of people can be represented as an uneven shape with small blobs on top to indicate the heads. Legs may not be seen, hidden in the shadows.

Cars and other vehicles can contribute to the authenticity of a street scene, and can be indicated roughly or exactly, but if you feel that this may tax your ability put them in as accents of colour in the middle distance. Cars drawn from memory may surprise; they will probably be lower in height than you think (a man of average height can lean his elbows on the top of a saloon), and the top section of a car is far less important and will stand out less than the body. The windows may be opaque rather than transparent, dependent on the way the light is coming, and as cars are taken for granted they should be looked at afresh, as ingredients in a picture not a means of transport. As shadows often block off part of the wheels, you may not

have to draw freehand curves, a difficult task for some, and a suggestion of curvature may be sufficient.

You may be happy with your landscape or townscape, the subjects are behaving themselves and are sitting nicely in space with the right kind of shadows, and you have taken the orthodox road of painting from dark to light, not as in watercolour, light to dark. But perhaps it is not 'hanging together', there are too many elements fighting for supremacy, even if you have got the tones right. Perhaps you have got the technique; but perhaps you have not composed a picture. You have let colour take the upper hand. The answer is simple – tone it down or tone it up, toning it down being usually the most advisable.

In oils there are several ways of doing this. The simplest is to use a transparent glaze to subdue the whole picture; another way is to apply a scumble of dry paint. Another, which involves more repainting, is to look at the picture again, see if the focal point is well accentuated – and if it is a worthy focal point – and decide to modify the colours. What is the highest colour you have? There is no question that it is white. And white must be reserved for special occasions, such as highlights. In a landscape this can be a window which is striking the light; or it can be a splash on water; but clouds are white, the old whitewashed barn you have so diligently put in is white. What do you do?

If you want to reserve your white for the highlights, you have to put grey into the clouds and the barn, so that they are not competing for attention. With the very light tones lowered, others have to be adjusted accordingly, with yellows being blended to greens or, maybe, if a warm feel is wanted, a touch of orange; with greens sobered down by adding red, and perhaps a blue sky retouched with yellow ochre. The degree of dilution depends very much on how important you want your focal point to be, and whether it shares top billing with something else. Naturally you can take all the tones down drastically, perhaps with a very pronounced dark, and then bring up certain of the tones you want, so that they glow.

Landscape and townscape are perfect for palette knife work. Painting with the palette knife should be tried at an early stage, and the process has something in common with pastels in that you create a complete picture in a few minutes. Many newcomers to oils, people who are perhaps adept at watercolours, are reluctant to use too much colour, and get into the habit of using very diluted paint. There is nothing wrong with this, but if it is done continually it can become automatic, and the painter never

304

Left: In this, the final stage, build up thick layers of paint, working on the picture as a whole rather than concentrating on unnecessary details.

Right: Detail of clock tower.

Below: This impressionistic view of King's Cross, London, was painted almost entirely with a palette knife and the artist has used subtle colour to convey the mood of this wet November day.

gets the kick out of handling thick luscious paint. With a palette knife you have to use thick paint, for otherwise you get an oozing uncontrollable mass dribbling off the knife. But when using the palette knife there is no need to be dogmatic, and for fine details a fine pointed brush can be employed, perhaps nylon rather than sable because of its long-wearing attributes. And, of course, you can carry through a picture using palette knife and bristle brushes, changing from one to the other as the need arises.

Preliminary sketching is usually dispensed with, and the masses are applied directly with the knife, holding it sideways and using a broad sweep, which will lay the paint down in a curve with a straight edge. Vary the sizes of the palette knife to suit. It is advisable to have a clean unmuddied palette, leaving plenty of room to mix colours. Palette-knife painting is best with a bold approach, knowledge of what you are going to do, and a willingness to wipe paint off in one fell swoop if the picture is getting out of control and the colours have lost their crispness.

Some artists advise the use of two palettes, one for the basic construction, one for the lights and extras. The basic colours are first mixed on the palette; mix plenty of it. Construct your shapes with this. The 'incidental' colours can be mixed later when you have become certain of the tones. Bear in mind the solids themselves and the spaces they form outside themselves. This is important in all painting in oils but especially so with palette-knife work. When the basic tones have been put in, the filling-in can take place, using the knife flat for smooth effects, the point for detail, before taking up the brush. As with all painting, you do not have to stop at an 'edge'; you can bite into the previous layer at any time. The brush can also be used to give texture to the paint spread down with the knife.

The palette knife is often used for sea pictures; it is impossible to better when building up waves, and the very stroke of a loaded knife wielded horizontally can create convincing waves immediately, down to the flecks of foam. The open quality of sea pictures means that the palette knife does not have to be poked into little corners which it does not quite fit, and the knife is perfect for huge expanses of sky.

Sea pictures are a favourite non-professional art form, but their apparent easiness is deceptive. Waves are so distinctive a subject that they can be recognized immediately (whereas a stream may look like a path and a tree might look like a floorcloth on a stick); but because waves are recognizable it does not mean to say that they are good waves.

Sea Pictures

There are numerous methods. Here is one, traditional but not unadventurous. The subject involves rocks and a raging sea with plenty of spume and spray. Five mixtures are made, each for a specific purpose:

Sky: ivory black, titanium white, green oxide, mixed to make a cold grey.

White surf: Mostly titanium white with a little of the sky grey.

Green water: viridian with a little of the white surf mix.

Light rocks: burnt sienna and viridian.

Dark rocks: ivory black and cadmium red to make a greyish-violet mix.

This way of dealing with colours, mixing them deliberately for a set purpose and not deviating from the pre-arranged plan, is very useful in all subjects, not just sea pictures. When there are so many colours to choose from, it prevents chaos. L. S. Lowry did much the same thing, using a very restrained and limited palette, as you will read in the section on colour schemes near the end of this book.

The canvas is first of all painted with raw umber and turpentine rubbed on with a rag and then wiped off until the canvas has taken a stain, which will be approximately the same density as the sky. With a piece of cheese cloth the light areas of surf and splash are then wiped off. The rock area is then roughed-in with a large brush, then gone over with a smaller brush emphasizing the darker tones and outlining the various planes or sides of the rocks. The movement of the water is then tentatively suggested with light use of the brush. At this stage the picture is more or less monochrome. The full colour is then applied, trying to express textures and movement with direct brush strokes. Dark water in the distance and dark lines in the foreground rocks are added near the end; and finally light touches and highlights, and a final going over with dark rock mixture to suggest wetness on the rocks.

Another method is to apply a thin stain to the canvas, which serves to take off the glare of white. Draw in the design with charcoal, and then spray with a fixative. Begin with thin turpentine glazes, using brilliant colour, until you are satisfied, and then let the canvas dry completely. Finish with thick paint, guided by the underpainting.

A further method involves painting the canvas in one basic grey, with tone, detail, the highlights taken out with a cloth, until you have what is virtually a picture in monochrome. You then work on this with heavier paint, building up on the underpainting. If you are experienced with watercolour, look on this method as tinting.

306

Step 1: In this seascape the canvas is first of all painted with raw umber and turpentine rubbed on with a rag. Some areas have been wiped away to suggest surf and spray.

Step 2: The rocks are painted in with a one-inch flat brush. The movements of the waves are then sketched in very loosely with blues and whites.

Overleaf: Step 3: The finished picture. Full colour is now applied and the rocks are made to look wet. Surf and spray is painted with blues and greens mixed with white to achieve the desired effect.

307

In 'pure' sea pictures there are three basic elements – the sky, the sea, and the rocks. Movement is the most distinguishing feature of sea pictures. Clouds play a very important part, with regard to colour and shape, and these are flexible which you can adjust any time. Although the sky may be only a small strip at the top of the picture, even outside the picture, the artist must be always aware of its effect on the water. Sometimes the sky is too brilliant or too light in tone, in which case it is transposed down a tone or two to make a picture which hangs together. Water can be divided into three divisions – that in the foreground, that in the middle distance, and that in the distance. The water in the foreground is the most difficult to paint, that in the middle distance the most important, and distant water the easiest because it appears the most placid. It is generally found most convenient to paint the middle distance and distance first, leaving the foreground, both rocks and water, last.

Many marine painters find their focal point in the central section of the canvas; the central section can be defined as the space inside an imaginary line drawn all round the picture a quarter of the way inside the canvas and it does not have to be an imaginary line; if the paint is wet, you can pick out the central area with a pointed instrument or the handle of the brush. The main feature of the picture may be a breaker coming in, a wave breaking, or a wet rock gleaming in the sun, and everything else may be subordinated to this. A common fault of novice pictures is that there is no focal point; each item in the picture has equal prominence. Whether it is a landscape, a sea picture, a still life, or a portrait, the technique is the same for bringing it out – lessening the contrast of tones outside the main feature, lowering the tone of lights, raising the tone of darks, and softening any sharp edges which seem to grab the attention.

A way of looking at this focal point is to imagine a spotlight directed at it, with the illumination fading as it reaches the outer edges of the canvas. Forms inside the spotlight area will be sharp and contrasting. This principle has been practised by all the great artists of the past, including Rembrandt, Titian and Vermeer; it is often a good idea to look at reproductions of their work, forgetting the subjects which may be so familiar that we have ceased to examine the pictures objectively, and noticing how they employ the spotlight effect.

Many artists, whatever field they practise in, make small watercolour drawings before they set out on a time-consuming canvas, and it is always advisable to keep a sketchbook with you and when something strikes the eye jot it down.

Right: A portrait using a very simplified technique.

Life Drawing and Portraits

Oils are a marvellous medium for figure work and portraits. The painting of the human figure is unquestionably a challenge. If you can paint a nude you can paint almost anything. It is not difficult, though it is better to start off with charcoal and pencil than to launch straight away into oils. The best way to enter this area of painting is to join a life class, perhaps at a night school. Do not be embarrassed or alarmed that the standards may be too high. They will vary greatly. In any case most new-comers feel nervous at first. Students of all ages can learn from each other as well as from the teachers. Art classes usually last about two hours; this may not be long enough for some artists to carry out an oil painting, but does allow plenty of time to prepare sketches and crayon or pencil studies for taking back home, where you can complete the oil painting.

There are numerous ways to approach the task. A brief charcoal outline, building up with shadows, and then filling in with paint; putting the background shadows in first and laying out the figure against these; putting in the figure in a single neutral colour much diluted with turpentine and then overpainting with thicker paint; the same process using a palette knife instead of brushes; doing much the same thing with a neutral tint in acrylic and using oils over it at once as acrylic dries very rapidly; making a meticulous drawing in pencil and then filling in with soft brushes, the equivalent of tinting in watercolour.

Here is a straightforward and traditional method:
The colours are put on the palette – burnt sienna, burnt umber, ultramarine, yellow ochre, viridian, and flake white. Three further colours are prepared for the final stages – lamp black, vermilion, and crimson lake. The drawing is indicated in thin burnt umber using turpentine as a medium. Massed shading is added, using a larger brush, but still in burnt umber. The colours are added, rapidly, using plenty of turpentine. The canvas is toned down. The picture is built up with heavier pigment using a mixture of turpentine and linseed oil (or a prepared shop-bought medium). The drawing is corrected, and a small sable brush is used for the eyes, lips, and other detail, employing the additional colours. A soft clean brush is then applied, merging some tones and softening any hardness. The figure is in focus, the background is blurred. An oil painting of this kind, size 24 in. (61 cm) by 20 in. (51 cm), can be completed in two hours, just enough for a life class session.

How good must the drawing be? It depends on what sort of picture you want. If you can get

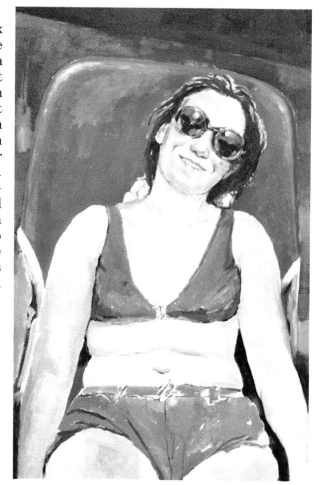

The nude study *(right, below)* by Henri Matisse is an excellent example of how effective simple brushwork can be.

310

the effect of solidity and flesh you are halfway there. A compact pose is easier than one all arms and legs. A seated figure is easier than a standing one. The main thing is to look and assess; how long is the arm? (Measure it against something else by holding a closed fist at arm's length, projecting the thumb, and using it as a measuring instrument. The arm may be three-quarters of a thumb; a leg may be a whole thumb; the head may be a thumb-nail.) Paint what you see not what you know is there; anybody can draw a mouth and have it recognized as such. But when a mouth is looked at in certain lighting conditions it may only be seen as a shadow beneath the lower lip and a thin line where the lips meet. If you are uncertain about your drawing abilities, mentally tone the whole thing down, as though the figure is in deep shadow, and bring out details here and there – a suggestion of the face for example. If you feel that you cannot handle perhaps the most demanding piece of anatomy, the hand, leave it in darkness. Do what you know you can do.

Where do you start? It is up to you. Some start with the head, some the torso, extending outwards to the arms and legs, indicating them at first tentatively, then more firmly. Remember the proportions: a man is eight heads tall, a woman six heads tall, a child of one four heads tall. The halfway point down of a man is the crutch. The neck does not sit on the shoulders but is inset; a man's neck slopes outwards, a woman's neck slopes inwards. The hand is not in one plane like a flatfish; the thumb droops unless the hand is outstretched. The eye consists of three parts, pupil, eyelids, eyelashes, plus a pouch beneath the eye. The most important part of the foot is the ankle; if it is badly placed a foot looks like a leg of lamb.

Solidity is more important than accuracy. If the body looks like it is made of plywood add shading, toning round the body, watching where the ribs make minor highlights, or take off colour with a rag, letting the canvas show through. If it is lightly tinted it will provide a mid-tone which you can work on. If, by using a brush, you are unable to get right the transition between the tones, use your finger tips.

When you are applying colour remember that you do not have to stop at the edges. You are not colouring an outline in a children's book. Outlines are a convenience. You use them when you want them, discard them without mercy when you do not.

Many artists when it comes to doing costume

311

312

figures often depict their models nude then add the clothes later. The pose of the figure does determine how the clothes hang. Folds in clothing come in four kinds – folds in hanging materials, folds in pulled materials, folds in heaped materials, and folds in crushed materials. All are expressed not with changes of colour but changes of tone. The local colour can be tinted with a grey or other neutral, depending on the overall colour scheme. Patterns, unless they are aggressive, should be suggested rather than copied.

Portraits have to be accurate, otherwise there is no point in doing them. When marking in the features, there are useful aids. The eyes are halfway down the head and the tops of the ears are at the level of the eyes. The distance between the top of the forehead and top of the nose is the same as that between the top of the nose and the bottom of the nose. The distance between the top of the upper lip and the bottom of the chin is the same as that between the top of the ear and the bottom of the ear. Of course there is some variation; otherwise we would look all the same.

Many portraitists start with the eyes, building from there. One standard method is this: Tint the canvas. Draw the outline of the head in charcoal, choosing a three-quarter view as this provides better shadows. Put in the features with a soft brush, using a brown such as burnt umber, well diluted with turpentine, and fix the shadows. Take the same tint lightly over the face, building up gradually, putting eyes, nose, mouth with heavier colour, and affirming the shadows. Indicate the lines of the neck, stressing the pit of the neck, vital for setting the head on the shoulders. The hair is put in lightly, stressing the direction of the growth and the way it is massed, and the colour added, but be careful not to overload the picture with too much dark. Put in the background. Work on where the face abuts the background, remembering you can go over the edges. Tone down where necessary, taking out pure whites and reserving them for highlights (tip of nose, bottom lip, highlight in eyes – same place each eye). Soften tone-edges which are too sharp with a soft brush. If the head is merging with the background take an off-white and go round the head with a soft slow brush.

This page and far left: Different portraits demonstrate a simplified method of painting. It is vital not to overwork the picture, which could end up as a muddy mess.

Painting a face in profile is a quick method of obtaining a good likeness.

A three-quarter view portrait creates its own problems.

314

Still Life and Flowers

Still life is a splendid 'starter' subject. You can make the selection as easy or as difficult as you wish. The main thing is to bring all the objects together to make a whole, so that the picture is not a mere catalogue; therefore, as with all other subjects, you need a focal point to which the eye is drawn. You can begin in many ways such as a charcoal outline, broad masses with the tones added later, shadows first, objects afterwards, speculative drawing in burnt umber with the brush, filling in first with thin paint then adding thick paint. But all subjects can be tackled in the way *you* prefer. When doing a still life think of the spotlight metaphor, picking out something with the light dissipating towards the edges of the canvas. Top colour, raw colour, is reserved for the featured object – a bottle, an apple, a jar, a bunch of flowers. The rest is sobered down, the background fades into insignificance. Use colour to suit yourself, tone it down so that you don't know whether it is greeny-grey or browny-purple. It is easy to paint brightly; not so easy to be subtle and evocative. It is simple to put paint on a canvas, simple even to depict articles so that they can be recognized. It is rather more difficult to put solid objects in space in such a way that they belong together and are not strewn across the picture surface; but not that much more difficult. Look, assess and paint. The secret of success is in your hands.

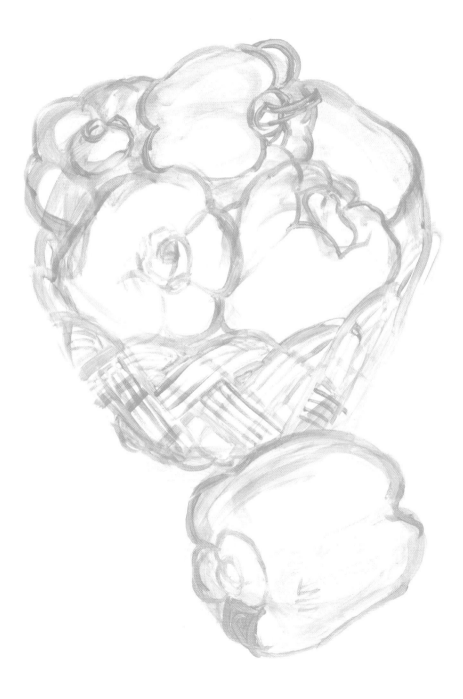

Left: Step 1: In this still life, the subject has been sketched directly onto the canvas using yellow ochre. This colour has been chosen because it is in sympathy with the colours that will be used in the finished painting.

Far left, bottom: It is not often that artists have the chance to paint a nude figure out of doors. In this picture, the artist has managed to capture the feeling of sunlight.

315

Step 2: Using a one-inch soft, flat brush, sketch in the main areas of colour and keep the brush strokes very loose.

Step 3: In the finished painting the contrasting highlights and shadow areas have been added.

Wherever you live you will always find something interesting to paint. Try to catch the subject matter when the light is at its most attractive.

Top right: This captures the effect of the birch tree in a strong autumn wind. Thick paint straight from the tube is applied with a stiff brush, allowing each successive layer of paint to dry before adding the next.

Bottom right: The vegetable garden can contain many attractive subjects to paint, such as these cabbages. This effect was achieved by thin scumbled layers of oil paint revealing the umber background colour.

Far right: Sunshine is not always vital to your painting. These geraniums were painted on a dull day using a combination of techniques. The background is scumbled and thinly painted while the foreground flowers and leaves are composed of thick layers of colour.

318

Far right: In this painting of a mill, the atmospheric quality is achieved by using only a very limited palette and simplified brush strokes.

Above: Detail of reflection.

Right: Only the merest suggestion of a change of colour and brush stroke is enough to indicate a figure.

Ronald Brown

Above: Detail of reflection in the water.

Left: Note how the artist has used aerial perspective to give the feeling of distance to the trees in this detail.

Far left: This winter landscape makes a satisfying composition. The dramatic lines of convergence give conviction to the perspective. Interestingly the vanishing point would be behind the tree.

323

There is interest even in
the most mundane of
subjects. There is no house or
garden, however small, which
cannot supply the observant
artist with an interesting
composition, as shown in the
collection of paintings on
these pages.

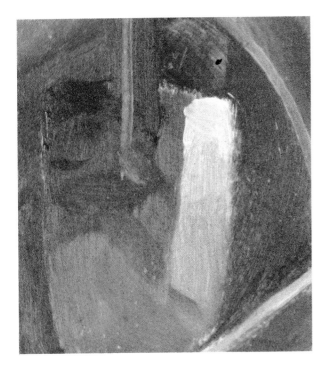

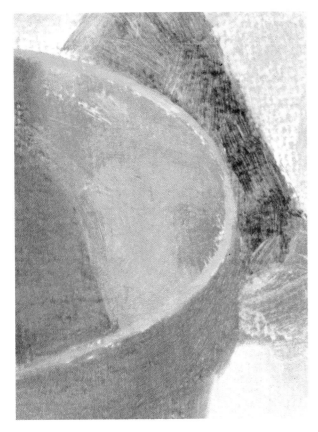

The painting on the facing
page has an interesting
composition which leads the
eye downwards in an S-shape,
from the top left to the fruit at
the bottom of the picture.

The details *(left)* of the basket
and the flowerpot show subtle
tonal shades where highlights
are accentuated by the depth
of the shadows.

Renaissance artists had to rely on good quality surfaces to enable them to paint in such exquisite detail. They had only canvas or walls on which to paint, thus paintings on wooden panels tended to be small as in this *Madonna and Child* of Filippo Lippi.

ADVANCED TECHNIQUES

There are basically two methods of painting, in whatever medium. There is the direct method, as advised by the Impressionists but not always practised by them, in which the paint, usually opaque, is put on in one application, and there is the building-up method, in which the paint is put on layer upon layer (in watercolour wash upon wash). The second method is the most time consuming, and an artist can spend months, even years, on a large picture, to the detriment of his output. These pictures may not be very good, but they certainly last, and any Italian Renaissance picture (say from the 14th to the middle of the 16th century) is sure of a warm welcome whatever the level of competence.

Painters of that time – and much later – had to be proficient in the art of colour-making as well as picture-making. In 1675 the competent but immensely boring portrait painter Sir Godfrey Kneller employed a man solely to make his colours. The artists' colourman dates from about the middle of the 18th century, and in 1776 a certain Matthew Darly was advertising 'transparent colours for staining drawings.' Reeves introduced small soluble cakes of watercolour in about 1820, followed 10 years or so later by Winsor and Newton, who put their watercolour into pans. In 1847 Winsor and Newton introduced watercolour in tubes.

Renaissance artists not only mixed their own colours, but they prepared their own surfaces, usually panel, often of poplar. They coated the panel with gesso, which provided a sound link between panel and paint, and provided brightness beneath the coats of paint. When this was not wanted, the white was toned down with a wash of transparent yellow (the 'imprimatura'). The main outlines of the forms were transferred from the drawing, using the 'pricking' method. At regular intervals holes were pricked into the drawing, and charcoal was dusted through these holes on to the panel, recreating the design. An alternative 'squaring-up' method much used today, is explained in the volume on Drawing. The Victorian Lord Leighton used the pricking method extensively.

The outlines were then emphasized with grey, black or brown ink or paint using a fine brush or a quill pen, with sometimes hatched strokes put in to indicate modelling. In the 15th century a monochrome wash of grey or brown was applied as an underpainting. Then the successive layers of transparent colour were applied. Duccio (c. 1260–1320) used green underpainting for his flesh sections. Green is

the complementary colour of the flesh tints, and when the local colour (the 'real' colour) was introduced this green came through the layer above and provided shadow. It was found that adding grey or brown to the flesh tint could result in a muddy colour. This green wash was allowed to dry, and then overpainted with a transparent wash of 'verdaccio', a mixture of black and ochre. This wash, in turn, was then left to dry.

The green method was very popular among the Italian artists (but not elsewhere). The next stage was the application of the local colours. The flesh tints were applied in separate hatched strokes, starting with a middle tone, white being added for the lighter parts, and the shadows added last. Hatching was used elsewhere, along with evenly graduated washes. Blues in drapery and skies were underpainted in a light dim blue, and the vivid reds were applied over a wash of red ochre and white. This first wash was deliberately uneven, adding variety to the final overpainting.

Above: Here, in total contrast to the previous old master painting, the artist has made a quick sketch of the two children having a bath, and he pays no attention to technique or method and even allows the white canvas to show through in places.

Elsewhere in Europe similar techniques were being employed. The Flemish painters used a lot of ultramarine in their shadow areas, and a soft green was used under blue, particularly when the draperies were of this colour. Titian (*c.* 1487–1576) came more than two centuries after Duccio, but he still followed the sequence of underpaintings, except that his handling was far freer, and his underpainting of the flesh (except in the deepest shadow) was *darker* than the overpainting. The underpainting served as a foil to the later layers, and washes of blue and red were applied seemingly at random. In the 16th century there came a demand for clever effects and dramatic light and shade. Instead of an underpainting in transparent browns and greys the whole of the canvas was primed with brown, sometimes verging on black (El Greco was particularly keen on this). The local colours were put in light and weakly, built up with brighter colour in a dashing manner. The flesh was begun in pink, modelled with madder and black so that the effect was greyish, then boldly overpainted with light flesh colour. El Greco often dragged a dry brush of the light colour over the underpainting so that contrast is

heightened. To give brilliance to his draperies, the underpainting was very light, with a good deal of white mixed in with the local colour.

Rubens (1577–1640) came a century after Titian, and was in a position to see that oil paint becomes transparent in time and that the Italian style of brown underpainting had unforeseen consequences as it was coming through the upper layers. Rubens used a brilliant white ground, toned down with yellow imprimatura, and then he applied a grey underpainting, probably using a sponge dipped in size and ground charcoal. He dragged this across the panel in parallel strokes, not completely covering the imprimatura, so that light paint would stand out better than an all-over grey wash. The underpainting was then carried out in transparent brown.

The flesh tint was laid out thickly on the part to be light, and dragged thinly on the shadow areas, and highlights were applied with pure white. Rubens worked fast, and achieved spontaneity, and may be said to have found a formula that suited him perfectly. Rembrandt (1606–1669) had a formula too – lots of shadow, not much light. He used a medium-brown priming on his grounds, modelling in a greeny-grey colour, much darker than the final light tone, not so dark as the final shadows, and this gloom obliged Rembrandt to rely heavily on the medium and light colours in the concluding stages.

Rembrandt and painters like him paved the way to direct painting ('alla prima'), and after the orthodoxy of the early Italian Renaissance painters there was an eagerness to experiment. Caravaggio (1573–1610), although a generation before Rembrandt, looks forward in his theatricality and tight control to a later age, and he was one of the first to be preoccupied with a perfectly smooth finish, using soft brushes and a thin medium, a technique also used by Velazquez (1599–1660). Vermeer (1632–1675) primed his canvas with a brown-grey mixture made from chalk, lead white, umber and charcoal, and it is possible that instead of the traditional underpainting he began by putting in flat areas of colour.

329

To speed up the drying process he mixed wax with his paints, and some of his pictures have six or seven layers, put on in any order, each with a different drying rate. No wonder that after 200 years the surface of his pictures looks like crazy paving. Reynolds was primarily a portraitist, and he began his work by putting in a rough circle of white on the grey priming of his canvas. Onto the white he placed his head, working rapidly and not waiting for the colours to dry before applying further paint, either solid or in transparent glazes. After he had done the face, and probably the hands, he would pass the picture to assistants to do the drapery and background, adding the final touches himself. Reynolds could do a face in a day, and charged on average £210 a picture, the equivalent of close on £5000 or $8500 today.

While Thomas Gainsborough (1727–1788) is rated higher now, his pictures averaged £168 each, and although he seems to have painted with sump oil he did have some regard for his public, careful in his choice of paints, and not having his pictures brought back to him by his clients for repainting – one of Reynold's tiresome chores. Gainsborough blocked in his portraits with thin highly diluted paint, completing the face before turning to the drapery and background. He painted with great freedom and bravura, but kept his methods sound and

Above: A Child's Portrait in Different Views: 'Angels' Heads by Sir Joshua Reynolds.

Right: Portrait of Edward Richard Gardiner by Thomas Gainsborough. This is a fine demonstration of how the artist used thin glazes to build up such a marvellous translucent quality.

Watteau (1684–1721) often worked directly on to the canvas, making amendments and alterations as he went along, and working at great speed, using too much medium with his paint, which resulted in the deterioration of his paintings. Many 18th-century painters also wished to work rapidly, especially those society painters for whom the commissions were piling up and for whom guineas were more important than the verdict of posterity. Among these was Sir Joshua Reynolds (1723–1792), whose personal motto should have been 'Anything for Money', and whose influential *Discourses on Art* he disregarded completely.

rarely bodged the resulting picture.

John Constable (1776–1837) had a different technique altogether. He began with pencil and oil sketches, and when he worked he put in his main masses in an undercoat, bringing in the detail gradually. In order to make certain the painting would hang together, he drastically altered major portions. Often accused of leaving his pictures unfinished, Constable would round off the painting with flecks and stabs of highlight, sometimes applied with the palette knife. Glazes of reds and browns were used to add substance to the foreground, and he paid great attention to his clouds. If you visit the Victoria and Albert Museum in London you can see a large number of his cloud studies: he was one of the first artists to actually look at them. No one merits such close study as Constable. He used the technique of scumbling (dragging a nearly dry brush loaded with white over a layer of paint to get sea or sky effects) extensively. His colour seems so natural and realistic that it is sometimes a shock to realize that the accents in the foreground are in pure vermilion and that the shadows are in fact green. It must be admitted that he sometimes overworked his paintings and that the oil studies have more

Left: Detail of sky in the painting *(below)*.

Below: A sketch for 'Hadleigh Castle' by John Constable. In complete contrast to the way Gainsborough painted, Constable appeared to attack his canvas. This is particularly evident in his smaller paintings which were often painted on site. Constable's larger works such as *The Hay Wain* would have been painted in his studio from smaller sketches made out of doors.

freshness and verve.

J. M. W. Turner (1775–1851) was the great adventurer in English oil painting, and there is a world of difference between his early prim architectural subjects and the mystery of his later light-bathed paintings. He was very keen on colour theories, which have worked to the detriment of his paintings as his yellows have proved fugitive and some of his pictures have taken on an arcane quality due to colour changes. In many of his pictures he returned to the white ground of earlier painters, putting in his underpainting in bright pastel colours much diluted with turpentine, applying thick or thin paint on top to get his effect. For Turner effect was all, and he employed any technique to get it – scumbling, glazing, palette-knife, scratching, diluting thick paint already on the canvas, and even mixing his colours on the canvas rather than on the palette. Often he laid his pure colours down side by side, and it is no wonder that the Impressionists in France claimed Turner as their own. It is difficult to think of any other artist who has exploited the qualities of oil paints so completely as Turner, and if he did have a weak point it was his figures.

It was in figure painting that William Etty (1787–1849) was supreme. The nude was Etty's subject and obsession, and he was probably the most 'painterly' specialist artist of the period. Known as the English Titian, Etty was a master of his medium, and in his flesh tints managed to produce a pearly glow so distinctive that it was said that he used a 'secret medium'. Unlike other classically trained painters, Etty employed any technique that occurred to him, taking off glazes with his thumb, dabbing at the paint surface with his pocket handkerchief, and scratching with his thumb nail when it seemed that this was what was wanted. He achieved a pearly glow through tiny specks of black and white.

With the increasing number of art schools and the growing influence of the Royal Academy Schools, there was an emphasis on formula painting, tight control, and no improvising. To escape this formal training, many students went to Paris to study in the studios of the famous French artists of the time, only to find that they too were hard taskmasters, though there was

Above: Walton on the Naze by Ford Madox Brown. The Pre-Raphaelites were famous as colourists and for their attention to detail. This is an excellent example of aerial perspective.

Left: The Dogana, San Giorgio Citella, from the Steps of the Europa by J. M. W. Turner. Because Turner was so preoccupied with light, his brush work had to have a translucent quality. He created his effects by building up thin glazes of oil medium.

333

The Winnower by Jean-François Millet. His paintings were recognized as being dark and sombre, but nevertheless he still managed to convey a marvellous illusion of light.

Below: Mariana by John Everett Millais. Millais was completely captivated by detail as this painting aptly illustrates.

always the odd eccentric.

Typical of the 19th-century French painters was Jean Millet (1814–1875), one of a group known disparagingly as the Dismals on account of their subject matter and not their personalities. Millet's picture *The Angelus* was probably the most famous painting in the world. Unending toil was the theme of Millet's work, which was subdued in colour (browns, blue/green, black, white, iron oxide red), and dramatic in lighting. Millet used an off-white priming, and he established his design with charcoal or chalk, using a wash to establish outlines and masses. Shadows were added, leaving the underpainting for the half-tints, and the highlights were added, fairly heavily. The background was often colour-scumbled, letting the underpainting show through, and he strengthened his outlines with a soft brush which, although effective at times, gives his figures the appearance of cut-outs or cartoon characters; not the kind of thing the Paris art schools liked at all. The texture of Millet's paint closely resembles plaster, but his vigorous handling and unconcern for the proprieties had a powerful effect on subsequent painters, such as van Gogh. He also made gloom and the downtrodden peasantry fashionable. The handling of paint, clotted and earthy, is akin to the techniques used by the 'Kitchen Sink' English school of the 1950s and 1960s. There is no doubt that Millet is an important figure and well worth more than a cursory glance. It is the kind of painting which is not too difficult to do and which always makes a dramatic impact on the spectator.

It is a world away from the academically trained British artists of the period, who thrived on patience and perseverance and techniques of a high order, not afraid to spend weeks on some tiny detail and who used brushes with one or two hairs only. The ultimate in this kind of highly-detailed work is Richard Dadd's *Titania*, which became the highest priced British painting of all time in March 1983 at £500,000 ($1,000,000).

You can still hear modern artists sneering at the Victorian painters, even though their work now regularly commands five and six figure sums in the sale room. This may be due to sour grapes because these modern artists cannot emulate the skill and artistry of Victorian painters. You can fudge a Millet, a Constable, or a van Gogh; you cannot fudge a Lord Leighton, an Alma-Tadema, or a Poynter.

Lord Leighton (1830–1896) was typical of them and his nudes created something of a scandal when they were exhibited at the Royal Academy. Leighton made many thumb-nail sketches before he began, and then laid out his

design on paper, squaring it up for transfer to canvas or, if the design was full-size, using the pricking method. A small oil-sketch was made to establish the colour scheme, and then Leighton put in his underpainting in a warm monochrome. If it was a nude the nude was painted first, and the draperies were added later, from separate studies. Leighton used a flat translucent wash for the draperies so that the modelling of the nude would show through, and he then began to apply the thicker colour, preferring stiff paint with very little medium. He kept the surface 'dead' until the latter stages, when he would add more medium to liven the painting up. His colour scheme, about which he was careful, was ultramarine, yellow, cadmium red, scarlet madder, yellow ochre, burnt sienna, indigo, rose madder, madder carmine, black and white. He and his contemporaries preferred a white priming, as this was what his clients liked, as a reaction against the 'Black Masters' (the old painters whose work could barely be discerned beneath their coatings of heavy varnish and dirt). The sparkling character of much Victorian

painting owes everything to precise and well-understood techniques, which are still evident.

The Victorian academic painters based their pictures on good drawings; oil paintings were regarded largely as tinted drawings, and the greatest public acclaim came for those pictures which were as near to reality as possible, and had finish. There was little wilful distortion, except for comic effect: this was left to the cartoonists and caricaturists. Of course there were some painters, such as Rossetti, who had not trained at the art-world establishments, and others who pursued their ways oblivious to public opinion. G. F. Watts was more concerned with the message and not the medium, and his vast allegorical pictures are still out of fashion. When he felt that he had made his point, Watts stopped painting his particular picture, and the rough coarse canvas he preferred was left with blank spaces showing through, so sparse was the paint. He laid on pure colours without mixing on the palette, he ignored detail, and did not like objects to have firm outlines, preferring them to melt into the background.

Our English Coasts by William Holman Hunt. As a Pre-Raphaelite, Hunt was much preoccupied with realism and attention to detail as well as with quality of light, which is evident in all his paintings.

There were always painters who broke with the establishment, either from inner compulsion to do their own thing or from the awareness that there was no one best way to paint. Edouard Manet (1832–1883) combined traditional and experimental techniques. He was influenced by Velazquez, and wished to reduce half-tone in his pictures and thus stress the contrast between lights and darks. He used off-white canvases, painted wet-on-wet, mixing his colours on the canvas, and when he had painted his main groups he defined them by going over the outlines with a pointed brush. His main objects he painted with thick rich pigment, but his backgrounds were often scumbled. Sometimes he would scrape down his day's work, leaving the merest vestiges, and evolve anew from these. Although often lumped in with Impressionists such as Monet, Manet was a supreme virtuoso, knowing instinctively when to leave off, and how to suggest texture without being too specific. If you want an English equivalent, there is no more suitable candidate than John Singer Sargent (who as it happens was American).

Why Manet is still described as an Impressionist is something of a mystery; probably because he gets muddled with Claude Monet (1840–1926), a painter preoccupied with catching the fleeting effects of light, and who thus had to work fast and on the spot. He used a weak see-through priming, and blocked in his main features with thin scumbled paint, over which he applied opaque paint very dry, dragging the brush across the underpainting in strokes so that the previous layer showed through. There are very few absolute darks in Monet's paintings, for he usually mixed his colours with white. He was good on shimmering effects, and creating texture through his brushwork, often drawing through the paint with the handle of his brush to reveal the colour beneath. Viewing a Monet painting at close range is a meaningless exercise, for we see only dabs and blotches of colour. Despite the speed at which he worked, Monet was always careful with technique, and despite his mixtures of wet-on-wet and wet-on-dry and his indifference to outline, especially in his later work, he managed to avoid muddiness, a constant menace to those who paint in dabs rather than areas of colour.

Le déjeuner sur l'herbe à Chailly by Claude Monet. In this sketch, inspired by Manet's picture, and in direct emulation, Monet determined to show how open-air painting should be done. Manet's *Déjeuner* is obviously of models posed in a studio against a painted backdrop, resulting in a highly artificial picture. Monet worked from sketches and figure studies made on the spot. This sketch for the life-size work shows what Monet intended but never completed.

Above: La Grenouillère by Auguste Renoir. Renoir, who had developed a delicate touch as a china decorator, is more fluid than Monet, who is quite rough in his efforts to achieve freedom.

Left: Waterloo Bridge. Cloudy Weather by Claude Monet. The bridge, crowded with traffic, stands dark and brooding over the fast-running Thames. Monet praised the London fog for eliminating details. When the weather changed with spring, he left London.

Georges Seurat (1859–1891) became concerned with colour and optical theory, and introduced the 'pointillist' technique, covering the painted areas with tiny dots of different colours, which, in theory, merge in the viewer's eye to become one. He painted wet-over-dry to retain the vivacity of the colours, and in his underpainting, carried out in the local colours of the objects, he outlined the objects with the brush. His object outlines are always immaculately defined, and his areas are never blurred and haphazard. His colour sense was incredibly subtle, which cannot be said of his almost exact contemporary Vincent van Gogh (1853–1890), whose *Sunflowers* has probably inspired many amateur artists, often with disastrous consequences. Van Gogh used coarse canvases, often painting directly on to them without a priming, and using opaque paint from the start, without any attempt at underpainting. The features of his pictures were worked over and outlined, usually in an unlikely colour such as blue or brown. The texture of van Gogh's paint has something of cream cheese, and to

build up his impasto he mixed in wax. There was no attempt at finish, and his vigorous and frenzied brushwork is everywhere evident. In his admirers this type of brushwork becomes scratchy and irritating.

In his way, van Gogh emancipated colour from the restrictions placed on it by reality, and in the beginning of the 20th century a group of painters known as the Fauves ('wild beasts') glorified paint, were not concerned with representation, painted directly, and, like van Gogh, drew lines around their subjects to define them rather than let the paint areas do this job. Characteristic of these painters was Henri Matisse, but it was probably the type of artist personified by Pierre Bonnard (1867–1947) who has had more influence on more recent representational art. Bonnard was not interested in building up solidity or creating an illusion of depth, but aimed at a tapestry effect. He used a fairly absorbent ground, applying thin scumbles of diluted paint which he then intensified with thicker dabs of dryish powdery paint, a subtle form of picture-making.

Jean-Francois Millet. Five- colour palette.

Titian. Nine colours.

Peter Paul Rubens. Thirteen colours.

Colour Schemes

Each painter has favourite colours and combinations of colours, and sometimes these are so personal to the artist that you can pick him out not by his style or subject matter but by the general colour scheme.

Many artists used a very limited range of colours. Jean Millet (1814–1875), whose painting *The Angelus* was once one of the half-dozen most famous paintings in the world, often used a palette of no more than five colours: iron oxide red or vermilion; a brown earth colour of the burnt sienna variety; a blue green; a black; and white.

A modern artist who imposed a similar restraint on his palette was L. S. Lowry. He said: 'I am a simple man, and I use simple materials: ivory black; vermilion; prussian blue; yellow ochre; flake white – and no medium. That's all I've ever used for my painting.'

The writer on art A. W. Rich advises a palette of five colours: light red; yellow ochre; cyanine blue; ivory black; burnt sienna. As a concession, the same authority allows five more colours: viridian; raw sienna; ultramarine; aureolin; rose madder. The great drawback of this palette is that it lacks a vivid red.

Many of the great artists used a very wide range of colours, though Titian maintained that a painter needed only three. Nevertheless, he used nine colours: lead white; ultramarine; madder lake; burnt sienna; malachite green; yellow ochre; red ochre; orpiment (literally translated as 'gold paint'); ivory black.

Van Eyck had a palette of eight colours: brown; madder; ultramarine; yellow ochre; terre verte (a green); orpiment; red ochre; peach black.

Rubens used many: lead white; orpiment; yellow ochre; yellow lake; madder; vermilion; red ochre; ultramarine; cobalt blue; terre verte; malachite green; burnt sienna; ivory black.

The writer on art Hilaire Hiler, whose *The Painter's Pocket Book* (1937) is the best book of its kind ever written, gives a choice of two palettes, one low-toned, the other high-toned. The low one was: titanium white; yellow ochre; light red; cobalt blue; ultramarine. The high-toned one was: titanium white; cadmium yellow; ultramarine; cadmium red; lamp black.

In 1876 the aesthete P. G. Hamerton (1834–1894) declared what he thought was a basic essential palette. Hamerton was an artist of a kind, but is best known as a moderately influential critic of the middle-of-the-road school. These are the colours a good Victorian would have used: flake white; pale cadmium yellow; vermilion; rose madder; ultramarine; emerald green; vandyke brown; black.

It is interesting to compare this palette with

David Hockney's
Mr. and Mrs. Ossie Clark and Percy. A masterful modern painting which uses light and shade to the utmost dramatic effect.

However, this is not an art history or a paean to selected artists. Can we learn from these techniques? Although many of us are too impatient to apply glaze after slow-drying glaze over a carefully designed underpainting, we can short-circuit the oil-painting process by using acrylic, in which five successive glazes will dry in a couple of hours. One of the virtues of the use of transparent glazes is that the picture comes along bit by bit, underpinned by the underpainting so that the artist who has some idea of the end product cannot come wholly to grief. Painting direct *can* be a hit-or-miss method, though it is unquestionably the method most practised today.

For those who wish to simplify their forms, or are more concerned with colour than with tone or reality, there is a lot to be said for the black-line method (outlining the objects in a picture, or some of the primary objects in a picture, with the point of a soft brush). At its most subtle, this method can be seen in the work of Matisse; at its most majestic and sombre in the work of Georges Rouault. Rouault painted in several layers, altering and amending, outlining his paint areas with thick black lines.

A modern art historian perceptively drew an analogy between Rouault's paintings and stained glass windows.

The black-line method need not be forceful

and attention-grabbing, but merely a faint line separating the various patches of colour, a process used for centuries, particularly in water-colour painting. There is no question that there are more technical variations possible in oil painting than in watercolours.

Below: The Inattentive Reader by Henri Matisse. In this painting, the artist appears totally preoccupied with the poetry of flat colours.

343

that of the great Impressionist artist Renoir (1841–1919) at the same time: flake white; Naples yellow; chrome yellow; cobalt or ultramarine; alizarin red; viridian; emerald green; vermilion. Notice that Renoir did not use blacks at this time.

Renoir's palette was not so different from that of Georges Seurat (1859–1891), who evolved the 'pointillist' technique, in which separate dots of primary colours such as blue and yellow were placed side by side and intended to be interpreted by the human eye as green: white; an orange; raw sienna; alizarin red; ultramarine; cobalt blue and perhaps cerulean blue; vermilion; emerald green; viridian; cadmium yellow; yellow ochre.

Vincent van Gogh also eschewed the use of black: lead white; red lake; vermilion; cadmium yellow; ultramarine; cobalt blue; cobalt violet; emerald green; viridian; an earth colour probably sienna, burnt or raw.

A palette suitable for acrylic painting could

Hilaire Hiler. Low-toned and high-toned palettes.

P. G. Hamerton. Eight colours.

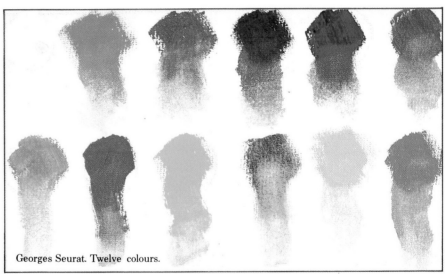

Georges Seurat. Twelve colours.

Auguste Renoir. Eight colours.

Vincent van Gogh. Eleven colours.

be made up of the following: a green; burnt and raw umber; cadmium yellow; cadmium red; crimson; raw sienna; ultramarine; cobalt blue; black; white.

Most of the palettes listed are general purpose ranges, but if you have in mind a green-based colour scheme you could restrict your choice to: black; white; burnt sienna; burnt umber; cadmium red; cadmium yellow; cobalt blue; chrome green; yellow ochre. Red mixed into a green is an admirable 'cooling down' colour. The chief fault of novice landscapists is to make the greens far too green and brash.

A rather cold colour scheme is: black; white; alizarin crimson; cadmium yellow; chrome green; monastral blue; violet.

A hot somewhat acid scheme is: black; white; burnt sienna; cadmium green; cadmium lemon; cadmium orange; cadmium red; cadmium yellow; cobalt blue; ultramarine; viridian; yellow ochre.

An interesting palette evolved by a pre-war chemist named Toch guaranteed permanency of pigments: Venetian or light red; medium cadmium; ultramarine; lamp black; zinc white; raw sienna; burnt umber; chromium oxide (yellow); madder lake.

These selections are only a handful of the hundreds of different schemes used by artists, and everyone will want to create their own. Some of the pigments used by the great painters of the past are not available at art-shops, perhaps fortunately, for many of the masterpieces we take so much for granted have been repainted so many times that they can hardly be called original works of art, since they have been repainted because the colour has literally disappeared or been transmuted. In Antwerp Museum there is a trunk containing the powdered colours used by Rubens (putting colour into tubes is fairly recent, dating back to the 1840s). The ultramarine, the madders, the lead white and all those browny colours known as earth colours have survived well, but the yellow lake, the vegetable greens and vermilion have almost entirely faded away. The ultramarine of the old painters was originally made from lapis lazuli, but even before the Second World War it cost more than a pound sterling for a tiny pan and is now virtually priceless. The modern equivalent is French ultramarine, the principal ingredients of which are sulphur and sodium.

Scientists have discovered (or decided) that there are 80,000 tints between white and black. Within a range of 20 colours or so most of us can get what we want.

FRAMING

Oil paintings are usually framed without glass, though if you wish they can be mounted and placed under glass, in the same way as water-colours, if they are painted on board, canvas paper, or card. If on canvas this is not possible. The mouldings of frames vary enormously; some are plain and some are intricate, and if you have no preferences a picture-framer is always the best person to advise.

Framing kits are readily available at reasonable prices, and it is always possible to find old frames, in second-hand shops and junk shops and at open markets, which may merely need a good clean up. In the old days frames for oil paintings were gilt and ornate, and often the mouldings of these were made of gesso, a mixture of plaster of Paris and glue which was subject to damp and time. If suitable frames are bought with peeling or damaged gesso it is better to strip the whole lot off to the bare frame, which can be gilded, painted, or waxed and polished. All second-hand frames should be freed of any backing paper, and all nails should be removed, as well as hanging cord, whether wire or cord.

If the moulding of the frame is in good condition, and if the design is 'built out' on wires coated with gesso, there is a chance that the frame may be worth a good deal of money. If the frame is carved, and if it is intricately carved with vine leaves, fruit, or other decorative devices, it could be worth not just a good deal of money but a fortune, so before you put your own picture in such a frame get expert advice. One wealthy collector who buys such frames, which are usually antique, displays them on the wall – by themselves, without a picture.

Oil paintings on card, board, or canvas paper can be cut down to fit an existing frame, but a painting on a stretched canvas must have the right size frame, though there can be a little leeway of a centimetre or so which can be wedged. Unless you are a skilled woodworker, do not try to cut frames down, as the merest error shows when the frame is reassembled.

Far left: Claude Monet's *Vase of Chrysanthemums.* Between 1878 and 1882 Monet painted some twenty still-life and flower paintings. Chrysanthemums were very much part of the vogue for things Japanese in Paris, and were a symbol of luxury and exoticism in the works of poets and novelists.

Left: A variety of frame designs suitable for oil paintings.

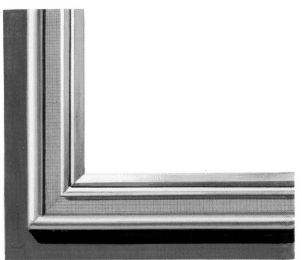

Far left below: Claude Monet's *Tulip Fields at Sassenheim.* When Monet revisited earlier haunts he seemed to revert partly to earlier styles: particular places, for Monet, called for a particular painting response.

347